The "War on Terror" Narrative

OXFORD STUDIES IN SOCIOLINGUISTICS

General Editors:

Nikolas Coupland
Adam Jaworski
Cardiff University

Recently Published in the Series:

Talking about Treatment: Recommendations for Breast Cancer Adjuvant Treatment
Felicia D. Roberts

Language in Time: The Rhythm and Tempo of Spoken Interaction
Peter Auer, Elizabeth Kuhlen, Frank Müller

Whales, Candlelight, and Stuff Like That: General Extenders in English Discourse
Maryann Overstreet

A Place to Stand: Politics and Persuasion in a Working-Class Bar
Julie Lindquist

Sociolinguistics Variation: Critical Reflections
Edited by Carmen Fought

Prescribing under Pressure: Parent-Physician Conversations and Antibiotics
Tanya Stivers

Discourse and Practice: New Tools for Critical Discourse Analysis
Theo van Leeuwen

The "War on Terror" Narrative: Discourse and Intertextuality in the Construction and Contestation of Sociopolitical Reality
Adam Hodges

The "War on Terror" Narrative

Discourse and Intertextuality in the Construction and Contestation of Sociopolitical Reality

Adam Hodges

OXFORD
UNIVERSITY PRESS

OXFORD
UNIVERSITY PRESS

Oxford University Press, Inc., publishes works that further
Oxford University's objective of excellence
in research, scholarship, and education.

Oxford   New York
Auckland   Cape Town   Dar es Salaam   Hong Kong   Karachi
Kuala Lumpur   Madrid   Melbourne   Mexico City   Nairobi
New Delhi   Shanghai   Taipei   Toronto

With offices in
Argentina   Austria   Brazil   Chile   Czech Republic   France   Greece
Guatemala   Hungary   Italy   Japan   Poland   Portugal   Singapore
South Korea   Switzerland   Thailand   Turkey   Ukraine   Vietnam

Library of Congress Cataloging-in-Publication Data
Hodges, Adam.
The "War on terror" narrative : discourse and intertextuality in the construction and
contestation of sociopolitical reality / Adam Hodges.
   p.   cm. — (Oxford studies in sociolinguistics)
Includes bibliographical references and index.
ISBN 978-0-19-975959-0 (hardcover : alk. paper) — ISBN 978-0-19-975958-3 (pbk. : alk. paper)
1. September 11 Terrorist Attacks, 2001. 2. War on Terrorism, 2001–2009. 3. Discourse analysis—
Political aspects. 4. Critical discourse analysis. 5. Sociolinguistics. 6. Intertexuality.
7. Bush, George W. (George Walker), 1946—Language. I. Title.
HV6432.7.H63   2011
909.83′1—dc22   2010017027

1 3 5 7 9 8 6 4 2

Printed in the United States of America
on acid-free paper

For the victims of 9/11 and the wars in Afghanistan and Iraq
Peace and justice begin with understanding.

Contents

Preface, ix
Acknowledgments, xi

1. Introduction, 3

2. The Characterization of 9/11 and America's Response to Terrorism, 18

3. The Narrative's Part-Whole Textual Interdependence, 41

4. The Construction of Al Qaeda and Iraq as Linked Antagonists, 64

5. Intertextual Series: Reproduction and Resistance in the Media, 84

6. Talking Politics: The Narrative's Reception among College Students, 112

7. Whose Vietnam? Discursive Competition over the Vietnam Analogy, 133

8. Conclusion, 153

   Appendix A. Corpus of Presidential Speeches, 161

   Appendix B. Transcription Conventions for Presidential Speeches, 164

Appendix C. Transcription Conventions for Focus Group Interviews, 165

Appendix D. Media Discourse Data, 166

References, 168

Index, 176

Preface

A *picture* held us captive. And we could not get outside of
it, for it lay in our language and language seemed to repeat
it to us inexorably.

—Ludwig Wittgenstein (2001: 41)

By now, much has been written about the events of 9/11, the invasion of Afghanistan, the war in Iraq, weapons of mass destruction, supposed links between Saddam Hussein and Al Qaeda, Joseph Wilson's trip to Niger, the torture of prisoners at Abu Ghraib and Bagram Air Force Base, the Downing Street minutes, the torture of "enemy combatants" at Guantanamo Bay, extraordinary rendition, the Geneva Convention deemed "quaint" by the Attorney General, the elimination of habeas corpus by Congress, waterboarding—in short, the multiple variations on the all-encompassing theme that Americans came to know as the "war on terror" during the Bush administration's tenure in the White House. Given that the sine qua non of democracy is transparency and accountability, one hopes that Americans will persist in the search for greater understanding of these issues and practice democracy by entering into a healthy conversation about the past in an attempt to create a better future.

I write this book from the perspective of a sociocultural linguist interested in the discursive details of political interaction, but I also write as an American citizen deeply concerned with the response to 9/11 orchestrated by the Bush administration and the policy it pursued during its two terms in the White House. My position as a scholar cannot be decoupled from my position as an intellectual in a democratic society. Although this book is primarily aimed at an academic audience familiar with and interested in the empirical study of political discourse and concomitant theoretical issues, the impetus for the investigation stems from my position as a member of a society that has been engaged in an ongoing debate about an appropriate response to terrorism and America's role in the world. As a citizen, I watched the horrifying scenes of 9/11 beamed via television into my home, and became further horrified as my government turned to war as the answer. My horror turned to incredulity as I witnessed the Bush administration plan and execute the selling of a second war in Iraq, using 9/11 as the pretext for its marketing campaign. How could the administration be so effective in convincing so many Americans that war with Iraq was justified and necessary? Arguably, the mobilization against the war prior to its start was unprecedented. Millions of concerned citizens, myself included, joined campaigns and street protests to voice opposition to what we saw as an ill-conceived and illegitimate invasion. Yet, the "marketing campaign" succeeded, and the war in Iraq became just another "front" in the "war on terror," according to the narrative. In short, the Bush administration succeeded in painting a vision of the world that seemed to hold a nation captive. With that vision of the world, the Bush administration succeeded in gaining consent for its foreign policy.

This book is a scholarly investigation guided by the big picture question of how language use shapes and influences sociopolitical reality. It is also a critical inquiry into how political rhetoric can pave the way for justifying war in the hope that such an understanding might raise awareness and develop the critical ethos needed to avoid future wars. In broad terms, both critical scholarship and democratic participation rely on such a critical ethos where the aim is, as Foucault writes, "to question over and over again what is postulated as self-evident, to disturb people's mental habits, the way they do and think things, to dissipate what is familiar and accepted, to reexamine rules and institutions" (Foucault and Kritzman 1988: 265). In the case of this book's investigation, the task is to get outside the "picture" (to use the imagery Wittgenstein provides in the epigraph) that the Bush administration has presented to us about 9/11 and America's response to terrorism. Even political opponents of the Bush administration have been held more or less captive by the picture that is the Bush "War on Terror" Narrative, and were hard pressed to completely rupture its dominance in American public discourse while he was in office. The aim of this book is to examine why that might be the case from a linguistic perspective, and to expose the Bush "War on Terror" Narrative for what it is: only one story (among other potential possibilities) about the world since September 11, 2001.

Acknowledgments

In true Bakhtinian form, this book builds upon countless prior interactions. Although it would be impossible to name every individual here who has impacted this project, there are several people who bear special mention. First and foremost, I owe my deep gratitude to Kira Hall whose enthusiastic encouragement and incisive feedback made this book possible. Karen Tracy, Ira Chernus, Andy Cowell, and Barbara Fox have also been instrumental with their time and comments as I brought this project to fruition. Chad Nilep has been a true colleague and I owe many thanks to him for his readings of earlier drafts of this work. Special thanks are also due to Adam Jaworski and Nikolas Coupland for their feedback and encouragement on the manuscript. There are, of course, many others who I cannot mention by name, but their influence has impacted this work all the same. Whatever shortcomings that may remain are, of course, my sole responsibility.

The "War on Terror" Narrative

Introduction

At 8:46 on the morning of September 11, 2001, the
United States became a nation transformed.

—9/11 Commission (NC 2004a: 1)

DISCOURSE AND THE "WAR ON TERROR"

Immediately upon the impact of the first plane into the north tower of the
World Trade Center on September 11, 2001, people began talking. Live
images of lower Manhattan and accompanying words were broadcast
across the nation and around the world. Journalists began to ask questions,
bystanders recounted their personal experience of the events, and the nation (and broader world) entered into a conversation about the nature and
meaning of what would come to be known as "9/11" and its aftermath. The
events of 9/11 have produced an abundance of reactions, among scholars
in particular and the nation in general. Regardless of the specific details of
those reactions, they all have one thing in common: they are interpretive
acts achieved through discourse. Although the events of 9/11 are actual
happenings in the world, those events do not intrinsically contain their
own interpretation. Only through language are such events turned into a
full account of that experience. Through language, we name protagonists,

ascribe motivations, and provide explanations. Through language, we construct a narrative.

This book provides a comprehensive treatment of the discourse of the George W. Bush administration in the years after 9/11. In particular, I focus on the formation and recontextualization of what I term the Bush "War on Terror" Narrative (henceforth, the Narrative), which forwards a powerful set of assumptions and explanations about America's struggle against terrorism since September 11, 2001. Although much narrative research has been done on personal narratives—that is, narratives told by individuals about personal experiences (e.g., Heintzelman 2009, Linde 1993, Ochs and Capps 2001, Riessman 1993, Young 1989, inter alia)—I focus here on political narrative (e.g., Martin and Wodak 2003, Wodak and van Dijk 2000).

The empirical investigation is divided into two parts. The first part examines speeches delivered by President Bush over a time period of nearly seven years, stretching from September 11, 2001 through March 19, 2008. I analyze these speeches to examine how basic elements of the Narrative are discursively established. Although the analysis focuses on a narrative told by an individual speaker on specific occasions, the result is to distill from these representative examples the macrolevel discourse about the "war on terror." In this way, the repeated narrations by the president of the United States effectively accumulate into a larger cultural narrative shared by many within the nation (and beyond)—what Bruner (1991) terms "narrative accrual." Importantly, the power of the president (and the story he tells) is, as Gal (1991) says of power more generally: "more than an authoritative voice in decision making; its strongest form may well be the ability to define social reality, to impose visions of the world" (197).

The second part of the analysis examines the process of recontextualization that takes place as the Narrative enters into the media and is taken up by citizens in their conversations with each other. The representation of issues is an ongoing process always subject to challenges and new *re-presentations*. More pointedly, it is through multiple, overlapping discursive encounters that the social practice of meaning making occurs. As fragments of discourse, once spoken, enter into subsequent contexts, their recontextualization involves reshaping to some degree. I examine the intertextual connections in American public discourse about the "war on terror" to understand how the Narrative is not only reproduced but also reshaped and resisted across multiple discursive settings. The overarching aim of the two-part analysis is to illuminate the connection between micro-level discursive action and macrolevel cultural understandings. I argue that applying ideas on intertextuality to the analysis of political discourse is central to understanding this micro/macro connection.

As widely recognized by language scholars, language—and more specifically, discourse—does not simply reflect events that take place in the world. Discourse infuses events with meaning, establishes widespread social understandings, and constitutes social reality. The beginning of the 9/11 Commission's Executive Summary states, "At 8:46 on the morning of September 11, 2001, the United States became a nation transformed" (NC 2004a: 1). Yet any transformation that may have occurred was realized through discourse and the stories told about the experience. As Bruner (1991) notes, "we organize our experience and our memory of human happenings mainly in the form of narrative—stories, excuses, myths, reasons for doing and not doing, and so on" (4). The Bush "War on Terror" Narrative has provided "the official story, the dominant frame" (Chernus 2006: 4) for understanding 9/11 and America's response to terrorism. It has allowed for the discursive justification not just of a metaphorical "war on terror" but of the very real wars in Afghanistan and Iraq.

At the outset, it is worth emphasizing both what this book is about and what it is not about. I am not attempting to assess the truth of the statements that underlie the Bush "War on Terror" Narrative. That is, I am not attempting to assess the Narrative's adequacy (or lack thereof) for accurately describing and explaining the world. Instead, the point is to focus on the way discourse effectively brings into existence a "truth" with real world consequences rather than to evaluate that truth against a supposedly more objective body of knowledge.[1] In Foucault's (1980) terms, the Bush "War on Terror" Narrative is a type of discursive formation that sustains a *regime of truth*. It places boundaries around what can meaningfully be said and understood about the subject. As Blommaert (2005) summarizes, "Whenever we speak, we speak from within a particular *regime of language* (the title of Kroskrity 2000)" (102; italics in original). The Narrative has provided that regime from within which supporters and critics of the Bush administration have operated.

Regardless of the accuracy of the assumptions and explanations that the Narrative forwards about America's struggle against terrorism since September 11, 2001, the knowledge that it spawns serves as the truth in the sense that it produces real effects in the world. Although it may or may not

---

1. Although events and objects certainly exist in the world regardless of whether or how they are talked about, following Foucault, my aim here is to place primary importance on the meanings given to those events and objects. Such meanings—in effect, social realities—are brought into existence through discourse.

be empirically valid that Saddam Hussein had ties to Al Qaeda and possessed weapons of mass destruction, if a significant number of people believe it to be true, real consequences result.[2] Thus, truth is not simply an object external to social interaction; but rather, a form of knowledge emergent from that interaction. In this book, I highlight the textual and intertextual nature of the process that makes it possible for the powerful discursive formation that is the Bush "War on Terror" Narrative to gain significant traction in public understandings since 9/11. By examining the formation and circulation of such powerful narratives, we gain insight into the social effects that text production and circulation can have in sustaining regimes of truth and producing real world actions.

DISCOURSE AND DISCOURSES

Central to the analysis in this book is a broad understanding of discourse, which takes into account Foucault's (1972) conception of the term. Thus, it is important to lay some definitional groundwork by differentiating between discourse in the linguistic sense and discourses in the Foucauldian sense. Most simply, the term *discourse* refers to language use; and the study of discourse from a sociolinguistic perspective deals with the situated use of language, or language use in context (Brown and Yule 1983). Yet Foucault's notion of discourse adds a different understanding. Foucault speaks not just of discourse, but of "a discourse" or "discourses" (as a count noun). A discourse is a "way of representing the knowledge about [. . .] a particular topic at a particular historical moment" (Hall 1997: 44). It refers to the "forms of knowledge or powerful sets of assumptions, expectations and explanations, governing mainstream social and cultural practices" (Baxter 2003: 7). In other words, a discourse regulates the way a topic can be talked about meaningfully in a particular culture at a particular point in history. For example, Foucault (1978) examines the discourse of sexuality, which provides a way for talking about and governing forms of sexual behavior. As Foucault describes, it only makes sense to talk about certain social subjects (e.g., the "homosexual") within this particular discourse, or discursive formation. Moreover, for Foucault, *discourse* not

---

2. One could innumerate those consequences in the countless lives lost and dollars spent since the U.S. invasion of Iraq in 2003, which the discourse surrounding the "war on terror" helped justify. What I wish to underscore is the importance of language in the manufacturing of consent for war in a democratic society. As Nelson (2003) emphasizes, "Human conflict begins and ends via talk and text. [. . .] It is discourse that prepares for sacrifice, justifies inhumanity, absolves from guilt, and demonizes the enemy" (449).

only refers to objects of knowledge, but constitutes those objects of knowledge. Thus, "'the homosexual' as a specific kind of social subject, was *produced*, and could only make its appearance" (Hall 1997: 46; italics in original) within the discourse of sexuality that arose, as Foucault (1978) documents, in the late nineteenth century.

Within the context of this book's topic, the Bush "War on Terror" Narrative provides a way for talking about America's response to terrorism after September 11, 2001. This discourse, in the Foucauldian sense, governs public discussion and debate on the topic. It provides a common language to refer to objects of knowledge. For example, the crashing of airplanes into the World Trade Center becomes an "act of war" that launches a "war on terror." Moreover, this discourse effectively constitutes these and other understandings of the world. Instead of being seen as one among several possible interpretations, the "war on terror" discourse becomes naturalized as a widely accepted, "common sense" way for viewing and talking about 9/11 and America's response to terrorism. In Foucauldian terms, the Narrative represents the knowledge about this topic and thereby constrains what can be meaningfully said about it.

Gee (1996, 2005) provides a helpful way of thinking about these different notions of discourse with his labels "little d" discourse versus "big D" discourse. By "little d" discourse, Gee (2005) means discourse in the linguistic sense, that is, "language-in-use, or stretches of language" (26). In contrast, "big D" discourse encompasses the forms of cultural knowledge bound up in specific domains of language use—that is, discourse in the Foucauldian sense.

Fairclough (1992a, 1992b, 2000, inter alia) brings both the linguistic (i.e., "little d") and Foucauldian (i.e., "big D") notions of discourse into Critical Discourse Analysis (CDA). Whereas Foucault primarily deals with discourse in the macrolevel sense of the term, Fairclough and others attempt to provide analysis of microlevel discursive action to illustrate how that situated use of language relates to larger discourses. Phillips (1996), for example, operates from a CDA perspective to examine the connection between "little d" discursive action (in the form of political speeches, press reportage, and interviews) and the "big D" discourse of Thatcherism that arose during her tenure as prime minister of the UK. In linguistic anthropology, Inoue (2006) examines a similar type of connection between "little d" discourse and the larger discourse about Japanese women's language, which, as Inoue shows, arose as "an obligatory cultural category and an unavoidable part of practical social knowledge" in Japan (1). In a similar vein, the goal of this book is to examine the relationship between microlevel discursive action—in the form of presidential speeches and public discourse—and the shared cultural understandings bound up in the macrolevel Bush "War on Terror" Narrative.

TEXT AND INTERTEXTUALITY

In his discussion of text and power, Hanks (1989) notes how text production and reception impact perceptions of social reality. In many ways, this describes the Bush "War on Terror" Narrative qua text, which is, as Hanks (1989) describes of text more generally, "a powerful mode of naturalizing social reality" (Hanks 1989: 118). Through the production and circulation of text, "historically specific social facts become invisible and unquestionable" (Hanks 1989: 118). In the Narrative, the events of 9/11 become "acts of war" invisible to alternative interpretations and America's response to terrorism unquestionably becomes a "war on terror." Even for those who oppose the policy and actions that the Narrative justifies, they cannot help but acknowledge and interact with this powerful text as they resist the policy it entails. Importantly, the production and reception of the Narrative, as with any text that accrues into a shared cultural narrative, cannot take place unless it is subject to an iterative process—an *intertextuality*—whereby it is reinscribed across different interactional contexts.

The notion of intertextuality—a term associated with Kristeva's (1980) articulation of Bakhtin's (1981, 1986) dialogism and widely taken up by sociocultural linguists (note, for example, A.L. Becker's role in introducing intertextuality to sociolinguistics as well as its influential use by Richard Bauman and Charles Briggs within linguistic anthropology)—is useful for the analysis of political discourse because it emphasizes the connections across multiple discursive encounters where issues are formulated and contested. Intertextual connections involve a process whereby a given piece of discourse is lifted from one setting—that is, it is *decontextualized*—and is inserted into another setting where it is *recontextualized* (Bauman and Briggs 1990). When a piece of discourse is moved from one context to another, it carries along aspects of the earlier context; but it is also transformed in the new context.

In the perspective on language forwarded by Bakhtin (1981, 1986; see also, Voloshinov 1973), any use of language is effectively implicated in a wider dialogue where "the utterance is related not only to preceding, but also to subsequent links in the chain of speech communion" (Bakhtin 1986: 94). For example, within the context of a political speech where the audience is primarily limited to nonverbal responses (i.e., applause, cheers, jeers), the speaker must account for both the immediate audience and "an indefinite, unconcretized *other*" (Bakhtin 1986: 95). That political speech builds upon what has previously been said (e.g., in media commentary) and anticipates potential responses of the present audience as well as the wider public.[3] President Bush's speeches about the "war on terror" enter into a chain of connections whereby language from the speeches is taken up and recontextualized in the media and in public interactions. In turn, Bush's speeches may themselves be shaped by pressures from the responses that take place in these contexts.

Whereas the concept of intertextuality applies to both spoken and written discourse, the use of this term among literary theorists such as Kristeva (see also Barthes 1967, 1974, 1977) has mainly been associated with the study of written texts.[4] Given linguistic anthropologists' focus on spoken interaction, the term *interdiscursivity* has been used within that field to refer to the same phenomena but with a focus on spoken discourse. In his commentary on the papers in Agha and Wortham (2005), Bauman (2005) echoes many of the contributors in voicing a preference for the term interdiscursivity: "*Interdiscursive*, I would submit, is a better general term, as various members of the panel have suggested, reserving *intertextuality* for matters having to do with [written] texts" (146).

Yet this consensus does not necessarily hold across the broader coalition of sociocultural linguistics.[5] Notably, within CDA, Fairclough (1992a) keeps intertextuality as a general term but, following French discourse analysts (Authier-Révuz 1982, Maingueneau 1987), provides finer level distinctions between what he terms *manifest intertextuality* and *constitutive intertextuality*. "In manifest intertextuality, other texts are explicitly present in the text under analysis; they are 'manifestly' marked or cued by features on the surface of the text, such as quotation marks" (Fairclough 1992a: 104). Constitutive intertextuality, on the other hand, refers to the confluence of discourse conventions—including genres, voices, and types of discourse—that weave together to form a text. In this typology, Fairclough uses *interdiscursivity* as a synonym for *constitutive intertextuality*.

For the framework forwarded in this book, I have chosen to adopt the term *intertextuality*. Although I am primarily, but not exclusively, dealing

---

3. To underscore this notion of *dialogism*, Jakobson (1953) notes that "dialogue underlies even inner speech" (15; quoted in Mannheim and Tedlock 1995: 7).

4. In fact, Bakhtin (1981, 1986) himself often articulated his ideas in reference to spoken discourse.

5. I follow Bucholtz and Hall (2005, 2008) in using the term *sociocultural linguistics* to refer to the broad coalition of scholars centrally concerned with the role language plays in social and cultural life, which includes linguistic anthropologists, sociolinguists, and discourse analysts.

with spoken discourse throughout my analysis, the term *intertextuality* is preferable for several reasons. As is widely recognized within sociocultural linguistics, a text, whether written or spoken, simply refers to a product of discursive action (Hanks 1989: 95). A large focus of the book is on the construction of the textual product that is the Bush "War on Terror" Narrative. This product then becomes, in Gal's (2006) words, an "objectified unit of discourse that is lifted from its interactional setting" (178). Given the focus in this book on the lifting of such discourse units from one setting and their reinsertion into another, the notion of a "permutation of texts, an intertextuality," as conveyed by Kristeva (1980: 36), seems wholly appropriate. Moreover, in light of Fairclough's narrow definition of interdiscursivity, my choice of the term *intertextuality* avoids introducing any unnecessary confusion to audiences that use the term *interdiscursivity* in different ways.

With my use of intertextuality in this book I have in mind the types of intertextual connections that can be captured under Derrida's (1977) terms *iterability* and *citationality*. Iterability refers to the general repetition of texts across different contexts. As a result, an intertextual series (Hanks 1986) may form where a particular text, introduced in one context, is repeatedly inscribed in subsequent contexts. The texts are reiterated without acknowledging a source for the text. A common example of iterability in political discourse is the use of slogans. The repetition of such texts in various contexts by a "permutation of individuals across speech-act roles" (Agha 2003: 247) works to establish and reinforce a message across overlapping settings. For example, during the 2004 U.S. presidential elections, the Bush campaign introduced the phrase "flip flopper" to characterize Democratic candidate John Kerry. As Bush supporters and campaign officials reiterated this slogan across multiple encounters, it helped to reinforce a negative characterization of Kerry as indecisive. The iteration of the Narrative across the numerous contexts of presidential speeches is another example. Frequently, however, when a text is brought into a new context, overt attention is drawn to the context from which it was lifted. This notion is captured with Derrida's (1977) *citationality*. Citationality is often achieved through reported speech frames where prior text is directly or indirectly quoted. In political debates, for example, candidates frequently quote words previously uttered by an opponent. Such quotations of prior words draw attention to the previous context in which those words were spoken while reinterpreting them within the current interactional setting.

Any use of language, or what Becker (1995) terms *languaging*, involves a certain amount of "diachronic repetition" (Tannen 1989), which involves "taking old language. . .and pushing. . .it into new contexts" (Becker 1995: 185). Prior text is inevitably reshaped in this process where it is not simply repeated, but effectively reworked. Drawing from Goffman (1974), Tannen (2006) discusses this process in terms of "recycling," "re-keying," or "reframing" prior text (see also, Gordon 2006 and Tovares 2005). Or, as Kristeva (1980) points out, imitation may be done "seriously, claiming and appropriating it [prior text] without relativizing it" or the process of recontextualization may introduce "a signification opposed to that of the other's word" (73). In its extreme, resignification may move into the realm of parody (Bakhtin 1981: 340, Coupland 2007: 175, Álvarez-Cáccamo 1996: 38). The key point is that the reshaping of prior text may occur with varying degrees of fidelity to its meaning in the originating context.[6]

PRESIDENTIAL SPEECHES, MEDIA DISCOURSE AND FOCUS GROUP DATA

Data for this study come from three primary domains: presidential speeches, media discourse, and focus group interviews with politically active college students. These different types of data work together to provide a holistic picture of the way the Bush "War on Terror" Narrative is both constructed and recontextualized across different settings.

First, presidential speeches provide a prime means for conveying the Bush administration's official narrative about the "war on terror" (Klocke 2004: 31). Given the rehearsed nature of these speeches, they articulate a perspective that has been well thought out and is representative of a larger set of ideas that underlies much of the administration's discourse and policies. For this reason, I examine a large corpus of presidential speeches to analyze key elements of the Narrative and show how it is discursively achieved. These speeches comprise the bulk of the data drawn on in chapters 2–4, where the focus is on the construction of the Narrative by the President.

The speeches come from a large body of addresses delivered throughout George W. Bush's tenure in the White House, stretching from September 11, 2001 through March 19, 2008. I collected these publicly available speeches from the White House web site (www.whitehouse.gov).[7] My initial collection netted 315 public speeches; I then looked through the

6. I use the term *originating* rather than *original* because, as pointed out by literary theorists (e.g., Kristeva 1980, Barthes 1977, Derrida 1976, inter alia), any text is always comprised of prior texts so that it is misleading to speak of an "original" context (Allen 2000: 36; see also, Derrida's 1978 notion of *différance*).

7. The archived web site for the Bush White House is available at http://georgewbush-whitehouse.archives.gov.

White House transcripts of these speeches and pulled out 70 speeches that focused significantly on 9/11 and the "war on terror." These 70 speeches, although not inclusive of every speech touching upon 9/11 during Bush's tenure, provide a comprehensive corpus on that topic. They consist of major public addresses that include State of the Union speeches, prime-time addresses to the nation, speeches that mark salient events (e.g., the anniversaries of 9/11, the "end of combat operations in Iraq"), and policy speeches on the "war on terror" (a complete listing can be found in appendix A). Moreover, I chose speeches that also had publicly available video (or audio) recordings, which I watched and/or listened to as I prepared excerpts for the analysis so that the transcriptions capture the discursive details of Bush's delivery. The resulting data are representative of the larger patterns that can be found across the corpus of presidential speeches, in particular, and the Bush administration discourse on the "war on terror," in general.

Although I use a standard prosaic representation of the data in the first part of chapter 2 and chapter 3, I adopt a poetic representation of the data for the second part of chapter 2 and chapter 4. In the latter case, I adapt Gee's (1986) poetic structural approach and represent the data in lines and stanzas. Line breaks represent rhetorical pauses in the delivery and help portray the flow of the speech. An advantage of this transcription technique is a better visual representation of rhetorical parallelism and the juxtaposition of elements in the narrative. The lines are grouped into stanzas based on their representation of a narrow topic within the broader theme (transcription conventions for the speeches are provided in appendix B).

Presidential speeches are a type of public performance, generally written and rehearsed in advance of their delivery. Other than televised addresses to the nation, most presidential speeches are typically delivered live to a limited audience of mainly partisan supporters and later recontextualized in media coverage for playback to the nation. Thus, the speech giver is speaking to multiple audiences at once; and importantly, is implicated in a wider dialogue with those audiences in the Bakhtinian sense of dialogism. The speech may react to previous commentary and anticipate future reactions in the national dialogue.[8]

---

8. In addition, the role of the President and others in crafting and delivering the speech may be elaborated upon with Goffman's (1981) notion of the participation framework. When the President delivers a speech, he is both the *animator* and *principal* of a message that is formulated along with the help of other *strategists* (Goffman 1974). In addition, the speech itself is written by at least one *author* (Goffman 1981; Bell 1991) with varying levels of input given by the President and strategists in this process.

Whereas presidential speeches provide a means for isolating the macrolevel Bush "War on Terror" Narrative, additional forms of media discourse are needed to examine ways in which the Narrative is recontextualized across different settings. For this reason, media discourse data figure prominently in chapter 5, where I focus on how language associated with the Narrative is reshaped.

The media discourse data were collected via the Google search engine. As Hill (2005) illustrates in her examination of intertextual series of mock Spanish items, "Google technology provides a powerful new avenue for exploring dimensions of indexicality and for modeling intertextual series" (123). Taking her cue, I employed the Google News Archive Search to examine key phrases associated with the Narrative. The Google News Archive searches content from major newspapers and magazines as well as news and legal archives. The search can specify dates (or ranges of dates) as well as sources (e.g., *New York Times, Washington Post, Wall Street Journal*, Fox News, CNN, CBS, MSNBC). Google News Archive can sort results both according to relevance and according to a chronological time line. In the search results, it recommends the most significant year for the search item and provides a time-line graphic to represent the relative distribution of articles found over the specified date range. Effectively, the Google News Archive Search provides a chronological snapshot of an intertextual series. One can gain an idea of when a key phrase first enters into significant circulation in the media and how its use evolves over time.

After analyzing the construction of the Narrative in presidential speeches, I pulled out several key phrases associated with it—that is, what are often referred to as sound bites or talking points. These included phrases such as "war on terror," "central front in the war on terror," "terrorists and tyrants," "weapons of mass destruction" (and permutations such as "weapons of mass distraction" or "weapons of mass deception"), "stay on the offense," "fighting the terrorists in Iraq," and "either you are with us or with the terrorists/the enemy/against us." I also included searches with combined terms such as "war on terror" and World War II, "war on terror" and Vietnam, as well as Iraq and Vietnam. In examining the search results, I ignored results that were merely reprinted transcripts of Bush's speeches and focused on results from major media outlets in the United States. These sources include newspapers of record and news wires—the *New York Times, Washington Post, Wall Street Journal*, and Associated Press—as well as the web sites of broadcast media—CNN, Fox News, MSNBC, CBS, ABC, NPR, and PBS. As I went through the results, I saved articles from these sources at different points along the time line, which allowed me to compile a corpus of about 330 articles. Given the search tool and method, this corpus provides a representative sample of the way language associated with the Narrative was recontextualized across the major U.S. media between September 11, 2001 and March 2008.

As an example, a search for the phrase "central front in the war on terror" returned approximately 1,600 results. The first occurrences in the archive began to appear in September 2003, after Bush began using the phrase in speeches about Iraq and the "war on terror." Examining the results by year shows the phrase returning more results as the intertextual series becomes better established in the media. The various permutations of the phrase include direct and indirect quotations of Bush in reportage, and iterations of the phrase by others in the media without directly citing the President. In the analysis, I follow such phrases across different contexts to examine the reification and resistance of the Narrative in public discourse. I represent these data as found, and the features of written representation chosen by the journalists and used in the reportage (e.g., presence or absence of quotations marks or capitalization patterns) figure into the analysis.

The final piece of data comes from discussions I held between February 2007 and April 2008 with politically involved college students who attended school in the western United States. Although the media play a significant role in how the nation talks about political issues, it is also important to understand how citizens view and discuss politics in discussions with each other (van Leeuwen 2005). These data are important because they illustrate the way individuals who are not in the media spotlight understand America's response to terrorism and recontextualize the language associated with the Narrative when they talk politics.

In collecting the focus group data, I talked with twenty-six college Democrats and Republicans. The students' involvement in politics included membership in their political party's campus chapter and/or participation in their party's 2008 caucuses. I attended meetings of both the college Democrats and Republicans during the spring of 2007 where I recruited my initial pool of participants. I recruited additional participants at the Democratic and Republican caucuses in 2008. Most of the students ranged in age from 18 to 24 with one student who was 32 years of age. Their position in school varied from first year students to seniors, and also included one first-year graduate student. Their majors encompassed the social sciences (e.g., political science, international affairs, economics), the natural sciences (e.g., engineering, computer science, environmental science), and the humanities (e.g., music, classics, literature). Except for two who identified as Hispanic and one as South Asian, the rest identified as white or Caucasian, a racial make-up representative of the broader campus community. The pool included twenty men and six women. This lack of gender parity was primarily due to the composition of the political groups from which I recruited participants. I encountered more men at the meetings I attended, especially among the campus Republicans. Although the resulting subject pool, therefore, provides a decidedly male bias, this bias is representative of the groups more generally. Politically, fourteen identified as Democrats and twelve identified as Republicans. However, two of those Republicans qualified their self-identification by noting that they were more closely aligned with the Libertarian party and had only recently registered as Republicans to caucus for presidential candidate Ron Paul.

I met with these students individually or in small groups of two to four. In an attempt to lessen the formality of the audio-recorded interview situation, I framed our meetings as informal conversations over coffee, and most of the discussions took place in the student union, a place where students gather at tables to eat, talk, or study. Given these students' interest in politics, they were keen to discuss their views. I started off each interview by asking them what they saw as some of the more important issues facing the nation. Eventually, we made our way through a gamut of core issues covered in all of the discussions, including the Bush administration's response to 9/11 and terrorism, the "war on terror," the war in Iraq, media bias, and their thoughts on particular politicians. They also talked about additional issues, such as health care, the economy, and the environment, as their interests dictated. In the end, I conducted fifteen sessions; the average time of each meeting was slightly over an hour. This gave me a total of sixteen hours of focus group data for the analysis (see transcription conventions in appendix C).

OVERVIEW OF THE CHAPTERS

The chapters that follow provide a two-part analysis of the formation (chapters 2–4) and recontextualization (chapters 5–7) of the Bush "War on Terror" Narrative. Chapter 2, "The Characterization of 9/11 and America's Response to Terrorism," examines the central element of the Narrative: the plight of a nation at war. Along with the basic use of the war metaphor, the Narrative draws from past conflicts in the nation's history to position the "war on terror" as one with parallels to World War II and the Cold War.

Chapter 3, "The Narrative's Part-Whole Textual Interdependence," provides a schematic overview of the constituent elements that make up the Narrative and shows how they fit together to form a coherent text. Although I take my examples from specific speeches, these examples are representative of the larger body of speeches about the "war on terror" delivered by George W. Bush during the last seven years of his presidency. Thus, although the analysis draws from situated narrative performances, the result is to distill from these representative examples the larger cultural narrative about the "war on terror" shared by the nation as a whole.

Chapter 4, "The Construction of Al Qaeda and Iraq as Linked Antagonists," focuses on the process of constructing an enemy in times of war. Central to any narrative are the principal characters, and this chapter uses data from presidential speeches to illustrate the way two disparate enemies of the United States—Iraq and Al Qaeda—are discursively positioned as interchangeable adversaries in the "war on terror." The "socially recognized sameness" (Bucholtz and Hall 2004: 383) of these otherwise disparate entities is a discursive achievement that allows the war in Iraq to be but a battle in the broader "war on terror." It also establishes a powerful understanding about the nation's enemy and the role of the United States in Iraq. These aspects find their way into subsequent recontextualizations explored in the remaining chapters.

Chapter 5, "Intertextual Series: Reproduction and Resistance in the Media," shifts the analytic focus to the recontextualization of the Narrative in national discourse where the media play an important role in its circulation. The chapter begins by exploring "strategies of entextualization" (Wilce 2005) that make later quotations of discourse highly likely. Such strategies include the formulation of catchy phrases (i.e., sound bites) and easily repeatable articulations of political positions (i.e., talking points) that work to assert control over the way pieces of discourse enter into subsequent settings. As key phrases enter into circulation, they form the basis of an intertextual series. One effect of this reiteration across contexts is to further solidify the larger narrative with which they are associated. However, while reiteration of prior text may maintain fidelity to a meaning already established, it may also introduce "a signification opposed to that of the other's word" (Kristeva 1980: 73). Challenge and resistance may occur through metapragmatic comments that overtly evaluate prior text (Buttny 1997, 1998) or through the simple refraction of meaning that takes place anytime prior text is introduced into a new context (Voloshinov 1971). In examining these strategies, I illustrate the way key phrases associated with the Narrative (e.g., "central front in the war on terror") are reshaped and given new social meanings.

Chapter 6, "Talking Politics: The Narrative's Reception among College Students," continues to explore the themes developed in chapter 5.

Here, instead of focusing on media discourse, I look at the language used by politically active college students to discuss politics and their own views about terrorism and the war in Iraq. By examining focus group data, the aim is to understand how these students receive and reshape the discourse of the "war on terror" as they interact with each other. As Foucault (1972) notes, "there can be no statement that in one way or another does not reactualize others" (98). This chapter illustrates the way social actors draw upon a reservoir of words in social circulation to reinscribe, resist and (re)interpret the Narrative.

Chapter 7, "Whose Vietnam?: Discursive Competition over the Vietnam Analogy," explores an important aspect of the Narrative: its ability to subsume disparate foreign policy objectives under the rubric of the "war on terror." For the Bush administration, Iraq has become the "central front in the war on terror," even though critics of the administration resist this categorization of sociopolitical reality and work to define Iraq and the "war on terror" (or more specifically, the conflict in Afghanistan) as unrelated ventures. Moreover, in voicing opposition to the Iraq war, many opponents have made analogies between Iraq and Vietnam. This chapter takes data from media discourse, focus group interviews, and presidential speeches to examine the way Bush has attempted to appropriate the Vietnam analogy from his critics and reshape it for use within the Narrative. Although critics use the Vietnam analogy to represent Iraq as a messy quagmire that lacks a broader strategic objective, Bush repositions Vietnam as central to the Cold War's struggle against Communism just as Iraq is said to be central to the broader war against terrorism. The chapter provides a fitting end to the analysis by illustrating that even dominant macrolevel narratives are dialogically revised amidst pressures from oppositional voices.

Chapter 8 concludes by discussing the implications of the book's analysis. Importantly, sociopolitical reality requires more than a single authoritative pronouncement to be established. It is through multiple, overlapping discursive encounters that social meanings are constructed and contested. Understanding the power of political discourse to shape sociopolitical reality, therefore, requires a focus on intertextuality. Moreover, because any piece of discourse is exposed to potential resignification in new settings, the examination of the intertextual connections in political discourse also holds the key to understanding the roots of social transformation. The chapter closes this comprehensive look at the Bush administration's discourse about terrorism in light of the shifting rhetorical landscape brought on by the new Obama administration.

The Characterization of 9/11 and America's Response to Terrorism

I stand before you as a wartime president. I wish I
didn't have to say that, but an enemy that attacked us
on September the 11th, 2001, declared war on the
United States of America. And war is what we're
engaged in.

—George W. Bush (2007, August 22)

INTRODUCTION

The focus on the textual elements of the Narrative in the first part of the
analysis (chapters 2–4) starts with two key premises. First, language is
not a transparent medium of communication that simply mirrors the
world and denotes presumably stable meanings. Rather, as discourse
scholars widely recognize, the constitutive dimension of language (Taylor 1985) sets up relations among individuals, establishes shared meanings, and constructs the social reality in which we live. Second, as
Riessman (1993) notes, "narratives structure perceptual experience"
(2). There is nothing inherent in the events of 9/11 that demanded the
interpretation forwarded in the Bush "War on Terror" Narrative. Yet this

particular narrative has effectively organized a collective reaction to the events shared by many Americans.

In this chapter, I examine how the generic framework of a nation at war provides a highly recognizable template for narrating the "war on terror." The interpretation of 9/11 as an act of war flows from the linguistic realization of the war metaphor, which helps situate the Narrative within the genre of war. The details of the "war on terror" are then fleshed out through the use of analogies with past conflicts in the nation's history. These historical precedents, namely, World War II and the Cold War, act as exploitable source domains in the formulation of new understandings about the struggle against terrorism. They provide exemplars of the generic war script, and comparisons with these models work to naturalize America's response to terrorism as a "war on terror."

GENRE AND THE INTERTEXTUAL GAP

Bruner (1991) outlines several features involved in the narrative construction of reality, including *genericness* and *particularity*. He reminds us that we know how to recognize different kinds of narrative, such as tragedy or comedy or romance. Genres such as these provide conventionalized expectations that guide the interpretation of particular narratives. The narrator draws from a generic precedent to frame a text; then the particulars of a narrative are mapped onto these generic frameworks. The result, Bruner (1991) summarizes, is to "provide both writer and reader with commodious and conventional 'models' for limiting the hermeneutic task of making sense of human happenings" (14).

In Hanks's (1987) words, genres provide "orienting frameworks, interpretive procedures, and sets of expectations that are not part of discourse structure, but of the way actors relate to and use languages" (670; see also, Bauman 1986). In many ways, genre is similar to Goffman's (1974) notion of a *primary framework*, which "allows its user to locate, perceive, identify, and label a seemingly infinite number of concrete occurrences defined in its terms" (21). Like a Goffmanian frame, genre plays an important role in text interpretation and in regulating intertextual relations by patterning discourse into culturally recognized types and thereby providing expectations associated with those types.

In their discussion of genre, Briggs and Bauman (1992) introduce the notion of an *intertextual gap*, referring to the distance between a text and the genre conventions associated with it. The fidelity of a given text to appropriate genre conventions can be manipulated by social actors to create certain effects. Importantly, "texts framed in some genres attempt to achieve generic transparency by *minimizing* the distance between texts and genres, thus rendering the discourse maximally interpretable through the use of generic precedents" (Briggs and Bauman 1992: 149).

In the Bush "War on Terror" Narrative, the particulars of 9/11 and America's response to terrorism are mapped onto the familiar human plight of a nation at war. The generic script of a nation at war provides a ready-made cultural framework to aid in both telling and interpreting the Narrative. Alternative generic scripts certainly exist and can be seen operating in public discussion of terrorist acts. Instead of the plight of a nation at war, for example, we could instead hear the tale of a horrific crime. In such a narrative, the events of 9/11 would alternatively be framed as a criminal act instead of an act of war. In both of these possible formulations, generic precedents provide the basic foundation upon which the particulars are laid and thereby interpreted.

Notably, metaphor and analogy play a central role in minimizing the intertextual gap in the Narrative. Metaphor aids the mapping of particulars onto a generic script by connecting the particulars (e.g., 9/11 and terrorism) to the genre (e.g., the war genre) through the comparison of different domains of experience. Like a generic script, a metaphor's source domain acts as a basis for making the novel, unfamiliar, and incomprehensible seem familiar, understandable, and easily identifiable. Therefore, the use of metaphor can effectively suppress the *intertextual gap* (Briggs and Bauman 1992) between *particularity* and *genericness* (Bruner 1991), making the text easily interpretable. Moreover, although the war metaphor represents a particular ideological perspective on how to deal with terrorism, this ideological dimension gets erased when alternative perspectives no longer sound as plausible due to their incongruity with the established framework of a nation at war.

METAPHOR AND IDEOLOGY

A great deal of contemporary scholarship exists on the topic of metaphor (Lakoff 1993; Lakoff and Johnson 1980, 1999; Lakoff and Turner 1989; Ortony 1993; inter alia), and many insights from this research have been applied to the arena of politics (Chilton and Lakoff 1995; Zinken 2003; Musolff 2004; inter alia) and the study of discourse more generally (Corts and Pollio 1999; Koller 2003; Cameron and Stelma 2004; Musolff 2006; Semino 2008; inter alia). The theory of conceptual metaphor forwarded by Lakoff (1993; Lakoff and Johnson 1980, 1999) provides a basic starting point for this research, including the current chapter, even though I diverge from the Lakovian emphasis on cognition to focus on the linguistic realization of metaphor in discourse and its connection with ideology. Furthermore, I broaden my focus to look at explicit historical comparisons, or analogies.

In Lakoff and Johnson's (1980) words, *"The essence of metaphor is understanding and experiencing one kind of thing in terms of another"* (5; italics in original). Accordingly, language users utilize a source domain as the basis of comparison for a target domain. Fillmore's (1982, 1985) notion of a semantic frame (see also, Lakoff's 1987 idealized cognitive model) is helpful for fleshing out the conceptual nature of metaphor. A frame, according to Fillmore (1985), refers to "specific unified frameworks of knowledge, or coherent schematizations of experience" (Fillmore 1985: 23; see also Chilton and Schäffner 2002: 26, Werth 1999: 107; compare to Tannen and Wallat 1987). In other words, a frame comprises the background knowledge that is called upon to provide context for a word's usage and meaning in a given situation. For example, the family frame is accessed when the words *father, mother, sister,* and *brother* are used. Without the underlying area of experience provided by the family frame, these particular words would make little sense. Thus, frames are intimately tied into sociocultural context and built from the knowledge derived through an individual's interaction with society.[1]

In the Lakovian framework, metaphorical language is the surface manifestation of cross-domain mappings at the cognitive level. Thus, metaphors are not just poetical devices but are integral to the way we experience and conceptualize the world. In one example, Lakoff and Johnson (1980) point out that we talk about—and also conceptualize and reason about—arguments in terms of war. This conceptual metaphor, ARGUMENT IS WAR, is realized linguistically when we say things such as, "He attacked my arguments" or "She shot down all of my arguments." They explain that "we don't just talk about arguments in terms of war," but the metaphor actually "structures the actions we perform in arguing" (Lakoff and Johnson 1980: 4).

The Lakovian view on metaphor holds important similarities with the perspective on narrative forwarded by Bruner (1991). As Lakoff and Johnson (1980) remark, metaphors "play a central role in the construction of

---

1. Lakoff's model focuses more on bodily experience than cultural experience. Zinken (2003), therefore, distinguishes between *correlational metaphors*, which result from embodied physical experience, and *intertextual metaphors*, which "are the product of a specific cultural situatedness" (509). Importantly, the metaphors and analogies discussed in this chapter all rely on cultural experience to a large degree.

social and political reality" (159). After all, metaphor is a linguistic device used in the representation of the world. Compare this to the way Semino (2008) connects metaphor and representation via Halliday's *ideational function* of language. For Halliday (1973), the ideational function of language represents reality and expresses meaning "in terms of the speaker's experience and that of the speech community" (37). Metaphor plays a notable role in mapping a speaker's (and community's) experience from a source domain onto a target domain. Although metaphors may be conventionalized to a large degree within a given culture (as Lakoff and Johnson describe earlier), metaphors also play an important role in constructing understandings of novel events, like 9/11.

Importantly, metaphors—and more broadly, the explicit comparisons in analogies—work to frame[2] an issue under discussion; and the way an issue is framed varies with the ideological position of the speaker. In this way, critical discourse analysts (e.g., Fairclough 1989) have examined metaphors for what they convey about the ideological underpinnings of discourse. As Chilton and Schäffner (2002) explain, "Metaphor can provide a conceptual structure for a systematized ideology that is expressed in many texts and much talk" (29). In short, "different metaphors have different ideological attachments" (Fairclough 1989: 119).

Ideology, simply defined, "involves the representation of 'the world' from the perspective of a particular interest" (Fairclough 1995a: 44). It involves the "mental frameworks" (Hall 1996: 26) or shared "social beliefs that organize and coordinate the social interpretations and practices of groups and their members" (van Dijk 1998: 8). As critical linguists have widely pointed out, language use is never neutral. It always conveys some ideological perspective on the world.

Voloshinov (1973) emphasizes the point that all language use is ideological in his discussion of what he calls "one of the most important problems in the science of meanings, the problem of the *interrelationship between meaning and evaluation*" (103; italics in original). He speaks of the "evaluative accent" of words and representations. As he explains, "No utterance can be put together without value judgment. Every utterance is above all an *evaluative orientation*" (Voloshinov 1973: 105; italics in original). The ideological underpinnings of language manifest themselves in

2. In *Frame Analysis*, Goffman (1974) discusses the issue of framing in detail. A Goffmanian frame (as opposed to the semantic frame described by Fillmore), refers to the "basic frameworks of understanding in our society for making sense out of events" (10). As described by Entman (1993), "To frame is to select some aspects of a perceived reality and make them more salient" (52; see also Tannen and Wallat 1987).

the everyday use of language to describe events and represent reality. "Because of the way language inevitably passes judgment on the world, even as it describes it, Voloshinov argues that rather than reflecting reality, language should be seen as 'refracting' it through the lens of social struggle" (Maybin 2001: 65). Put another way, language represents reality from the particular perspective of a speaker, and metaphors are a potent means to represent that perspective.

THE "WAR" AGAINST TERRORISM

Since 9/11, the Bush administration's response to terrorism has primarily been formulated within the framework of war. The administration argues that the "war on terror" is not merely a metaphorical war but a real war waged on many fronts (more on these "fronts" in chapter 3). Yet there are nevertheless metaphorical underpinnings to the "war on terror." The characterization of 9/11 as an act of war (rather than, as others have argued, a criminal act) and the response to terrorism as a "war on terror" (rather than an investigation into terrorist crimes) is a discursive achievement. This achievement has naturalized one characterization of 9/11 and America's response to terrorism as the dominant way to talk about the issue. Moreover, it has laid the groundwork for launching the very real military campaigns in Afghanistan and Iraq.

Here, I examine the metaphors used in the first three public speeches delivered by Bush after the events of 9/11: his televised address to the nation on the evening of September 11, a statement he made to the press after meeting with his national security team in the White House on September 12, and his address at the National Cathedral to mark the national day of prayer and remembrance on September 14. These speeches provide a glimpse into the initial discursive moves that formulated the "war on terror."

In the excerpts that follow, I have highlighted in italics the lexical correspondences associated with the two conceptual metaphors that are most ubiquitous in these speeches: TERRORISM IS WAR and TERRORISM IS CRIME (see appendix B for full transcription conventions). Other metaphors certainly exist, but these two represent important ideological positions in the debate over how to deal with terrorism.[3] Both are

---

3. Note, for example, the hunting metaphor used in excerpt 4 where the "enemy" is represented as an animal who hunts or "preys." The hunting metaphor is also used elsewhere in Bush's speeches—most notably, in lines that assert America's resolve in "hunting down the terrorists." See Silberstein (2002) for more on this metaphor within the framework of war.

present in Bush's characterization of 9/11, especially in his initial public reactions to the events. However, as the week unfolds, the war metaphor is put to greater use so that it dominates the crime frame in his speeches. In the following excerpt, we see Bush address the nation on the evening of September 11 when the interpretation of the events is incipient.

Excerpt 1. (Bush 2001, September 11)

Good evening. Today our fellow citizens, our way of life, our very freedom came under attack in a series of deliberate and deadly terrorist acts. The *victims* were in airplanes, or in their offices, secretaries, businessmen and women, military and federal workers, moms and dads, friends and neighbors. Thousands of lives were suddenly ended by evil, despicable acts of terror. The pictures of airplanes flying into buildings, fires burning, huge- huge structures collapsing, have filled us with disbelief, terrible sadness, and a quiet, unyielding anger. These *acts of mass murder* were intended to frighten our nation into chaos and *retreat*.

As Lakoff (2001) points out, "The crime frame entails law, courts, lawyers, trials, sentencing, appeals, and so on." It also entails "victims," a lexical correspondence seen in excerpt 1 (highlighted in italics). Also seen in excerpt 1 is reference to "acts of mass murder." Murder fits within the crime frame, but "mass murder" is less clear because such acts are often carried out by state actors who hold a monopoly on force. At the end of the excerpt, the word *retreat* corresponds to a war frame where the armies of nation-states are attacked and driven into retreat. Elsewhere in the speech, as seen in the next excerpt, additional lexical correspondences to the crime frame are present.

Excerpt 2. (Bush 2001, September 11)

The *search is underway* for those who are behind these evil acts. I've directed the full resources of our intelligence and law enforcement communities to find those responsible and to *bring them to justice*.

Criminals are the subject of a search, and in excerpt 2 Bush declares "the search is underway." He makes explicit reference to the use of law enforcement "to bring them to justice." Yet the characterization shifts significantly toward the end of the speech, as seen in the next excerpt.

Excerpt 3. (Bush 2001, September 11)

America and our friends and allies join with all those who want peace and security in the world, and we stand together to win the *war against terrorism*.

In excerpt 3, we see the first reference to "the war against terrorism." This characterization of an act of terrorism is very different from the more neutral descriptor used by President Bill Clinton in a speech given on August 27, 1998 in the wake of the terrorist bombings of the American embassies in Kenya and Tanzania. In the speech, Clinton references "our struggle against terrorism." Moreover, in his radio address to the nation on August 8, 1998, immediately after those bombings, Clinton clearly invokes the crime frame in his response: "No matter how long it takes or where it takes us, we will pursue terrorists until the cases are solved and justice is done." Whereas crimes are "solved," wars are either "won" or "lost." Moreover, wars involve "attacks" by an "enemy" (as opposed to a "suspect") and "battles." These lexical correspondences of the war frame dominate the speech given by Bush on September 12, as seen in excerpts 4 and 5

Excerpt 4. (Bush 2001, September 12)

I've just completed a meeting with my national security team, and we've received um the latest intelligence updates. The deliberate and deadly *attacks* which were carried out yesterday against our country were more than acts of terror. They were *acts of war*. This will require our country to unite in steadfast determination and resolve. Freedom and democracy are *under attack*. The American people need to know that we're facing a different *enemy* than we have ever faced. This *enemy* hides in shadows, and has no regard for human life. This is an *enemy* who preys on innocent and unsuspecting people, then runs for cover. But it won't be able to run for cover forever. This is an *enemy* that tries to hide. But it won't be able to hide forever. This is an *enemy* that thinks its harbors are safe. But they won't be safe forever. This *enemy attacked* not just our people, but all freedom-loving people everywhere in the world. The United States of America will use all our resources to conquer this *enemy*. We will rally the world. We will be patient, we will be focused, and we will be steadfast in our determination. This *battle* will take time and resolve. But make no mistake about it, *we will win*.

Excerpt 5. (Bush 2001, September 12)

But we will not allow this *enemy* to *win the war* by changing our way
of life, or restricting our freedoms.

Leudar, Marsland and Nekvapil (2004) discuss the use of pronouns in
these speeches along with the reference to the nation as a whole rather than
"just those in the World Trade Center" (246). This works to conceptualize
the entire nation as under attack, which is consonant with the war frame. In
the speech on September 14, shown in the following excerpts 6–8, the con-
ceptualization of the events as war also dominates over the crime frame.

Excerpt 6. (Bush 2001, September 14)

On Tuesday *our country was attacked* with deliberate and massive cru-
elty. We have seen the images of fire and ashes, and bent steel. Now come
the names, the list of *casualties* we are only beginning to read. They are
the names of men and women who began their day at a desk or in an air-
port, busy with life. They are the names of people who faced death, and in
their last moments called home to say be brave, and I love you. They are
the names of passengers who defied their *murderers*, and *prevented the
murder* of others on the ground. They are the names of men and women
who *wore the uniform of the United States*, and *died at their posts*.

Excerpt 7. (Bush 2001, September 14)

War has been waged against us by stealth and deceit and murder.

Excerpt 8. (Bush 2001, September 14)

Our unity is a kinship of grief, and a steadfast resolve to prevail against
our enemies. And this unity against terror is now extending across the
world. America is a nation full of good fortune, with so much to be grate-
ful for. But we are not spared from suffering. In every generation, the
world has produced enemies of human freedom. *They have attacked
America*, because we are freedom's home and defender, and the commitment of our fathers is now the calling of our time.

In these excerpts, no longer do we hear of "victims" but rather of "casualties" as would be heard in news reports from a war zone. Among those
highlighted in the list of casualties are "the men and women who wore the

Table 2.1. Lexical correspondences associated with war frame and crime frame

War Frame	Crime Frame
Bush (2001, September 11)	Bush (2001, September 11)
1. retreat	1. victims
2. peace	2. acts of mass murder
3. war against terrorism	3. search is underway
	4. law enforcement communities
	5. bring them to justice
Bush (2001, September 12)	Bush (2001, September 12)
4. intelligence updates	—
5. acts of war	
6. under attack	
7. enemy (7 references)	
8. enemy attacked	
9. battle	
10. we will win	
11. win the war	
Bush (2001, September 14)	Bush (2001, September 14)
12. our country was attacked	6. murderers
13. casualties	7. prevented the murder
14. wore the uniform of the United States	
15. died at their posts	
16. war has been waged against us	
17. our enemies	
18. they have attacked America	

uniform of the United States." The nation as a whole is further invoked as the recipient of a foreign invader's actions: "war has been waged against us" (where "us" indexes the nation) and "they have attacked America" (where "they" indexes the foreign other).

In Table 2.1, I provide a comparative summary of the lexical correspondences from these three speeches associated with the conceptual metaphors TERRORISM IS WAR (left column) versus TERRORISM IS CRIME (right column). As can be seen, the war frame dominates the crime frame for characterizing 9/11 and America's response to terrorism.

Critically, the underlying conceptual metaphors used to represent 9/11 also represent a particular ideological perspective on how to deal with terrorism. As Fairclough (1989) notes, "Different metaphors imply different ways of dealing with things: one does not arrive at a negotiated settlement with cancer, though one might with an opponent in an argument. Cancer has to be eliminated, cut out" (120). Likewise, although one launches a criminal investigation in response to a criminal act, one wages a military campaign in response to an act of war.

The Narrative's interpretation of events is but one among other viable interpretations. Yet, as the Narrative continues to minimize the intertextual gap between the generic war schema and the particulars of 9/11, the premise that countering terrorism necessitates a "war on terror" becomes more plausible—and hence, more widely accepted in American society. Competing frameworks are pushed aside and the Narrative's call for a highly militarized foreign policy in response to terrorism becomes opaque to the underlying ideological position it represents. It is simply seen as a "common sense" interpretation or just "the way things are."

"Ideological dominance and hegemony is 'perfect' when dominated groups are unable to distinguish between their own interests and attitudes and those of dominant groups" (van Dijk 1998: 102; Gramsci 1971). Yet where there are differing ideological positions on an issue, resistance remains. Despite the prominence of the Narrative in American political life, Bush has had to defend its premise on how to deal with terrorism against competing ideological perspectives.

Amidst political resistance to the metaphorical "war on terror" and the militarized policy it entails, talk of the "war on terror" sometimes rises to the level of metadiscourse in the Narrative. In these moments, the ideological struggle underlying the characterization of terrorism becomes explicit (compare to Musolff 2004: 61, and Chilton 2004: 202 on metarepresentation). The next excerpt comes from Bush's 2004 State of the Union address where he lays out these different ideological positions.

Excerpt 9. (Bush 2004, January 20)

I know that some people question if America is really in a war at all. *They view terrorism more as a crime*, a problem to be solved mainly with *law enforcement* and *indictments*. After the World Trade Center was first attacked in 1993, some of *the guilty* were *indicted*, and *tried*, and *convicted*, and *sent to prison*. But the matter was not settled. The terrorists were still training and plotting in other nations, and drawing up more ambitious plans. After the chaos and carnage of September the 11th, *it is not enough to serve our enemies with legal papers*. The terrorists and their supporters *declared war* on the United States, and *war* is what they got.

The Bush "War on Terror" Narrative is certainly not formulated within a vacuum, unaffected by discourse taking place within the nation.

Rather, it exists, like any discourse, "on moving discursive ground" (Inoue 2006: 32). Importantly, the numerous speeches that contribute to the Narrative exist as part of a wider *dialogical network* (Leudar, Marsland and Nekvapil 2004). In excerpt 9, Bush takes account of what Bakhtin (1986) calls "an indefinite, unconcretized *other*." That "other" is those who oppose his characterization of the response to terrorism as a war in favor of a different ideological position that views a more appropriate response to terrorism through the use of law enforcement tools.[4]

In excerpt 9, Bush characterizes the position of his opponents as inadequate given his definition of the issue through the framework of war. In a line that brings together the lexical correspondences of the war and crime frames, he states that "it is not enough to serve our enemies with legal papers." The power of this utterance derives from the incongruence of "enemies" with "legal papers." Only criminals can be served "legal papers" in line with the crime frame. Consonant with the war frame, "enemies" should be dealt with on the battlefield. The mixing of the lexical correspondences of these two frames leads to a mismatch. Whereas serving a criminal with legal papers would seem wholly appropriate, the placement of "enemies" into this frame leaves the impression of an inadequate response. The implication is that the terrorists can only be dealt with militarily.

At the end of excerpt 9, Bush concludes by arguing that war is the only possible response: "The terrorists and their supporters declared war on the United States, and war is what they got." Presupposed in this statement is the proposition that the events of 9/11 indubitably constitute war on par with the type of military campaigns waged by one nation-state against another. If this presupposition is accepted, then the only logical reaction would be to adopt a war stance and wage a full-scale war in return. Here we see how the response to terrorism as a war is presented as flowing naturally from the events themselves as if the events provide their own interpretation. In this way, a particular ideological position is presented simply as the way things are, whereas the opposing ideological position is painted as wholly outside the realm of "common sense."

In excerpt 10, taken from a speech given on the anniversary of the Iraq invasion, Bush reinforces his meaning of the "war on terror" as a real military campaign.

---

4. See Chang and Mehan (2006) for more on the "legal mode of discourse" used to characterize the response to terrorism.

Excerpt 10. (Bush 2004, March 19)

The war on terror is not a figure of speech. It is an inescapable calling of our generation.

For Bush, "the war on terror is not a figure of speech." It is not merely a rhetorical trope. Rather than a metaphor, it is the moniker for a very real military campaign waged on numerous fronts including Iraq and Afghanistan. As he emphasizes in the Narrative, the real wars in Iraq and Afghanistan are not separate and unrelated, but together comprise the "war on terror." That is, they are separate battlefields of a single war. To reiterate Fairclough's (1989) point, "Different metaphors imply different ways of dealing with things" (120). In the case of the Bush administration's response to terrorism, the implications of the war metaphor for characterizing 9/11 have produced very real consequences.

In excerpt 10, Bush notes that the "war on terror" is "an inescapable calling of our generation." I discuss this "calling of our generation" in more detail in the next section, as I turn to an exploration of the way past wars act as important source domains for representing the "war on terror."

LESSONS OF HISTORY

Generic precedents of the nation at war provide ready-made cultural frameworks to aid in the interpretation of the particulars of 9/11 and America's response to terrorism. Whereas shared background knowledge is the basis of any communicative act, the comparisons with World War II and the Cold War draw upon a particular type of background knowledge: a nation's shared history. National memories of the past are not merely individual memories, but rather collective memories. These collective memories form the basis of nationality and represent the nation's shared cultural canon. Insofar as culture can be thought of as an assemblage of texts (Geertz 1973),[5] a nation's *collective memory* (Halbwachs 1980) represents a type of text that can be mined as a source of meaning for new events that it experiences. It is a type of text best characterized in terms of what Barthes (1977) calls a *readerly text*. That is, it is a text that holds little interpretive challenge. In short, the collective memories drawn upon as source domains for understanding the "war on terror" represent canonical

5. Geertz (1973) writes, "Believing, with Max Weber, that man *[sic]* is an animal suspended in webs of significance he himself has spun, I take culture to be those webs" (5).

episodes from the nation's history and provide ready-made meanings for making sense of new issues.

The cross-domain mappings in these analogies are discursively manifested in several ways, starting with the mapping of precipitating events. In the "war on terror," 9/11 plays the function that Pearl Harbor did in World War II, as seen in excerpt 11, taken from Bush's address to Congress nine days after 9/11. In the excerpts appearing in the remainder of this chapter, I represent the data in lines and stanzas. Following Gee (1986), the line breaks represent rhetorical pauses, and help capture the poetic flow of the speech (full transcription conventions are provided in appendix B).

Excerpt 11. (Bush 2001, September 20)

1   On September the 11th,
2   enemies of freedom
3   committed an *act of war*
4   against our country.

5   Americans have known wars
6   but for the past 136 years,
7   they have been wars on foreign soil,
8   except for *one Sunday in 1941*.

9   Americans have known the *casualties of war*
10 but not at the center of a great city
11 on a peaceful morning.

12 Americans have known surprise attacks
13 but never before on thousands of civilians.

14 All of this was brought upon us in a single day,
15 and night fell on a different world,
16 a world where freedom itself is under attack.

As with any analogy, the correspondences between source and target are never identical. The cross-domain mapping inevitably involves a certain degree of *erasure* (Irvine and Gal 2000). "Facts that are inconsistent with the ideological scheme either go unnoticed or get explained away" (Irvine and Gal 2000: 38). In excerpt 11, the precipitating event of the Narrative is put forth as an act of war through its comparison with the act of war that began World War II. The incongruities between the two events are ignored. The facts that Pearl Harbor was bombed by the military of a nation-state whereas 9/11 was carried out by individuals associated with a nonstate terrorist group are erased. Instead, the nature of both as "surprise attacks" that took place on American soil is highlighted in excerpt 11. The next excerpt, taken from a speech given by Bush on Pearl Harbor Day in 2005, further illustrates this process.

Excerpt 12. (Bush 2005, December 7)

1   On *September the 11th 2001*,
2   our nation awoke to another sudden attack.

3   In the space of just one hundred and two minutes
4   more Americans were killed
5   than we lost at Pearl Harbor.

6   *Like generations before us we accepted new responsibilities* and we confronted new dangers with firm resolve.

7   Like generations before us, we're taking the fight to those who attacked us
8   and those who share their murderous vision for future attacks.

9   Like generations before us, we've faced setbacks
10 on the path to victory.
11 Yet we will fight this war without wavering.

12 And like the generations before us,
13 we will prevail.

Erasure is frequently accompanied by a process of focalization, which works to highlight similarities (Hodges 2008: 493). In excerpt 12, the analogy between "September the 11th 2001" and "Pearl Harbor" is strengthened through the parallel syntactic structure that highlights, in stepwise fashion, the correspondences drawn between the precipitating event in the Narrative and the collective memories of World War II. The comparative adjective "like" marks the beginning of each new analogical correspondence, while a prosodic break marks the end. The repetition of this structure accentuates the point of similarity. Focalization and erasure, therefore, work to strengthen the plausibility of the analogy.

Another cross-domain mapping that occurs in the Narrative is the mapping of antagonists from the source onto the target. In the next excerpt, the enemy in the "war on terror"—that is, the "terrorists"—is juxtaposed with enemies the nation has faced in past conflicts: Hitler from World War II and Lenin as a representative of the Communist ideology of the Cold War.

Excerpt 13. (Bush 2006, September 5)

1   Now I know some of our country hear *the terrorists' words*,
2   and hope that they will not, or cannot do what they say.

3 *History teaches* that understan- underestimating the words of evil and
   ambitious men
4 is a terrible mistake.

5 In the early 1900s,
6 an exiled lawyer in Europe
7 published a pamphlet called "What Is To Be Done?"
8 in which he laid out his plan to launch a communist revolution
9 in Russia.
10 The world did not heed *Lenin's words*,
11 and paid a terrible price.
12 The Soviet Empire he established killed tens of millions and brought the
   world to the brink of thermonuclear war.

13 In the 1920s,
14 a failed Austrian painter
15 published a book in which he explained his intention to build
16 an Aryan super-state in Germany
17 and take revenge on Europe and eradicate the Jews.
18 The world ignored *Hitler's words*,
19 and paid a terrible price.
20 His Nazi regime killed millions in the gas chambers,
21 and set the world aflame in war before it was finally defeated at a terrible
   cost in lives.

22 *Bin Laden* and his terrorist allies have made their intentions
23 as clear as Lenin and Hitler before them.
24 The question is will we listen?
25 Will we pay attention to what these evil men say?

26 America and our coalition partners
27 have made our choice.
28 We're taking the words of the enemy seriously.
29 We're on the offensive, we will not rest, we will not retreat, and we will
   not withdraw from the fight until this threat to civilization has been
   removed. ((applause))

Potter (1996) outlines several features involved in the discursive construction of reality, including the way facts can be personified to obscure
"the work of interpretation and construction done by the description's
producer" (158). In excerpt 13, the lessons of history are forwarded by
history itself so that "history teaches." This personification gives history
its own agency, and erases the interpretive role Bush plays in the (re)
writing of history according to his own ideological perspective. In other
words, Bush's agency in this narrative act is backgrounded and the facts

are said to "do their own showing" (Potter 1996: 158; see also, Hodges 2010: 318).

Bush as narrator is further removed from the interpretive process by representing the historical events as flowing directly from the "words" of key antagonists. The naming of Lenin and Hitler simplifies a complex set of historical conditions and embodies those events in these two iconic figures. "History teaches" that the actions spawned by the rise of Lenin and Hitler were plainly recognizable in advance and foretold in their own "words." As evidence, Bush cites two texts where "Lenin's words" and "Hitler's words" were spelled out. Elsewhere in this speech, Bush makes extensive use of reported speech frames to represent Bin Laden and "the terrorists' words." The juxtaposition of "Lenin's words" and "Hitler's words" with "the terrorists' words" strengthens the analogy and works to present the parallels as objective lessons of history.

In these analogical comparisons, the antagonists of the Narrative are positioned as "heirs" or "successors" to the ideologies spawned by Lenin and Hitler mentioned in excerpt 13, as seen in the next two excerpts.

Excerpt 14. (Bush 2001, September 20)

1 We are not deceived by their pretenses to piety.
2 We have seen their kind before.
3 They are the heirs of all the murderous ideologies of the twentieth century.
4 By sacrificing human life to serve their radical visions,
5 by abandoning every value except the will to power,
6 they follow in the path of
7 fascism,
8 Nazism,
9 and totalitarianism.
10 And they will follow that path all the way to where it ends,
11 in history's unmarked grave of discarded lies. ((applause))

Excerpt 15. (Bush 2006, August 31)

1 The war we fight today is more than a military conflict,
2 it is the decisive ideological struggle of the 21st century. ((applause))

3 On one side are those who believe in the values of freedom and moderation
4 the right of all people to speak,

5   and worship,
6   and live in liberty.

7   And on the other side are those driven by the values of tyranny and
    extremism
8   the right of a self-appointed few
9   to impose their fanatical views
10 on all the rest.

11 As veterans, you have seen this kind of enemy before.
12 They're successors to fascists,
13 to Nazis,
14 to Communists,
15 and other totalitarians of the 20th century.

16 And history shows
17 what the outcome will be:
18 This war will be difficult; this war will be long; and this war will end in
    the defeat of the terrorists and tolatalitar- totalitarians, and a victory for
    the cause of freedom and liberty. ((applause))

The natural progression presented in these excerpts from fascists to
Communists to terrorists can be viewed in terms of a Vygotskian (1987: 139-
141) *chain-complex*. Meanings from the historical source domains are carried over to the domain of terrorism by connecting one to the next as links in
a chain. As Silverstein (2005) explains, these "tropic leaps" make "an equivalence class" (16). Thus, fascists and Communists yield terrorists as their
"heirs" (excerpt 14) and "successors" (excerpt 15) in the historical narrative
forwarded by Bush. The equivalence class is further strengthened through the
device of alliteration that binds together "terrorists and totalitarians" (excerpt
15). Elsewhere in the corpus of presidential speeches, Bush talks of "terrorists and tyrants" (see chapter 5; see also, Klocke 2004). Crucially, this alliter-
ative connection links together the disparate nation-state actors represented
by the Soviet Union, Nazi Germany, and (in the Narrative) Saddam Hussein's
Iraq with the nonstate actors of Bin Laden's Al Qaeda network.

    In Bush's analogies, both World War II and the Cold War represent
exploitable source domains for several reasons. The World War II era
holds the nation's imagination as a time of glory when the "greatest generation"[6] succeeded in an epic triumph of good over evil.[7] As Bakhtin (1981)

    6. This popular appellation for the World War II generation also acts as the title of a
book by the journalist Tom Brokaw (1998).
    7. I cannot begin to do justice to the religious undertones of Bush's discourse within
the scope of the current analysis. For more on this issue, see Chernus (2006) as well as
Chang and Mehan (2006).

writes in his discussion of epic narrative, the past is "the source of all authentic reality and value" (18). In the Narrative, the heroes and villains of the present "are woven by various intermediate links and connective tissue into the unified fabric of the heroic past" (Bakhtin 1981: 18). Whereas the present involves inconclusiveness and openness to interpretation and evaluation, the collective memory about the "good war"[8] provides a readerly text that supplies ready-made understandings.[9] In this way, the past is both represented and representing (Bakhtin 1981: 45). That is, mythologized images of the past are both illuminated in the Narrative and are used to interpret the present.

The canonical nature of World War II as a war between nation-states with concrete battles and clearly defined measures of success provides a stable base of meaning for the "war on terror." It also supplies language with which to talk about it; that is, as a "war" with "battles" and "fronts" and "enemies" and "casualties" and "wins" and "losses," as already illustrated. Yet, as Bush points out in his speeches, the "war on terror" is also "a different kind of war." In many ways, the Cold War provides a better source domain for understanding the "war on terror," as Bush articulates in the next excerpt.

Excerpt 16. (Bush 2007, July 26)

1 It's akin to the Cold War in some ways,
2 where we had an ideological struggle.

Here, and across his speeches, Bush positions the "war on terror" not just as a traditional hot war but as an "ideological struggle." As seen earlier in excerpt 14, the terrorists are the "heirs of all the murderous ideologies of the twentieth century." This includes Communism as well as fascism, Nazism, and totalitarianism (excerpts 14 and 15). In making the link between the ideologies of terrorists and their supposed predecessors, Bush makes use of a parallel rhetorical structure to map the similarities between source and target. The next excerpt further illustrates this process.

Excerpt 17. (Bush 2001, December 7)

1 Our war against terror is not a war against one terrorist leader,
2 or one terrorist group.

8. This designation has been canonized in Studs Terkel's (1984) *The Good War: An Oral History of World War Two*.
9. According to Barthes (1975), a readerly text reinforces the *doxa*, or "stereotypical meaning" (29; Allen 2000: 79).

3   Terrorism is a movement,
4   an ideology that respects no boundary of nationality,
5   or decency.

6   *The terrorists despise creative societies,*
7   and individual choice.
8   And thus they bear a special hatred for America.

9   *They desire to concentrate power in the hands of a few,*
10 and to force every life into grim and joyless conformity.

11 *They celebrate death,*
12 making a mission of murder and a sacrament
13 of suicide.

14 Yet for some reason,
15 for some reason,
16 only young followers
17 are ushered down this deadly path to paradise while terrorist leaders run
    into caves
18 to save their own hides. ((applause))

19 We've seen their kind before.

20 *The terrorists*
21 are the heirs to fascism.

22 *They* have *the same* will to power,
23 *the same* disdain for the individual,
24 *the same* mad global ambitions.

25 *And they* will be dealt with in just *the same* way. ((applause))

26 Like all fascists
27 the terrorists cannot be appeased,
28 they must be defeated.

29 This struggle will not end in a truce or treaty.
30 It will end in victory for the United States, our friends, and for the cause
    of freedom. ((applause))

As van Dijk (1991) points out, a common function of parallelism is to emphasize "negative properties of opponents" (219). In excerpt 17, this is accomplished through the use of a clausal pattern that repeats, in parallel steps, different attributes of "the terrorists." Lines 6, 9, and 11 open parallel stanzas with the same subject-verb frame. Line 6 begins with the nominal referent "the terrorists" and lines 9 and 11 refer back to this antecedent with the pronominal referent "they." With this refrain established, the remainder of these three stanzas elaborates upon their negative properties—or more precisely, develops an argument detailing the negative aspects of their "ideology." The same structure of three parallel stanzas is repeated again beginning in line 20. In the second of these stanzas, beginning in line 22, a refrain within the refrain emerges. The phrase "the same" is repeated in each of the three lines of this stanza, which works to highlight the similarities between "the terrorists" and "fascism." Line 25 ends the pattern with a note of contrast. Whereas the previous lines contained active constructions, line 25 shifts to a passive construction so that "they" (i.e., the terrorists) are the goal of the described action: "they will be dealt with." The agent of this action is not provided in this line, although the referent is clearly implied and spelled out in line 30: "the United States."

The structure used in excerpt 17 can also be applied to the other, in Bush's terms, "murderous ideology of the twentieth century."[10] Instead of "fascism," simply insert "Communism" into the refrain. This is illustrated in excerpt 18:

Excerpt 18. (Bush 2005, October 6)

1 The *murderous ideology of the Islamic radicals* is the great challenge of our new century.
2 Yet in many ways, this fight resembles the struggle against *Communism* in the last century.

3 *Like the ideology of Communism,*
4 Islamic radicalism is elitist,
5 led by a self-appointed vanguard that presumes to speak for the Muslim masses. ((point further developed in an additional six lines))

6 *Like the ideology of Communism,*
7 our new enemy teaches that innocent individuals can be sacrificed
8 to serve a political vision. ((point further developed in an additional twenty-three lines))

9 *Like the ideology of Communism,* our new enemy pursues totalitarian aims. ((point further developed in an additional twelve lines))

10 *Like the ideology of Communism,* our new enemy is dismissive of free peoples,
11 claiming that men and women who live in liberty are weak and decadent. ((point further developed in an additional nine lines))

12 *And Islamic radicalism like the ideology of Communism,*
13 contains inherent contradictions that doom it to failure.

10. The phrase "murderous ideology" (e.g., excerpt 14 and line 1 of excerpt 18) varies with "hateful ideology" elsewhere in the corpus of speeches. "Islamic radicalism" (line 12 of excerpt 18) has also been termed "Islamic extremism," "militant Jihadism," and "Islamo-fascism" in the corpus.

As seen earlier in excerpt 12, excerpt 18 makes use of the comparative adjective "like" to mark the parallels between "the ideology of Communism" and "Islamic radicalism." The parallel structure is marked off with the same line at the beginning of the main stanzas in the excerpt: "like the ideology of Communism." The last stanza, which begins in line 12, then reiterates the source and target domains of the analogy in close juxtaposition to one another to reinforce their link—that is, Communism as the source domain for understanding the target domain of Islamic radicalism.

In the preceding excerpts, it is not the attributes drawn from the source domains (i.e., Communism, fascism, etc.) that are developed; rather, it is the properties given to "the terrorists" that are highlighted and developed underneath the opening line of each stanza. In other words, the attributes of the source domains remain largely implicit and vague. But this is possible in the Narrative because it is not the details of these past wars that matter. Rather, it is the image of the past that resides in the "national consciousness" (Anderson 1983) that is drawn upon. Moreover, the logical soundness of the comparisons also matters little. As Bruner (1991) notes, narratives provide "a version of reality whose acceptability is governed by convention and 'narrative necessity' rather than by empirical verification and logical requiredness" (4–5). Wittgenstein (1969) reminds us that "one is sometimes convinced of the *correctness* of a view by its *simplicity* or *symmetry*, i.e., these are what induce one to go over to this point of view. One then simply says something like: '*That's* how it must be" (14; italics in original).

WAR AND TERRORISM

The present, like history, is not simply about the events that happen but the interpretations they are given. As seen in this chapter, the organization of the unique experience of 9/11 in the Narrative draws heavily on domains of prior experience and collective memory shared by the nation. Although numerous potential frameworks exist for making sense of the events that took place on 9/11, the Narrative adopts the framework of war to categorize the issue. The language of war that underpins this categorization represents the Bush administration's ideological position on how to respond to terrorism. In the ideological struggle over the characterization of terrorism, alternative framings, such as viewing terrorism as a crime, sometimes rise to the metadiscursive level. In such instances, alternative framings are positioned as standing outside the realm of "common sense," and the framing provided by the Narrative is positioned as the only obvious interpretation dictated by the events of 9/11 themselves. The characterization of the struggle against terrorism as a "war on terror" is further aided by the use of analogies with the nation's past wars. These historical precedents flesh out the generic template of a nation at war upon which the Narrative is constructed. Suppression of the intertextual gap (Briggs and Bauman 1992) between the Narrative and this generic template helps create, in Barthes' (1977) terms, a readerly text. It is a text that invites "some well-rehearsed and virtually automatic interpretive routine" (Bruner 1991: 9). Through this process of text production, the Narrative becomes naturalized to a large extent as a conventional means for discussing America's struggle against terrorism. The next chapter continues to explore this process of text production by examining how the organizational structure of the Narrative contributes to its coherence as a text that subsumes diverse elements.

3

The Narrative's Part-Whole
Textual Interdependence

A long year has passed since enemies attacked
our country.

—George W. Bush (2002, September 11)

INTRODUCTION

Much of the political usefulness of the Narrative lies in its ability to subsume a variety of foreign policy objectives under the rubric of the "war on
terror." The war in Iraq is a case in point. Arguably, the invasion of Iraq in
2003 had nothing to do with 9/11 and the struggle against Al Qaeda. Nevertheless, Iraq exists as a fully developed episode within the Narrative
where it is presented as the "central front in the war on terror." Although
the textual details of how this particular episode is woven into the Narrative are not presented until chapter 4, in this chapter I provide a general
look at how disparate elements such as Iraq fit within the narrative whole.

In his discussion of *hermeneutic composability*, Bruner (1991) emphasizes the interrelationship between the whole text and its constituent
parts. To explain, he cites Taylor (1979), who notes that "expressions only
make sense or not in relation to others, [thus] the readings of partial
expressions depend on those of others, and ultimately of the whole" (28,

cited in Bruner 1991: 8). In other words, the text as a whole is interpreted in light of the components of which it is comprised. In turn, however, the meaning assigned to the text as a whole shapes the reading of its individual components. Bruner (1991) describes this paradox as "part-whole textual interdependence" (8). He applies this concept to narrative as follows:

> This is probably nowhere better illustrated than in narrative. The accounts of protagonists and events that constitute a narrative are selected and shaped in terms of a putative story or plot that then "contains" them. At the same time, the "whole" . . . is dependent for its formation on a supply of possible constituent parts. In this sense, as we have already noted, parts and wholes in a narrative rely on each other for their viability.

The key point to take away from this explication is that a narrative's constituent elements depend on an overarching plot to organize them. The organization of a narrative around a central plot, therefore, works to bring in diverse elements so that these elements, no matter how diverse, form a coherent whole. To an extent, the viability of the Iraq war as "the central front in the war on terror" follows from how the Narrative is structurally organized. When a narrative is skillfully told and organized, the result is what Bruner (1991) terms "narrative seduction" so that the "telling preempts momentarily the possibility of any but a single interpretation—however bizarre it may be" (9; see also, Hanks 1989 on textuality and coherence).

The aim of this chapter, therefore, is to provide a schematic overview of the constituent elements that make up the Narrative and to show how they fit together to form a coherent text. Although I take my examples from specific speeches, these examples are representative of the larger body of speeches about the "war on terror" delivered by George W. Bush over a period of nearly seven years. Thus, although the analysis focuses on a narrative told by an individual speaker on specific occasions, the result is to extract from these representative examples a template indicative of the "big D" discourse about the "war on terror." As outlined in the list that follows, the Narrative consists of six main components:

1. *Precipitating Event*: Reference to 9/11, the precipitating event that began the "war on terror"
2. *America's Response*: Discussion of America's response to terrorism in general terms, often mentioning that the fight is waged with many tools in many places
3. *"Battle" of Afghanistan*: Discussion of the first "battle" of the "war on terror" in Afghanistan

4. *Numerous Fronts*: Naming of several "fronts" to detail the global and ongoing nature of the war waged across the world
5. *"Battle" of Iraq*: Discussion of the "front" in Iraq
6. *Challenges and Commitment*: Discussion of the challenges faced in the "war on terror" and America's commitment to continue amidst adversity

Following Gee (1986), I refer to these six components as *sections*, or *episodes*. As detailed in the discussion that follows, each episode is more or less "defined by its consistency of topic/theme, character, and location" (400). (Transcription conventions are provided in appendix B.)

CONSTITUENT EPISODES OF THE NARRATIVE

The precipitating event

In his discussion of *canonicity and breach*, Bruner (1991) points out that narratives are told against the background of shared cultural scripts that define canonical behavior. The canonical elements of life are then breached in a way that makes a narrative worth telling. Bruner (1991) draws upon Labov and Waletzky's (1967) notion of a "precipitating event" to make this point about tellability. A precipitating event acts as the starting point for a story. In the Narrative, that starting point is 9/11, which becomes a crucial reference point in the Narrative. It acts as the pivot around which the rest of the Narrative is organized. The excerpt that follows is taken from Bush's address to the nation at a joint session of Congress nine days after 9/11. Here, reference to the date of "September the 11th" and description of the precipitating event that took place on that date—"an act of war against our country"—opens the Narrative. This breach is positioned against the backdrop of quotidian life in New York City, described as "a peaceful morning."

Excerpt 1. (Bush 2001, September 20)

On September the 11th, enemies of freedom committed an act of war against our country. Americans have known wars but for the past one hundred and thirty-six years, they have been wars on foreign soil, except for one Sunday in 1941. Americans have known the casualties of war but not at the center of a great city on a peaceful morning. Americans have known surprise attacks but never before on thousands of civilians. All of this was brought upon us in a single day, and night fell on a different world, a world where freedom itself is under attack.

The contrast between *pre-* and *postprecipitating event* is brought into stark relief through the description of 9/11 provided in excerpt 1. The "peaceful morning" of pre-9/11 gives way to the "surprise attacks" that mark the dividing line with the post-9/11 world. The contrast is summarized in Bush's assessment that "night fell on a different world." This contrast is further illustrated in the next excerpt, taken from Bush's address to the nation two months after 9/11.

Excerpt 2. (Bush 2001, November 8)

We meet tonight after two of the most difficult and most inspiring months in our nation's history. We have endured the shock of watching so many innocent lives ended in acts of unimaginable horror. We have endured the sadness of so many funerals. We have faced unprecedented bioterrorist attack delivered in our mail. Tonight many thousands of children are tragically learning to live without one of their parents. And the rest of us are learning to live in a world that seems very different than it was on September the 10th. The moment the second plane hit the second building, when we knew it was a terrorist attack, many felt that our lives would never be the same.

Labov (1972) discusses the importance of evaluation in narrative where he characterizes it as "waves of evaluation that penetrate the narrative" (369). Evaluations can occur in different ways. They can be external to the recounting of sequentially ordered events so that the narrator takes a pause from the complicating action to subjectively evaluate the meaning or significance of those events. In addition, evaluations can be embedded within the complicating action by using descriptions or reported speech to attribute sentiments as occurring to characters as events unfold (Labov 1972: 372). In excerpt 2, evaluations that make the pre- and post-9/11 contrast are provided in both these ways. First, Bush steps outside of the recounting of past events to evaluate the impact of those events on the present context of the speech, stating that "the rest of us are learning to live in a world that seems very different than it was on September the 10th." Next, Bush embeds this same evaluation within the complicating action itself by ascribing the sentiment to those who were witness to "the moment the second plane hit the second building." As that happened, he recounts how "many felt that our lives would never be the same." Critical linguists widely emphasize that language is never neutral. It is impossible to simply describe events without conveying those events from a particular perspective—i.e., without in effect providing an evaluation of them. Narrative provides different means by which these evaluations can be conveyed, as seen here.

Importantly, the precipitating event becomes codified in the Narrative through reference to the date of September 11, 2001. Sometimes this date is mentioned explicitly, as in excerpt 1. Other times it is referenced deictically, as in excerpt 2. Excerpts 3–5 further illustrate this variation:

Excerpt 3. (Bush 2002, September 11)

A long year has passed since enemies attacked our country.

Excerpt 4. (Bush 2003, September 12)

Two years ago yesterday we were attacked.

Excerpt 5. (Bush 2003, April 16)

On September the 11th 2001, America found that we are not immune to the threats that gather for years across the oceans. Threats that can arrive in sudden tragedy. Since September the 11th we've been engaged in a global war against terror, a war being waged on many fronts. That war continues, and we are winning. ((applause))

In each of these instances, the Narrative opens by directing attention back to the date of September 11, 2001. Following Ricoeur (1984), this time is not just "clock time" but "human time." "It is time whose significance is given by the meaning assigned to events within its compass" (Bruner 1991: 6). In other words, September 11, 2001 is more than just a historical date; and the span of time between that date and any given telling of the Narrative (e.g., one year in excerpt 3 or two years and one day in excerpt 4) is more than the simple measurement of years and days on a calendar. The very concept of 9/11 is anchored to this date. The meaning of 9/11 builds upon the division of historical time into a "before" and an "after," which creates a frame, or enclosure, for the narrative realm (Young 1989). In this way, clock time becomes human time. Within the world of the narrative, reference to this date comes to signify the precipitating event from which the other episodes of the Narrative flow. The precipitating event marked by 9/11, therefore, works to contextualize the diverse episodes placed within the bounds of the Narrative, from the war in Afghanistan to the war in Iraq. It provides the common thread that weaves together the other constituent episodes of the Narrative into the tissue of the text.

America's response

From the mentioning of the precipitating event, the narrative typically moves next into a discussion of America's response to terrorism in general terms. In some ways, this episode of the Narrative acts as a type of abstract or orientation (Labov 1972) for the rest of the narrative insofar as it recounts responses taken against terrorism without going into too much detail. The following excerpt, from a speech given at the National Guard Building in Washington, DC, begins right after the precipitating event is discussed, which is indexed again with reference to "that day."

Excerpt 6. (Bush 2006, February 9)

And since that day we've taken decisive action to protect our citizens against new dangers. We're hunting down the terrorists, using every element of our national power, military, intelligence, law enforcement, diplomatic, and financial. We're clarifying the choice facing every nation. In this struggle between freedom and terror, every nation has responsibilities. And no one can remain neutral. Since September the 11th we've led a broad coalition to confront the terrorist threat.

As seen in excerpt 6, the response against terrorism is often detailed as a listing of actions or methods used "to confront the terrorist threat." As Bush describes, the United States is "using every element of our national power." He then lists these elements as "military, intelligence, law enforcement, diplomatic, and financial." The metaphorical nature of a "war on terror" is evident in statements such as these. Like a "war on drugs," the "war on terror" adopts a whole host of responsive actions against terrorism. Bush often describes these elements as the "many tools" that complement the actual military campaigns being fought on "many fronts," as seen in the next excerpt taken from a speech at Fort Hood, Texas.

Excerpt 7. (Bush 2003, January 3)

And we're not quitting. We'll fight this war on many fronts, with many tools. Our intelligence operations are tracking the terrorists. We're sharing intelligence with other countries that share our desire for peace. Our allies are keeping the peace and helping us keep the peace in Afghanistan. We're hunting the terrorists on every continent. See they're in over sixty different countries. We've got a vast coalition of people bound by this principle, either you're with us, or you're with the enemy. Either you're with those who love freedom, or you're with those who hate innocent life. Our coalition is strong, and we're keeping it strong. And we're on the hunt. We're chasing them down one by one.

Even with the panoply of non-military "tools" available, the general parameters of the military response are frequently emphasized in this episode of the Narrative. This works to develop the metaphorical "war on terror" into "a new kind of war." That new war, of course, is based on the generic concept of war found in Bush's lessons of history, as discussed in chapter 2. The next excerpt, from a speech at Fort Stewart, Georgia, illustrates this general focus on a military response.

Excerpt 8. (Bush 2003, September 12)

In this new kind of war America has followed a new strategy. We are not waiting for further attacks on our citizens. We are striking our enemies before they can strike us again. ((applause)) As all of you know, wars are fought on the offensive. The war on terror will be won on the offensive. And America and our friends are staying on the offensive. We're rolling back- ((applause)) We're rolling back the terrorist threat, not on the fringes of its influence, but at the heart of its power. ((applause))

Evaluations are heavily embedded in these examples. These evaluative components of the narrative lay out several doctrines important in Bush administration policy. In excerpt 7, for example, we learn that "either you're with us, or you're with the enemy; either you're with those who love freedom, or you're with those who hate innocent life." Not only does this rhetorically impose an either-or choice, or false dilemma, onto the reading of the situation, but it also works to define the protagonists in the Narrative in terms of "us" versus "them." This is part of the discursive process of *distinction* discussed by Bucholtz and Hall (2004, inter alia) in their model of identity formation (to be discussed in more detail in chapter 4). Here, Bush distinguishes between "us" and "them" in a highly dichotomous manner. Through the evaluative component in excerpt 8, we learn of another Bush administration doctrine: "We are not waiting for further attacks on our citizens. We are striking our enemies before they can strike us again." This doctrine of so-called preemptive, or, more accurately termed, preventive[1] war paves the way for justifying the actions described in the fifth episode of the Narrative, the "battle" of Iraq (detailed later). In this way, another thread is put in place to weave additional elements of the plot into the fabric of the text.

The "battle" of Afghanistan

The general introduction to the wide range of "tools" used in America's response to terrorism, seen in the previous section of the Narrative, moves into a detailed section on what Bush variously terms the "the first theater in the war against terror" or the "battle of Afghanistan," as seen in excerpts 9 and 10, which follow. Excerpt 11 illustrates in more detail how that "first battle" is recounted in the narrative.

Excerpt 9. (Bush 2002, February 16)

But there's more to do in Afghanistan. We're entering a difficult phase of the first theater in the war against terror.

Excerpt 10. (Bush 2003, May 1)

In the battle of Afghanistan, we destroyed the Taliban, many terrorists, and the camps where they trained.

Excerpt 11. (Bush 2006, February 9)

Four weeks after the attacks America and our allies launched military operations, to eliminate the terrorists' principal sanctuary in the nation of Afghanistan. I told the world that if you harbor a terrorist you're equally as guilty as the terrorists. And when an American President says something, he better mean what he said. I meant what I said. ((applause)) We removed a cruel regime that oppressed its people, brutalized women and girls, and gave safe haven to the terrorists who attacked America. Because we acted the terror camps in Afghanistan have been shut down. And twenty-five million people have tasted freedom. Many for the first time in their lives.

---

1. Chomsky (2003) points out that the Bush administration's policy of "preemptive" war is in actuality a policy of *preventive* war, as it allows for "the use of military force to eliminate an invented or imagined threat." See Dunmire (2009) for more on the way the Bush administration adopted the language of preemptive war to justify a policy of preventive war.

The beginning of excerpt 11 provides another reference to the precipitating event. This helps to remind the audience of the common thread (i.e., 9/11) that ties together the various episodes of the Narrative. The implication is that each episode flows directly from that precipitating event. Here, Bush makes this connection explicit as he explains that "four weeks after the attacks" of 9/11, "America and our allies launched military operations" in Afghanistan. The deictic reference to 9/11 from the point in time at which America launched its invasion of Afghanistan ("four weeks after") works to establish the motivation for that invasion. Although this motivation for the military action taken in Afghanistan may seem patently obvious and beyond doubt, what should be noted is the precedent set here for the way this action is positioned as flowing naturally from the precipitating event. This point becomes more important in the Narrative's later episode of the "battle of Iraq," where the justification vis-à-vis 9/11 is less obvious outside the Narrative.

Excerpt 11 also illustrates the interleaving of evaluations within the recounting of events. For example, an action ("America and our allies launched military operations") is introduced along with a preferred reading of why it took place: "to eliminate the terrorists' principal sanctuary in the nation of Afghanistan." Different political commentators have provided alternative explanations for why the invasion of Afghanistan took place. Notably, oil always seems to be a popular alternative explanation for opponents of the administration. Seth Stevenson, a writer on Slate.com, documents this alternative theory, which "claims that the bombing of the Taliban has nothing to do with a 'war on terrorism' but everything to do with the oil pipeline the West wants to build through Afghanistan" (Stevenson 2001). In Bush's account, however, this and other potential motivations are preempted by the logic of the Narrative's structure in which all actions are positioned as responses to terrorism. In excerpt 11, evaluation also forwards another important doctrine of the "war on terror": "if you harbor a terrorist, you're equally guilty as the terrorists." This idea works to justify the incorporation of additional "fronts" in the "war on terror." Thus, it helps set the stage for the episodes that follow.

Although the discursive transformation of the military action in Afghanistan into a more legendary-sounding "battle of Afghanistan" (excerpt 10) in the "war on terror" can only be completed after that battle has been waged, this episode nevertheless appears in the Narrative before the invasion is launched. This, of course, is no surprise because ample discursive work is needed prior to any military venture to justify the action to the American public. The next excerpt is taken from Bush's address to the nation at a joint session of Congress nine days after 9/11 and seventeen days before the United States invaded Afghanistan.

Excerpt 12. (Bush 2001, September 20)

The leadership of Al Qaeda has great influence in Afghanistan, and supports the Taliban regime in controlling most of that country. In Afghanistan we see Al Qaeda's vision for the world. ((details enumerated)) The United States respects the people of Afghanistan. After all, we are currently its largest source of humanitarian aid. But we condemn the Taliban regime. ((applause)) It is not only repressing its own people, it is threatening people everywhere, by sponsoring and sheltering and supplying terrorists. By aiding and abetting murder, the Taliban regime is committing murder. And tonight, the United States of America makes the following demands on the Taliban. ((the demands are detailed)) These demands are not open to negotiation or discussion. ((applause)) The Taliban must act, and act immediately. They will hand over the terrorists, or they will share in their fate.

Importantly, the section on Afghanistan represents a well-formed episode within the Narrative even prior to the invasion, as seen in excerpt 12. Instead of being recounted as a past event in the "war on terror," the military campaign in Afghanistan is foreshadowed and presented as all but an inevitable event prior to the invasion. Excerpt 13, which follows, occurs once the war in Afghanistan is underway. These excerpts illustrate the importance of developing an episode within the Narrative, such as the episode about Afghanistan, both prior to, during, and after the waging of military action.

Excerpt 13. (Bush 2001, November 8)

We are at the beginning of our efforts in Afghanistan, and Afghanistan is only the beginning of our efforts in the world. No group or nation should mistake Americans' intentions. Where terrorist groups exist of global reach, the United States and our friends and allies will seek it out and we will destroy it.

The Narrative's episode on Afghanistan further demonstrates the way evaluations penetrate the Narrative so that general doctrines are conveyed amidst the unfolding complicating action. These doctrines, along with the precedent set with the use of military force, establish a pattern for future actions outlined in subsequent episodes of the Narrative. In excerpt 13, for example, Bush assesses the events taking place in Afghanistan at the time of his speech, noting that "Afghanistan is only the beginning." This evaluation paves the way for an open-ended "war on terror." The implication is that more "fronts" will be opened up. Indeed, the topic of numerous "fronts'" in the "war on terror" is detailed in the next episode of the Narrative.

Numerous "fronts"

Although the Narrative often focuses on one or both of what Bush variously terms the two major "battles," "fronts," or "theaters" in the "war on terror,"[2] he often lists numerous fronts in addition to Afghanistan and Iraq. The listing of these numerous fronts constructs the notion of a larger battlefield upon which the "war on terror" is waged and makes the "two major theaters" of Afghanistan and Iraq appear less disconnected than they otherwise might appear. In Gee's (1986) terms, new narrative episodes are marked by shifts in location. Here, Bush shifts from Afghanistan to a different location that might best be described as a global battlefield. Enlarging the geographical scope of the war in this manner lays the discursive groundwork for narrowing the focus back down on a specific nation—i.e., Iraq—in the subsequent episode. This "numerous fronts" episode therefore serves as a rhetorical transition from the discussion of Afghanistan to the discussion of Iraq. Despite their differences, Afghanistan and Iraq are more easily connected when presented as two members of a larger, global set of "fronts." The following excerpt, taken from the 2002 State of the Union speech, illustrates the shift in location from the episode on Afghanistan to the current episode that details numerous "fronts."

Excerpt 14. (Bush 2002, January 29)

While the most visible military action is in Afghanistan, America is acting elsewhere. We now have troops in the Philippines, helping to train that country's armed forces to go after terrorist cells that have executed an American, and still hold hostages. Our soldiers, working with the Bosnian government, seized terrorists who were plotting to bomb our

2. For example, from a speech in Philadelphia in 2007, Bush lays out these "two theaters" as follows: "And right now what you're seeing is this global war against these extremists and radicals unfolding in two major theaters, Afghanistan, where we liberated 25 million people from the clutches of a barbaric regime that had provided safe haven for Al Qaeda killers who plotted and planned and then killed 3,000 of our people, and in Iraq" (Bush 2007, July 26).

embassy. Our Navy is patrolling the coast of Africa to block the shipment of weapons and the establishment of terrorist camps in Somalia. My hope is that all nations will heed our call, and eliminate the terrorist parasites who threaten their countries and our own. Many nations are acting forcefully. Pakistan is now cracking down on terror, and I admire the strong leadership of President Musharraf. ((applause)) But some governments will be timid in the face of terror. And make no mistake about it, if they do not act, America will. ((applause))

In excerpt 14, the new location is marked by the general term "elsewhere" in "America is acting elsewhere." This introduces the global battlefield on which the "war on terror" is waged. Several specific locations within this global arena are then named: the Philippines, Bosnia, "the coast of Africa," "the terrorist camps in Somalia," and Pakistan. This episode of the Narrative supplies a section of complicating action that works to emphasize the global nature of the "war on terror."

Importantly, the global nature of the struggle against terrorism emphasized here also highlights the ongoing and open-ended nature of the war. It is open-ended both in space and time. That is, the "war on terror" is not confined to specific countries, such as Afghanistan, but involves a much larger geographical encompass as indicated through the naming of numerous geographical "fronts." Moreover, the "war on terror" is not limited in its temporal boundaries. Actions are recounted in the past (e.g., "our soldiers. . .seized terrorists who were plotting"), in the present (e.g., "our navy is patrolling"), and importantly, the global and ongoing nature of the war also leaves open the possibility for further actions in the future. This is made clear in Bush's evaluation of the actions already underway: "And make no mistake about it. If they do not act, America will." The future tense references actions to come and more "fronts" to be added to the list already established.

The movement in the Narrative from past to present to future actions not only foreshadows the opening of new fronts, but works to narrate any new fronts as flowing naturally from the past events. As discussed earlier, the ultimate point from which all these episodes flow is the precipitating event of 9/11. The naming of otherwise disparate places in the world works to stitch these places together within the realm of the narrative whole. In what Bruner (1991) terms "narrative necessity," the opening of future fronts can be interpreted as a necessary and natural consequence of the naming of past and present actions. As seen already in excerpt 14 and as further evidenced in excerpt 15, which follows, this episode of the Narrative makes heavy use of lists in these efforts.

Excerpt 15. (Bush 2002, June 6)

Tonight over sixty thousand American troops are deployed around the world in the war against terror. More than seven thousand in Afghanistan. Others in the Philippines, Yemen, and the Republic of Georgia, to train local forces.

As seen in excerpt 15, another effect of this episode of the Narrative is to provide an impression that a great deal of work is being done and to highlight accomplishments in the struggle against terrorism. To these ends, the use of numbers also adds facticity to the claims of actions being accomplished. Bush notes that "over *sixty thousand* American troops are deployed around the world in the war against terror." A list of their places of deployment then follows, and includes Afghanistan, the Philippines, Yemen, and Georgia. The numbers and locations establish the actions as concrete facts.

Quite frequently, the listing of the numerous fronts is accomplished by using a *from-to* syntactical frame. That is, the list begins with the word *from* and continues *to* one place and on *to* another, which helps discursively paint an image of an all-encompassing global war on numerous fronts. This device, highlighted in italics, is illustrated in the following excerpts.

Excerpt 16. (Bush 2003, May 1)

From Pakistan to the Philippines to the Horn of Africa, we are hunting down Al Qaeda killers. Nineteen months ago, I pledged that the terrorists would not escape the patient justice of the United States. And as of tonight, nearly one half of Al Qaeda's senior operatives have been captured or killed. ((applause))

Excerpt 17. (Bush 2003, October 9)

We're hunting the Al Qaeda terrorists wherever they hide. *From Pakistan, to the Philippines, to the Horn of Africa, to Iraq.* Nearly two-thirds of Al Qaeda's known leaders have been captured or killed. Our resolve is firm, our resolve is clear, no matter how long it takes all who plot against America will face the justice of America. We have sent a message understood throughout the world. If you harbor a terrorist, if you support a terrorist, if you feed a terrorist, you are just as guilty as the terrorists.

Excerpt 18. (Bush 2006, September 29)

From Afghanistan and Iraq, to Africa and Southeast Asia, we are
engaged in a struggle against violent extremists. A struggle which will
help determine the destiny of the civilized world.

As seen in these excerpts, the global engagement on numerous fronts
is often followed by an assessment of the accomplishments made on those
fronts. In excerpts 16 and 17, Bush quantifies the numbers of Al Qaeda's
leaders or operatives that "have been captured or killed." In excerpt 17, we
are also reminded of a key tenet of the Narrative: "If you harbor a terrorist,
if you support a terrorist, if you feed a terrorist, you are just as guilty as the
terrorists." This evaluation reiterates the doctrine spelled out frequently
(e.g., recall excerpt 11). The reiteration of this doctrine further entrenches
this rationale as an interpretive aid that helps cohere the various actions
taken on the "numerous fronts."

The generalities presented in this episode of the Narrative are similar
in many ways to those presented in the second section on "America's
response" to terrorism. Recall that that episode focuses on the response to
terrorism in general terms; but while vague reference to fronts may be
made, specific places are not generally named as they are in this episode
about "numerous fronts." Moreover, the episode on America's response
typically occurs at the beginning of the Narrative and acts as a type of introduction to more specific episodes that follow. In contrast, the "numerous
fronts" episode is canonically positioned between the episodes on Afghanistan and Iraq and acts as a rhetorical bridge between those episodes. With
this said, however, the distinction between these two episodes may not
always be clearly delineated in a given speech. As seen in the next excerpt,
taken from a speech given in Idaho to an audience of military families, the
episodes about America's response and the "numerous fronts" are merged
together.

Excerpt 19. (Bush 2005, August 24)

We're using all elements of our national power to achieve our objectives. Military power, diplomatic power, financial, intelligence and law
enforcement. We're fighting the enemy on many fronts, from the streets
of the Western capitals to the mountains of Afghanistan, to the tribal
regions of Pakistan, to the islands of Southeast Asia and the Horn of
Africa. You see this new kind of war, the first war of the 21st century, is
a war on a global scale. And to protect our people we've got to prevail

in every theater. And that's why it's important for us to call upon allies and friends to join with us. And they are.

In excerpt 19, the mentioning of the "elements of our national power" (i.e., "tools") used in the metaphorical "'war on terror'" is immediately followed by the specific listing of fronts, including "the streets of the Western capitals" (a reference to the bombings in London in July 2005), "the mountains of Afghanistan, to the tribal regions of Pakistan, to the islands of Southeast Asia and the Horn of Africa." As this illustrates, variability exists in the implementation of the canonical elements of the Narrative in any given speech, a point I return to later.

The "battle" of Iraq

Perhaps the most resisted element of the Narrative (i.e., resisted by opponents and critics of the Bush administration) is the inclusion of Iraq as but a "front," "battle," or "theater" within the broader "war on terror," The next chapter provides a more detailed look at how the conflation of Iraq and Al Qaeda is discursively achieved within the Narrative, and chapter 7 returns to this issue to examine the discursive competition between oppositional voices and the Bush administration over Iraq. Here, however, I illustrate how the Narrative incorporates the war in Iraq as a distinct, well-developed episode. Importantly, from the perspective of the Bush administration and its supporters, the war in Iraq is an integral part of the "war on terror." As with the episode on Afghanistan, the episode on Iraq is present in the Narrative well before the invasion to discursively prepare the ground (specific examples of this are detailed in chapter 4). After the declaration of the end of major combat operations in Iraq by Bush on May 1, 2003, the action in Iraq then becomes a critical "front" in the "war on terror," as illustrated in excerpts 20–23.

Excerpt 20. (Bush 2003, May 1)

The *battle of Iraq* is one victory in a war on terror that began on September the 11th 2001 and still goes on.

Excerpt 21. (Bush 2003, September 7)

Two years ago I told the Congress and the country that the war on terror would be a lengthy war, a different kind of war, fought on many fronts in many places. *Iraq is now the central front*. Enemies of freedom are making a desperate stand there. And there they must be defeated.

Excerpt 22. (Bush 2003, October 9)

We're fighting on many fronts and *Iraq is now the central front*. Saddam holdouts and foreign terrorists are trying desperately to undermine Iraq's progress and to throw that country into chaos. The terrorists in Iraq believe that their attacks on innocent people will weaken our resolve. That's what they believe. They believe that America will run from a challenge. They're mistaken. Americans are not the running kind.

Excerpt 23. (Bush 2007, February 15)

This war against the terrorists, this war to protect ourselves, takes place on many fronts. *One such front is Iraq.*

As explicitly illustrated in excerpt 20, the war in Iraq is narrated as flowing directly from the precipitating event of "September the 11th 2001." Thus it becomes the "battle of Iraq" within the broader "war on terror." The enemy in Iraq is often described as "terrorists" in the Narrative (see excerpts 22 and 23), which is a simple yet crucial way to connect the war in Iraq with the "war on terror." Arguments for the claim that Iraq is part of the "war on terror" may also be bolstered through the citation of the enemy's own perspective on the situation, as seen in excerpts 24 and 25.

Excerpt 24. (Bush 2005, October 6)

The terrorists regard Iraq as the central front in their war against humanity. And we must recognize Iraq as the central front in our war on terror.

Excerpt 25. (Bush 2004, March 18)

So the terrorists understand that Iraq is the central front in the war on terror. They're testing our will, and day by day they are learning our will is firm. Their cause will fail. We will stay on the offensive. Whatever it takes, we will seek and find and destroy the terrorists, so that we do not have to face them in our own country. ((applause))

In discussing the issue of context sensitivity and negotiability in narrative, Bruner (1991) notes, "We inevitably take the teller's intentions into account and do so in terms of our background knowledge (and, indeed, in the light of our presuppositions about the teller's background knowledge)" (17). In other words, "we assimilate narrative on our own terms" and according to our own ideological biases. Moreover, narrators intuitively understand this and know that, to make their story believable, outside corroboration may be needed. The citation of "the terrorists" in excerpts 24 and 25 effectively provides this outside corroboration. If one does not believe George W. Bush's assertion that Iraq is the "central front in the war on terror," then one only need listen to the terrorists themselves. So goes the implicit reasoning in these narrative excerpts.

An even stronger form of corroboration through citation is to represent the terrorists' position in their own words—that is, through the use of reported speech. In excerpts 26 and 27, Bush quotes Osama Bin Laden directly.

Excerpt 26. (Bush 2007, August 22)

We must remember the words of the enemy. We must listen to what they say. Bin Laden has declared that "the war in Iraq is for you or us to win. If we win it, it means your disgrace and defeat forever." Iraq is one of several fronts in the war on terror. But it's the central front. It's the central front for the enemy that attacked us and wants to attack us again, and it's the central front for the United States and to withdraw without getting the job done would be devastating. ((applause))

Excerpt 27. (Bush 2005, June 28)

Some wonder whether Iraq is a central front in the war on terror. Among the terrorists there is no debate. Hear the words of Osama Bin Laden. "This Third World War is raging in Iraq. The whole world is watching this war." He says, "It will end in victory and glory, or misery and humiliation." The terrorists know that the outcome will leave them emboldened, or defeated. So they are waging a campaign of murder and destruction. And there is no limit to the innocent lives they are willing to take.

After quoting Bin Laden in excerpt 26, Bush summarizes the interpretation to be drawn about Iraq: "It's the central front for the enemy that attacked us." Therefore, his evaluation concludes, "it's the central front for the United States." In excerpt 27, Bush directly responds to the words of his critics—i.e., in Bakhtin's (1986) terms, that "indefinite, unconcretized *other*" (95)—who "wonder whether Iraq is a central front in the war on terror." As in excerpt 26, he quotes "the words of Osama Bin Laden" to provide outside corroboration for his assertion that Iraq is indeed part of the "war on terror." The implicit assessment is that the inclusion of Iraq within the Narrative arises out of de facto necessity rather than the ideological bias of the narrator. That is, the decision to include Iraq within the framework of the "war on terror" supposedly stems from an "objective reality" external to the Narrative.

Moreover, the presence of terrorists in Iraq after the invasion further bolsters claims about a linkage between Iraq and terrorists prior to the invasion. Thus, as Bruner (1991) discusses, narrative explanations excel at "converting post hoc into propter hoc" (19). A strong counter-argument made by administration critics, backed up by a 2005 report by the National Intelligence Council (see NIC 2005 and Priest 2005), claims that Iraq had little to do with Al Qaeda prior to the U.S. invasion and that the American war has effectively turned Iraq into a haven for terrorists. Within the Narrative, however, the causal direction is flipped so that postinvasion terrorist activity works to prop up and further solidify the Iraq episode. The Narrative uses this evidence to interpret its claims made prior to the invasion as prescient foresight. "Truth" in narrative, as Bruner (1991) explains, does not "depend on its correctly referring to reality" but rather on its semblance to reality. "Narrative 'truth' is judged by its verisimilitude rather than its verifiability" (Bruner 1991: 13).

Challenges and commitment

The final section of the Narrative acts as a coda (Labov 1972). It sums up the challenges faced in the "war on terror" and concludes with a call to persevere amidst those challenges. It ends the Narrative by looking ahead to the future. As the concluding episode, it therefore bridges "the gap between the moment of time at the end of the narrative proper and the present" context of the speech (Labov 1972: 365). A simple example is seen in excerpt 28, taken from Bush's address to the nation two months after 9/11.

Excerpt 28. (Bush 2001, November 8)

Ours is the cause of freedom. We've defeated freedom's enemies before, and we will defeat them again. ((applause)) We cannot know every turn this battle will take. Yet we know our cause is just, and our ultimate victory is assured. We will no doubt face new challenges, but we have our marching orders. My fellow Americans, let's roll.

Here, Bush moves away from precise details about the "war on terror" (e.g., the naming of specific fronts, actions taken, etc.) to vague generalizations about "the cause of freedom" and "ultimate victory." Amidst these platitudes, he warns of uncertain challenges to come, "We cannot know every turn this battle will take." Any war, and especially a nebulous "war on terror," is sure to be fraught with unanticipated difficulties. One effect of acknowledging these difficulties is to further position the "war on terror" as an open-ended, malleable conflict. Despite whatever "turn this battle will take," the implication is that the "war on terror" will respond accordingly. This leaves open the possibility for opening new "fronts" under the rubric of fighting terrorism.

Moreover, as this lays the ground for expanding the "war on terror," it simultaneously works to *prejustify* any such expansion. The future possible actions, whatever they may be, are justified because "we know our cause is just, and our ultimate victory is assured." These global assertions—or "axiom markers" (Adams, Towns and Gavey 1995)—provide self-evident rationale for the unfettered continuation of the "war on terror." They work to replace legitimate debate on the wisdom and efficacy of policy choices with blind faith in the actions narrated by the President. If the wisdom of the Bush administration's course of action is accepted as self-evident, then, as Bush concludes, "we have our marching orders. My fellow Americans, let's roll." In other words, there is no other choice but for Americans to persevere down the path laid out in the Narrative.

Furthermore, as is often implied in this episode, a failure to faithfully commit to this path is depicted as "surrender" to the "enemy" given the characterization of America's response to terrorism as a "war." This view, which paints the world in black or white, is well summarized in the doctrine outlined earlier in excerpt 7: "either you're with us or you're with the enemy." This final episode of the Narrative concludes by intimating this Manichean vision of the world. As Bush alludes to the challenges that America faces in the "war on terror," the only choice in this either-or binary is to remain resolved in the "cause of freedom" in order to defeat "freedom's enemies." Although the particular details in this coda may take many forms across Bush's speeches, the theme of challenges and commitment remains consistent.

A CANONICAL EXAMPLE OF THE NARRATIVE

Here, I provide an example that illustrates the elements discussed above and how they flow together within a situated telling. This extended excerpt shows the unfolding of the Narrative in a concise rendition told in a speech by Bush to an audience of military personnel and families at Fort Stewart, Georgia in 2003. I have added labels for each episode in capitalized headings.

Excerpt 29. (Bush 2003, September 12)

((The Narrative begins 5:23 minutes into the speech after general opening remarks.))

PRECIPITATING EVENT

Two and a half years ago, or two years ago, this nation came under enemy attack. Two years ago yesterday, we were attacked. On a single morning, we suffered the highest casualties on our own soil since the Civil War. America saw the face of a new adversary. An enemy that plots in secret, an enemy that rejects the rules of war, an enemy that rejoices in the murder of the innocent. We made a pledge that day, and we have kept it. We are bringing the guilty to justice, we are taking the fight to the enemy. ((applause))

AMERICA'S RESPONSE

In this new kind of war America has followed a new strategy. We are not waiting for further attacks on our citizens. We are striking our enemies before they can strike us again. ((applause)) As all of you know, wars are fought on the offensive. The war on terror will be won on the offensive. And America and our friends are staying on the offensive. We're rolling back- ((applause)) We're rolling back the terrorist threat, not on the fringes of its influence, but at the heart of its power. ((applause))

BATTLE OF AFGHANISTAN

In Afghanistan America and our broad coalition acted against a regime that harbored Al Qaeda, and ruled by terror. We've sent a message that is now understood throughout the world. If you harbor a terrorist, if you support a terrorist, if you feed a terrorist, you're just as guilty as the terrorists, and the Taliban found out what we meant. ((applause)) Thanks to our men and women in uniform, Afghanistan is no longer a haven for terror, and as a result, the people of America are safer from attack. ((applause))

NUMEROUS FRONTS

We are hunting the Al Qaeda terrorists wherever they still hide, from Pakistan to the Philippines to the Horn of Africa. And we're making good progress. Nearly two-thirds of Al Qaeda's known leaders have been captured or killed. The rest of them are dangerous, but the rest of them can be certain we're on their trail. Our resolve is firm; the resolve of this nation is clear. No matter how long it takes, we will bring justice to those who plot against America. ((applause))

BATTLE OF IRAQ

And we have pursued the war on terror in Iraq. Our coalition enforced the demands of the UN Security Council, in one of the swiftest and most humane military campaigns in history. Because of our military, cata-strophic weapons will no longer be in the hands of a reckless dictator. ((applause)) Because of our military, Middle Eastern countries no longer fear subversion and attack by Saddam Hussein. Because of our military, the torture chambers in Iraq are closed, and people who speak their minds need not fear execution. Because of our military, the people of Iraq are free. ((applause))

((From 10:25 to 22:55 minutes into the speech, the Iraq episode is developed and discussed in more detail.))

CHALLENGES AND COMMITMENT

In meeting the dangers of a new era, the world looks to America for leadership. And America counts on the men and women who have stepped forward as volunteers in the cause of freedom. I want to thank you all for your good service. Thank you for the credit, and honor, you bring to our country every day. May God bless you, may God bless your families, and may God continue to bless America. ((applause))

((The speech ends here at 23:32 minutes.))

Overall, excerpt 29 provides a canonical example of the Narrative, although a differently situated telling may vary slightly from this typical form. As can be seen in this particular rendition, the bulk of the speech is dedicated to developing arguments within the Iraq episode (most of which I have elided from the excerpt). In any given telling, one or another episode may be developed more than others. For example, prior to or after the invasion of Afghanistan, that episode would be developed in more detail, just as the Iraq episode is developed here. And, of course, the section on Iraq does not enter into the narrative until 2002, about a year after 9/11, when the selling of that war began in earnest. Moreover, differently situated tellings of the Narrative may omit or combine sections, such as illustrated earlier in excerpt 19 where the episodes on America's response and the numerous global fronts were merged. Also, additional episodes infrequently appear, such as discussion of the history leading up to 9/11, yet I have not discussed them here because they are rare.

Despite subtle variations, the structure and organization I have sketched in this chapter is canonical of the Narrative text. It begins with the precipitating event of 9/11 and then alternates between general and specific episodes. That is, the precipitating event is followed by a general introduction to America's response to terrorism. The text then moves to specific details of the actions taken in Afghanistan, and then back to a more general listing of numerous global fronts. The listing of numerous fronts works to segue into the next episode, which provides specific details on the actions taken in Iraq. Finally, the coda anticipates, in general terms, the challenges that America faces and emphasizes its commitment to forge ahead.

This movement between general and specific episodes structurally connects the diverse elements. The specific details of the war in Afghanistan are connected with the specific details of the war in Iraq via a general episode that establishes the numerous global fronts on which the "war on terror" is waged. Moreover, the chronological ordering of the episodes, which moves from September 11, 2001 to the invasion of Afghanistan and on to the invasion of Iraq via the intermediary episode that details successes on the numerous global fronts, helps stitch together a timeline of historical events into a coherent narrative about those events. The common thread that unites everything within the narrative realm is the one that runs back to the precipitating event of 9/11. This thread weaves together the diverse episodes so that within the framework of the Narrative everything flows from 9/11 as actions that America has taken in the struggle against terrorism. This contextual domain of the Narrative thus provides a basis for interpreting the disparate foreign policy objectives of the Bush administration within its scope. I return to this point in the next chapter in a more detailed discussion of the Iraq context.

THE NARRATIVE CONSTRUCTION OF SOCIOPOLITICAL REALITY

The structure of the Narrative outlined in this chapter is representative of the macrolevel discourse about the "war on terror" found across Bush's speeches. As a narrative told on repeated occasions, the text has accrued into a shared cultural narrative. Bruner (1991) argues, "Once shared culturally [. . .] narrative accruals achieve, like Emile Durkheim's collective representation, 'exteriority' and the power of constraint" (19). The "war on terror" comes to exist and American actions at home and abroad are shaped accordingly. As a Foucauldian discourse, the Narrative represents knowledge about America's struggle against terrorism in the early part of the twenty-first century. It regulates the way this topic can be talked about meaningfully at this particular point in history.

The importance of narrative in constructing sociopolitical reality comes from its capacity to organize experience and human happenings. In many ways, narrative is a much more powerful device for doing this than "logical and scientific procedures that can be weeded out by falsification" (Bruner 1991: 3). As Bruner (1991) reminds us, "Narratives, then, are a version of reality whose acceptability is governed by convention and 'narrative necessity' rather than by empirical verification and logical requiredness, although ironically we have no compunction about calling stories true or false" (Bruner 1991: 4–5). Regardless of the objective "truth" about 9/11 and the various facets of America's response to terrorism—e.g., the logic of countering terrorism qua war (chapter 2), the nature of links between Iraq and Al Qaeda (chapter 4), and so forth—the Narrative has sustained a *regime of truth* (Foucault 1980) with real world consequences. It has effectively constructed a version of sociopolitical reality that even opponents of the Bush administration's policy live within and must adopt the language of in order to affect political change (the topic of chapters 5–7). The next chapter continues to explore the production of this text in terms of the connections it draws between the war in Iraq and the "war on terror."

4

The Construction of Al Qaeda
and Iraq as Linked Antagonists

> The terrorists regard Iraq as the central front in their
> war against humanity. And we must recognize Iraq as
> the central front in our war on terror.
>
> — George W. Bush (2005, October 6)

INTRODUCTION

As mentioned in the previous chapter, one of the most contested elements of the Narrative is the characterization of Iraq as an episode in America's war against terrorism. Central to this characterization is the claim of existential links between Saddam Hussein and Al Qaeda so that a strike against Iraq is viewed as equivalent to a strike against terrorists in the "war on terror." Despite evidence that no such links existed,[1] the Narrative succeeded in constructing a particular version of sociopolitical reality that profoundly shaped public understandings and helped justify the war in Iraq. Notably, a Pew Research Center poll conducted at the beginning of October 2002 showed that two-thirds of Americans believed "Saddam Hussein helped the terrorists in the September 11th attacks" (Pew 2002).

1. The final report of the 9/11 Commission released in 2004 states, "But to date we have seen no evidence that these or the earlier contacts ever developed into a collaborative

Similarly, an April 2004 study by the Program on International Policy Attitudes (PIPA) at the University of Maryland showed that 57 percent of Americans believed that Iraq had provided "substantial support to Al Qaeda, including 20 percent who believe[d] that Iraq was directly involved in the September 11 attacks" (PIPA 2004a).

The selling of the Iraq war and its incorporation into the Narrative was part of a concerted marketing campaign timed by the administration to begin in the fall of 2002. As White House chief of staff Andrew Card explained in a *New York Times* article, "From a marketing point of view, you don't introduce new products in August" (Bumiller 2002, September 7). With Congress back from its summer recess and Americans home from their summer vacations, administration figures began to weave the Iraq episode into the Narrative to make the case for opening another "front" in the "war on terror." In the week leading up to a planned congressional vote to authorize the use of military force against Iraq, Bush addressed Congress on October 2 and gave a notable speech to a public audience in Cincinnati on October 7. With congressional approval secured, the discursive build-up to war continued in an effort to convince skeptical members of the international community and unconvinced Americans. In this chapter, I examine Bush's speeches prior to the March 2003 invasion as well as those after the conflict began to examine how the "socially recognized sameness" (Bucholtz and Hall 2004: 383) of the otherwise disparate entities of Iraq and Al Qaeda is discursively achieved.[2] I draw from Bucholtz and Hall's (2004) work on language and identity to examine this process.

THE TACTICS OF INTERSUBJECTIVITY

Bucholtz and Hall's (2004) *tactics of intersubjectivity* provide a framework for understanding how "social identities come to be created through language" (370). Their model emphasizes the fluid and dynamic process of identity construction that variously emphasizes or downplays sameness and difference. Bucholtz and Hall explain as follows:

---

operational relationship. Nor have we seen evidence indicating that Iraq cooperated with Al Qaeda in the developing or carrying out any attacks against the United States" (NC 2004b: 83). A Senate Intelligence Committee (2006) report provides more details on the lack of a connection. Moreover, as pointed out by many critics (see, for example, Jhally and Earp 2004; Cirincione 2003), the goal of "regime change in Iraq" was part of the Bush administration foreign policy prior to taking office and well before the events of 9/11.

2. Earlier formulations of this analysis were developed in Hodges (2004) and Hodges (2007b).

Tactics of intersubjectivity are the relations that are created through identity work. We have chosen the term *tactics*, following Certeau (1984 [1974]), to invoke the local, situated, and often improvised quality of the everyday practices through which individuals, though restricted in their freedom to act by externally imposed constraints, accomplish their social goals. Our second term, *intersubjectivity*, is meant to highlight the place of agency and interactional negotiation in the formation of identity. (Bucholtz and Hall 2004: 383)

They present three pairs of complementary tactics: adequation / distinction, authentication / denaturalization, and authorization / illegitimation. Of particular concern for this chapter is the tactic of adequation, which establishes "socially recognized sameness" among individuals or groups.

The tactic of adequation can be seen, for example, within a nation during times of war when internal differences (e.g., between political parties) are suspended to form a united front. "In this relation, potentially salient differences are set aside in favor of perceived or asserted similarities that are taken to be more situationally relevant" (Bucholtz and Hall 2004: 383). The ubiquitous "United We Stand" bumper sticker seen on cars within the United States after the events of 9/11 is one example of how semiotic resources can be harnessed to create social cohesion. Differences within the polity are ignored and commonalities are brought to the forefront. In international relations, the tactic of adequation figures into alliances formed when nations face a common enemy (e.g., the United States and Soviet Union during World War II). *Adequation* works in contrast to the tactic of *distinction*, which "is the mechanism whereby salient difference is produced" (Bucholtz and Hall 2004: 384). In times of war, a nation sets up a binary opposition with the enemy "other" against which the nation fights. Through the tactic of distinction, the differences between "us" and "them" are highlighted and made salient.

Importantly, ideology undergirds these tactics of adequation and distinction. To achieve adequation, for example, differences may be erased. This *erasure*, captured in Irvine and Gal's (2000) use of the term, ensures that facts "inconsistent with the ideological scheme either go unnoticed or get explained away" (38). Therefore, as Bucholtz and Hall (2004) explain, identity "is a process not merely of discovering or acknowledging a similarity that precedes" a particular context, but of "inventing similarity and downplaying difference" (Bucholtz and Hall 2004: 371; see also Bourdieu 1984). Rather than existing prior to social interaction, identities are a social achievement emergent through interaction and shaped by ideology.

In the Narrative, the process of adequation is imposed from without, so that a connection between Iraq and Al Qaeda is created, not from the perspective of the two entities themselves, but from the perspective of the Bush administration. Potentially salient differences are erased on their behalf in order to position the two as a cohesive enemy alliance against which the United States wages its "war on terror." One difference potentially worth recognizing includes the animosity between Bin Laden's brand of Islamic fundamentalism and Saddam Hussein's secular dictatorship. In a tape released by Bin Laden on February 11, 2003, he emphasizes his "belief in the infidelity of socialists. [. . .] Socialists are infidels wherever they are, whether they are in Baghdad or Aden" (Bin Laden 2003). Notably, this difference is erased in the Narrative where Bin Laden's aims and ambitions are said to be shared by Saddam Hussein.

As Bucholtz and Hall (2004), note, "externally imposed identity categories generally have at least as much to do with the observer's own identity position and power stakes as with any sort of objectively describable social reality" (370). The capacity of narrative to define sociopolitical reality builds off the symbolic power of the speaker who imbues the message with credibility. According to Bourdieu (1987b), symbolic power is "worldmaking power" in that it can impose a "legitimate vision of the social world and of its divisions" (13). Thus, underlying the rhetorical strategies of the Narrative is the President's symbolic capital (Bourdieu 1991) as well as his related political capital. As Bush himself described in a November 4, 2004 press conference after winning a second term in office, "Let me put it to you this way: I earned capital in the campaign, political capital, and now I intend to spend it." In short, from his position of authority, the President wields "nomination power" (Bourdieu 1986, 1987a), or the power to impose a credible definition of sociopolitical identities on the world.

The nomination power wielded by President Bush in the categorization of Iraq and Al Qaeda as allies in the "war on terror" produces real world consequences regardless of the merit of the identification in actual fact. As a product of the situation, those identities may be taken up and given legitimacy by other social actors in a process of mutual social reinforcement. In the Narrative, the discursive construction of an Iraq/Al Qaeda alliance sets the stage for those entities to potentially orient to that imposed identity configuration. In the same February 2003 speech in which Bin Laden denounces Saddam Hussein as an infidel, he accedes to the adequation forced upon Al Qaeda and Iraq by Bush and states, "Under these circumstances, there will be no harm if the interests of Muslims converge with the interests of the socialists in the fight against the crusaders"

(Bin Laden 2003, February 12). As cited in chapter 3, the 2005 report by the National Intelligence Council details how the invasion of Iraq effectively carved out a space for Al Qaeda-linked terrorists in Iraq that did not previously exist (NIC 2005; Priest 2005[3]). Identity, therefore, is itself an effect of culture and sociopolitical interaction undergirded by relations of power.

HISTORICAL-CAUSAL ENTAILMENT

As discussed in chapter 3, the part-whole textual interdependence of the Narrative positions the wars in Afghanistan and Iraq as parts of the larger whole—that is, as "fronts" in the global "war on terror." Moreover, in Bruner's (1991) terms, the Narrative invokes a "historical-causal entailment" (19) so that the invasion of Iraq can be seen as following a natural historical progression that leads from 9/11 through the invasion of Afghanistan to Iraq. The following excerpts illustrate this progression. Excerpts 1 and 2 are taken from Bush's speech on May 1, 2003 to declare the end of combat operations in Iraq, given aboard an aircraft carrier off the coast of San Diego. Excerpt 3 comes from Bush's September 2003 address to the nation. As in the latter part of chapter 2, I follow Gee (1986) in representing the excerpts that follow in lines and stanzas to capture the poetic flow of the speech (see appendix B for full transcription conventions).

Excerpt 1. (Bush 2003, May 1)

1   The *battle of Iraq* is *one victory* in a *war on terror*
2   that began on September the 11th 2001
3   and still goes on.

Excerpt 2. (Bush 2003, May 1)

1   In the *battle of Afghanistan*
2   we destroyed the Taliban,
3   many terrorists,
4   and the camps where they trained.

3. In press coverage of the National Intelligence Council's report, Priest (2005) notes, "President Bush has frequently described the Iraq war as an integral part of U.S. efforts to combat terrorism. But the council's report suggests the conflict has also helped terrorists by creating a haven for them in the chaos of war."

Excerpt 3. (Bush 2003, September 7)

1   America and a broad coalition
2   acted first in Afghanistan,
3   by destroying the training camps of terror
4   and removing the regime
5   that harbored Al Qaeda.

The language in these excerpts assembles a series of events (i.e., 9/11, action in Afghanistan, action in Iraq) into the conceptual framework of a larger war. In excerpt 1, Bush refers to the war in Iraq as "the battle of Iraq" and calls it "one victory in a war on terror that began on September the 11th 2001 and still goes on." Here, 9/11 acts as the precipitating event from which "the battle of Iraq" eventually arises; but only after "the battle of Afghanistan" (line 1 of excerpt 2) has taken place. As Bush notes in excerpt 3, "America and a broad coalition acted first in Afghanistan." The description "acted first" (line 2 of excerpt 3) presupposes more actions to come after Afghanistan; and this promise bears fruit with the "battle of Iraq." Moreover, even after Iraq, the broader war "still goes on" (line 3 of excerpt 1).

Bruner (1991) discusses "the imposition of bogus *historical-causal entailment*" as a feature of narrative that works to frame events placed within the storyline. Through this feature, events may take on a causal re-lationship with other events in the story—for example, "the assassination of Archduke Ferdinand is seen as 'causing' the outbreak of the First World War" (Bruner 1991: 19). In a similar manner, the precipitating event of 9/11—which breaches the normalcy or canonicity of everyday life—acts as the originating causus belli for the invasions of both Afghanistan and Iraq. The natural progression from 9/11 to Afghanistan to Iraq is further illustrated in the following excerpt from a speech Bush gave in Saint Louis after the invasion of Iraq and before the "end of major combat operations." The excerpt provides a concise abstract of the progression of episodes within the Narrative.

Excerpt 4. (Bush 2003, April 16)

1   On September the 11th,
2   2001,
3   America found that we are not immune
4   to the threats
5   that gather for years

6   across the oceans.
7   Threats that can arrive in sudden tragedy.

8   Since September the 11th we've been engaged in a global war against terror,
9   a war being waged on many fronts.

10   That war continues,
11   and we are winning. ((applause))

12   In Afghanistan we and our allies ended the rule of the Taliban,
13   and closed down camps where terrorists plotted,
14   and trained
15   to attack us.

16   In Iraq,
17   our coalition has now removed an ally of terrorists,
18   and a producer of weapons of mass destruction.

19   In other nations we're hunting
20   and capturing members of Al Qaeda,
21   disrupting their plans before they can strike.

22   Across the world, terrorists
23   and tyrants
24   are learning this, that America and our friends and our allies will act in
      our own defense.
25   Instead of drifting toward tragedy,
26   we will protect our security,
27   and we will promote the peace in the world. ((applause))

The structure of the Narrative implies a historical-causal entailment so that the U.S. invasion of Iraq flows naturally from the events beginning with 9/11 and on through the invasion of Afghanistan. Bruner (1991) states that when the flow of such events fits seamlessly with the whole, the "telling preempts momentarily the possibility of any but a single interpretation" (9). Put another way, a key aim of narrative is achieved: plausibility. As described by Ochs and Capps (2001: 284), plausibility is important in narrative because it leads to credibility. Narrators embed their subjective evaluations within the naming of objective events that cannot be contradicted. For example, the recounting of events in excerpt 4 includes a description of the removal of Saddam Hussein from power in Iraq (lines 16–18). However, embedded within this description of these objective events is the evaluation that this means "our coalition has now removed an ally of terrorists" (line 17). Presupposed in this representation of Saddam Hussein is that he in fact was an "ally of terrorists." Although this presupposition has been widely contradicted outside the Narrative, within the

Narrative the positioning of such an evaluation among a series of objective events lends credence to the relationship between Iraq and the string of events in the surrounding text. Where an "unsubstantiated piece of interpretation is positioned after the carefully substantiated account," Fairclough (1995b) notes, "the aura of objectivity has been established, and interpretation now perhaps stands a good chance of passing as fact" (84). Moreover, the linkage between Iraq and Al Qaeda plays off of Bruner's (1991) notion of *coherence by contemporaneity*, which is "the belief that things happening at the same time must be connected" (19). Thus, an invasion of Iraq after a "war on terror" has been declared implies that the two events, which are happening within the same historical timeframe, must be related.

In his examination of presidential speeches, Silverstein (2003b) uses Vygotsky's notion of "thinking-in-complexes" to offer a comparable explanation (21–24). Similar to Bucholtz and Hall's (2004) focus on sameness in their *tactic of adequation*, a Vygotskian "complex" categorizes a series of items in terms of equivalence. Thinking-in-complexes, therefore, allows us to see "at least a local 'family resemblance'" when disparate items are juxtaposed, even when "the whole lot of things might still be very diverse overall" (Silverstein 2003b: 21). Especially in politics, Silverstein argues, "issues must be brought together—given plot and characters, rhyme if not reason" (Silverstein 2003b: 24). The merging of diverse foreign policy issues in the Narrative is exemplified by the transformation of the administration's pre-9/11 goal of regime change in Iraq into a central component of the fight against terrorism. Thus, "the battle of Iraq is one victory in a war on terror that began on September the 11th 2001 and still goes on" (excerpt 1). The "war on terror" label is a type of "captioning label or image," to use Silverstein's (2003b) words, which allows the entire analogical series to assume "a definitive identity—in fact retrospectively a *necessary* identity that we now recognize as so many examples of one underlying principle, conceptually implicit, even immanent" (23). This necessary identity structures the perceptual experience of a nation, and it does so in line with ideologically inspired policy objectives.

TERRORISM AS A CONCEPTUAL CATEGORY

Leading up to the invasion of Iraq on March 20, 2003, the Narrative pursues the *imposed adequation* of Iraq and Al Qaeda through their placement in the same conceptual category marked by lexical descriptors associated with the concept of terrorism (e.g., "terror," "terrorism," and "terrorist"). The remarkably different aims and aspirations of a nation-state (i.e., Iraq) and a militant terrorist group (i.e., Al Qaeda) are erased; and both entities are categorized in relation to terror, as illustrated in the excerpts that follow. Excerpt 5 is taken from Bush's October 2002 speech in Cincinnati prior to the Congressional vote on the Iraq War Resolution, which authorized the President's use of force against Iraq.

Excerpt 5. (Bush 2002, October 7)

1   Tonight I want to take a few minutes to discuss a grave threat to peace
2   and America's determination to lead the world
3   in confronting that threat.
4   The threat comes from Iraq.

5   It arises directly from the Iraqi regime's own actions,
6   its history of aggression,
7   and its drive
8   toward an *arsenal*
9   of *terror*.

10   Eleven years ago
11   as a condition for ending the Persian Gulf War,
12   the Iraqi regime was required to destroy its *weapons of mass destruction*,
13   to cease all development of such *weapons*,
14   and to stop all support for *terrorist groups*.

15   The Iraqi regime has violated
16   all of those obligations.
17   It possesses and produces chemical
18   and biological *weapons*,
19   it is seeking nuclear *weapons*,
20   it has given shelter and support to *terrorism*,
21   and practices *terror*
22   against its own people.

As seen in lines 8–9 of excerpt 5, the threat from Iraq is narrated as stemming from "its drive toward an arsenal of terror" rather than, say, a drive toward enhanced military capability to deter, defend or spread national interests as other nation-states do. As the excerpt continues, the notion of terrorism is repeatedly juxtaposed with an important rationale for waging war against Iraq: the possession, whether potential or real, of weapons of mass destruction (WMD). There is an alternation between "weapons" and lexical descriptors related to the notion of terror at the end of the lines, such as "terrorist groups" (line 14), "terrorism" (line 20), and "terror" (line 21). The rhetorical structure of the delivery weaves together an image of the two issues of "terrorist groups" and military "weapons of mass destruction" as inseparable so that the terror of 9/11 is positioned as morally equivalent to Iraq's "arsenal of terror." In this way, Al Qaeda's brand of terrorism is rhetorically constructed as a natural counterpart to Iraq's military actions and objectives.

The moral equivalence between the two is spelled out in excerpt 6, taken from remarks made by Bush at an appearance with Congressional leaders to discuss the upcoming vote on the Iraq War Resolution.

Excerpt 6. (Bush 2002, October 2)

1 Countering Iraq's threat is also a central commitment on the war on
  terror. ((six lines on Saddam Hussein's links to international terrorists))
2 We must confront both *terror cells* and *terror states*,
3 because they are different faces of the same evil.

The juxtaposition between "terror cells" and nation-states occurs in line 2 with the gratuitous modification of "states" as "terror states" (see also Fowler, Kress, Hodge and Trew's 1979 notion of "over-lexicalization"). Various modifiers can be used in the negative presentation of foreign enemies, overlexicalizing enemy states as "rogue states," "imperialist states," etc. Here, the choice of the modifier "terror" positions the nation-state of Iraq as morally equivalent to "terror cells." As Bush states in line 3, "they are different faces of the same evil." This coupling lays the foundation for a more direct link to Al Qaeda. That link is presented within the umbra of 9/11, the pivot around which the Narrative revolves, as seen in the excerpt below from Bush's Cincinnati speech prior to the Iraq War Resolution.

Excerpt 7. (Bush 2002, October 7)

1 The attacks of *September the 11th*
2 showed our country that vast oceans
3 no longer protect us from danger

4 Before that tragic date
5 we had only hints of *Al Qaeda's plans*
6 *and designs*

7 Today in Iraq
8 we see *a threat whose outlines*

9   are far more *clearly defined*
10 and whose consequences
11 could be far more deadly

12 Saddam Hussein's actions have put us on notice
13 and there is no refuge
14 from our responsibilities.

The threats posed by Al Qaeda and Iraq are positioned as sufficiently similar in the Narrative so that any potential difference is portrayed as one of degree, rather than of kind. In excerpt 7, "Al Qaeda's plans and designs" (lines 5–6) are juxtaposed with the "outlines" of a threat that are "clearly defined" in Iraq (lines 8–9). The structure in excerpt 7 moves from the precipitating event of 9/11 (line 1) to future possible events, and alternates between the two actors, Al Qaeda and Saddam Hussein. The parallelism that rhetorically juxtaposes the two actors reinforces the conceptual link between them. Here, parallelism is used to equate the negative properties of one opponent with another (van Dijk 1991: 219). The effect is that the devastation of 9/11 as embodied by the Al Qaeda hijackers subtly blurs with the hypothetical future actions of Saddam Hussein. Whereas Al Qaeda's plans have already been enacted in the "attacks of September the 11th" (line 1), the "consequences" (line 10) of the Iraqi threat have yet to be experienced. In this way, the Narrative links the lived past with the hypothetical future[4], and Al Qaeda's terrorist hijackers with Iraq's military.

THE LOGIC OF COMPLEMENTARITY

As Gal (2005) notes, "In general, erasures are forms of forgetting, denying, ignoring, or forcibly eliminating those distinctions or social facts that fail to fit the picture of the world presented by an ideology" (27). In the next excerpts from the Cincinnati speech, differences at odds with the ideological scheme are erased to set up a compatible relationship between nonstate terrorists and the nation-state of Iraq through the complementary roles each is capable of playing.

Excerpt 8. (Bush 2002, October 7)

1 All that might be required are a small container and *one terrorist*
2 or *Iraqi intelligence operative* to deliver it.

4. For more on the way political discourse projects the future, see Dunmire (2007).

3 And that is the source
4 of our urgent concern about *Saddam Hussein's links to international
   terrorist groups.*

5 Over the years
6 Iraq has provided *safe haven* to terrorists
7 such as Abu Nidal. ((eight lines on Abu Nidal))

8 Iraq has also provided *safe haven* to Abu Abbas. ((three lines on Abu
   Abbas))

9 And we know that Iraq is continuing to *finance terror*
10 and *gives assistance* to groups that use terrorism to undermine
11 Middle East peace.

In excerpt 8, Bush equates "one terrorist" (line 1) with an "Iraqi intelligence operative" (line 2). Either one or the other is deemed capable of an identical act of mass terror. Namely, in the scenario depicted, either "one terrorist or Iraqi intelligence operative" would release "a small container" (presumably of chemical or biological weapons in an American city). This image of a "terrorist" and an "Iraqi intelligence operative" using the same methods and operating with the same goals erases the different aims and motivations of the nonstate terrorist group and nation-state. Moreover, the existential presupposition in line 4 introduces a link between Saddam Hussein and "international terrorist groups" as a matter of fact. As pointed out by Lewis (1979), a fact embedded in a presupposition may be subject to "accommodation." That is, the "proposition may be added to the interpreter's memory as a 'fact' of reality" (Chilton 2004: 63). Given the presupposed nature of Saddam Hussein's links to terrorists, the hypothetical scenario spelled out in the first two lines through the modal "might" now morphs into a real concern. The imagined scene is thereby connected with what is presented as concrete reality.

As excerpt 8 continues, Iraq is positioned as a potential source of support (e.g., financing and assistance) for nonstate terrorist organizations; and terrorist groups are positioned as possible recipients or benefactors of that support. Beginning in line 4, Iraq's past support of individuals involved in acts of terror are enumerated. The use of the present perfect and present progressive in this excerpt—e.g., "has provided" (line 6), "has also provided" (line 8), "is continuing" (line 9)—leaves open the time frame of these actions. The use of the present progressive in line 9 ("we know that Iraq is continuing to finance terror") presupposes a past pattern of financing terror, which is pointed to with direct references to individual terrorists— "Abu Nidal" (line 7) and "Abu Abbas" (line 8). Moreover, it indicates "that Iraq is continuing" to act according to those precedents. Importantly, these established precedents are then used as a basis for inferring potential Iraqi support of Al Qaeda.

In their work on narrative, Ochs and Capps (2001) discuss the legal concept known as the *doctrine of precedent*, "the doctrine that decisions of earlier cases sufficiently like a new case should be repeated in the new case" (209). As they explain, we search for "familiar characteristics and analogies with previous situations that have come into public light and often pass judgment accordingly" (Ochs and Capps 2001: 209). Detailing the specific individuals who have carried out past acts classified as terrorism, e.g., Abu Nidal (line 7) and Abu Abbas (line 8), and their relation to Iraq establishes precedent. Their representation in this excerpt further strengthens the notion that these are but a few instances of an ongoing, established pattern of support for terrorism in the Middle East.

In legal proceedings, circumstantial evidence (i.e., facts used to infer other facts without direct evidence) also plays an important role in formulating judgments. Iraq's past ties to these individuals responsible for acts of violence throughout the Middle East authenticates a pattern that may plausibly be repeated in the case of Al Qaeda, which Bush turns to in excerpt 9.

Excerpt 9. (Bush 2002, October 7)

1 We know that Iraq and Al Qaeda have had *high level contacts*
2 that go back a decade.
3 Some Al Qaeda leaders who fled Afghanistan
4 went to Iraq.
5 These include one very senior Al Qaeda leader who *received medical treatment*
6 in Baghdad
7 this year.
8 And who has been associated with planning for chemical
9 and biological attacks.

In excerpt 9, Al Qaeda is directly referenced three times in a manner that fits with Iraq's supposed pattern of support for terrorists. The first piece of evidence is that "some Al Qaeda leaders who fled Afghanistan went to Iraq" (lines 3–4). Not only does this position Iraq as a potential provider of a safe haven to Al Qaeda leaders, but it also conceptually stitches together the war in Afghanistan with Iraq. The second piece of evidence is that one of those members of Al Qaeda who fled Afghanistan was "one very senior Al Qaeda leader who received medical treatment in

Baghdad" (lines 5–6). Thus, Iraq is said to provide both shelter and medical treatment to Al Qaeda, types of support in line with the previously established pattern. Moreover, the characterization of this support under the heading of "high level contacts" (line 1) builds upon the image of high level contacts in the realm of international relations where such contacts imply diplomatic ties between governments. Although the circumstantial evidence provided here does not completely bridge to the notion of a significant, let alone collaborative, relationship, it creates a well-built scaffold that allows listeners to make the leap.

Excerpt 10 is taken from a speech given by Bush the day after Secretary of State Colin Powell briefed the UN Security Council about the Iraqi threat.

Excerpt 10. (Bush 2003, February 6)

1 One of the greatest dangers we face is that weapons of mass destruction
   might be passed to terrorists,
2 who would not hesitate to use those weapons.

3 Saddam Hussein has longstanding, direct, and continuing ties
4 to terrorist networks.

5 Senior members of Iraqi intelligence
6 and Al Qaeda
7 have met at least eight times since the early 1990s.

8 Iraq has sent bomb-making and document forgery *experts* to work with
   Al Qaeda.
9 Iraq has also provided Al Qaeda with chemical and biological weapons
   training.

10 We also know that Iraq is *harboring* a terrorist network,
11 headed by a senior Al Qaeda terrorist planner.
12 The network runs a poison and explosive training center in northeast Iraq.
13 And many of its leaders are known to be in Baghdad.
14 The head of this network traveled to Baghdad for *medical treatment*
15 and stayed for months.
16 Nearly two dozen associates joined him there
17 and have been operating in Baghdad for more than eight months.
18 *The same terrorist network* operating out of Iraq is responsible
19 for the murder,
20 the recent murder,
21 of an American citizen,
22 an American diplomat,

23   Laurence Foley.

24   *The same network* has plotted terrorism against France,
25   Spain,
26   Italy,
27   Germany,
28   the Republic of Georgia,
29   and Russia.
30   And was caught producing poisons
31   in London.
32   *The danger Saddam Hussein po- poses* reaches across the world.

In excerpt 10, the ties to terrorists are elaborated through the *logic of complementarity*. Iraq is said to supply Al Qaeda with "experts" and "training" (lines 8–9), as well as "medical treatment" (line 14). These sources of support are interleaved with references to contacts made between "senior members of Iraqi intelligence and Al Qaeda" who "have met at least eight times since the early 1990s" (lines 5–7). The juxtaposition of contacts with these forms of support works to imply a relationship of active collaboration between Iraq and Al Qaeda.

As Bruner (1991) points out, the notion of *stare decisis* in jurisprudence guarantees "a tradition by assuring that once a 'case' has been interpreted in one way, future cases that are 'similar' shall be interpreted and decided equivalently" (18). As discussed in chapter 3, one of the doctrines in the Narrative is that no distinction will be made between terrorists and those who harbor them. This policy is first established in the episode about America's military campaign against Afghanistan where the Taliban harbored Al Qaeda, and it is now applied to the Iraq episode where Saddam Hussein is said to be "harboring a terrorist network headed by a senior Al Qaeda terrorist planner" (lines 10–11). The application of this doctrine, along with the enumerated links between Iraq and terrorists, positions Iraq within the rubric of the "war on terror."

The adequation of Saddam Hussein and the terrorist network said to be operating inside Iraq is completed in the evaluation provided in line 32. In the last two stanzas of the excerpt, the actions of the terrorist network are listed, and the description of those actions begins with reference to the "terrorist network" in the subject position of the narrative clauses (line 18 and line 24). However, this referent is replaced in the evaluative clause in line 32 where the focus on the actions of the terrorist network shifts to "the danger Saddam Hussein poses." The subtle shift of reference positions the danger from Saddam Hussein as flowing directly from the actions of terrorists around the world.

The precedent of Iraq as a source of safe haven, finances, and medical treatment for terrorists, on the one hand; and Al Qaeda as a terrorist group presumably looking for and benefiting from such types of support, depicts a synergistic relationship between the two. Such an alliance poses a threat to be feared. The potential consequences of this threat are spelled out in excerpt 11, taken from Bush's Cincinnati speech.

Excerpt 11. (Bush 2002, October 7)

1 Iraq could decide on any given day
2 to provide a biological or chemical weapon to a terrorist group
3 or individual terrorists.
4 Alliance with terrorists could allow the Iraqi regime to attack America
5 without leaving
6 any fingerprints.

Although the modal auxiliary "could" in lines 1 and 4 of excerpt 11 points to a hypothetical scenario, the plausibility of the Iraqi regime using terrorists "to attack America" follows naturally from the categorization of Iraq and Al Qaeda as entities of a similar kind with shared objectives. If not fully credible, their potential to fulfill complementary roles legitimizes the scenario as at least plausible. The logic of complementarity is spelled out in more detail in excerpts 12 and 13. Excerpt 12 is from Bush's remarks at an appearance with congressional leaders prior to the vote on the Iraq War Resolution. Excerpt 13 is from Bush's 2003 State of the Union address.

Excerpt 12. (Bush 2002, October 2)

1 With the support and shelter of a regime, terror groups become far more lethal.
2 Aided by a terrorist network, an outlaw regime can launch attacks
3 while concealing its involvement.

4 Even a dictator is not suicidal,
5 but he can make use of men who are.

Excerpt 13. (Bush 2003, January 28)

1 And this Congress and the American people must recognize another threat.

2 Evidence from intelligence sources, secret communications, and statements by people now in custody

3   reveal that Saddam Hussein aids and protects terrorists,
4   including members of Al Qaeda.
5   Secretly, and without fingerprints, he could provide one of his hidden
    weapons to terrorists,
6   or help them develop their own.

7   Before September the 11th, many in the world believed that Saddam
    Hussein could be contained.
8   But chemical agents,
9   lethal viruses and shadowy terrorist networks
10 are not easily contained.

11 Imagine those 19 hijackers with other weapons
12 and other plans.
13 This time armed by Saddam Hussein.

14 It would take one vial, one canister, one crate
15 slipped into this country to bring a day of horror like none we have ever
    known.

16 We will do everything in our power
17 to make sure that that day never comes. ((applause))

In these excerpts, the complementarity between Iraq and Al Qaeda moves beyond the mere provision of support into the realm of active collaboration. Yet the collaboration takes place in a possible world rather than the actual world. In line 11 of excerpt 13, the events of 9/11 are recreated within a hypothetical space. Here, we are invited to imagine the 9/11 "hijackers with other weapons and other plans. This time armed by Saddam Hussein" (lines 11–13). The counterfactual scenario paints a picture of Saddam Hussein using members of Al Qaeda as his own special agents. As Bush states in lines 4–5 of excerpt 12, "Even a dictator is not suicidal, but he can make use of men who are." The allusion to suicide bombers conveys how "a dictator" of a nation-state could employ the same tactics generally associated with nonstate terrorists.

The hypothetical, however, will never come to pass according to the Narrative because the United States will act against Iraq. Thus, as seen in excerpt 14 from Bush's speech the day after Powell spoke at the UN, the consequences of the active collaboration between Iraq and Al Qaeda will be averted.

Excerpt 14. (Bush 2003, February 6)

1   On September the 11th 2001,
2   the American people saw what terrorists could do

3   by turning four airplanes into weapons.

4   We will not wait
5   to see what terrorists or terrorist states could do
6   with chemical, biological, radiological or nuclear weapons.

Important in these excerpts is the erasure of the motivations and goals traditionally attributed to nation-states. The concept of deterrence, for example, does not enter into the picture of Saddam Hussein waging an attack on the United States via terrorist intermediaries. Although in the hypothetical scenario, Saddam Hussein would presumably act "secretly, and without fingerprints" (line 5 of excerpt 13), it is not clear, even if this were possible, how such an attack would forward a dictator's traditional ambitions of regional dominance and geopolitical influence. Such issues are conveniently ignored—that is, erased, in the sense of Irvine and Gal's (2000) notion of *erasure*—so that the adequation of the nation-state of Iraq with nonstate terrorists interested in destroying targets like the World Trade Center is presented as wholly plausible.

THE POWER OF NARRATIVE IN THE CONSTRUCTION OF SOCIOPOLITICAL REALITY

Any form of communication is a joint endeavor between speaker and hearer that relies on common ground to succeed. In this way, even one-way political speeches can be thought of as an interactive process; and in political discourse heavily laden with implicit meaning, the background an interpreter brings to the process is certainly vital to deriving intended (or unintended) messages. The effectiveness of the Narrative's *imposed adequation* of two disparate actors in world affairs can be seen in congressional approval for action against Iraq and the dominance of ideas from the Narrative in political debate in the United States. Notably, the lexeme "terror" appears nineteen times in the Iraq War Resolution. This resolution, legally referred to as the "Authorization for Use of Military Force against Iraq Resolution of 2002," passed the House of Representatives on October 10 and the Senate on October 11, and thereby authorized the war against Iraq. (NB: This resolution is different than the "Authorization for Use of Military Force against Terrorists," which was enacted by Congress on September 18, 2001 to authorize military action against those responsible for the events of 9/11.)

In addition, public opinion polls like those mentioned in the introduction to this chapter provide an interesting perspective on the uptake of ideas espoused (whether implicitly or explicitly) by the administration. Political discourse excels at providing listeners with an incomplete scaffold that requires further filling in through the use of "bridging assumptions" (Fairclough 1995b: 123; see also, Fairclough 1992a, Brown and Yule 1983). Although the organizational structure of the Narrative discussed in chapter 3 and the discursive moves highlighted in this chapter predispose the text to certain readings, the ideological assumptions an audience brings to the task of interpretation ultimately shape the meanings that are derived (a topic taken up in more detail in chapter 6). Therefore, it is no surprise that the results of polls such as those mentioned in the introduction to this chapter vary along partisan lines. For example, a study by PIPA in October 2004, just before the November presidential elections, found that 75 percent of Bush supporters versus 30 percent of Kerry supporters had the impression that Iraq "gave Al Qaeda substantial support," whereas 20 percent of Bush supporters versus 8 percent of Kerry supporters had the impression that Iraq was "directly involved in 9/11" (PIPA 2004b).

As Bruner (1991) notes in his discussion of *context sensitivity and negotiability*, "we assimilate narrative on our own terms" (17). This includes the ideological terms to which we are predisposed. Thus, depending on the bridging assumptions one brings to the interpretive task, the Narrative could be read as not only making the case for a significant relationship between Iraq and Al Qaeda, but also for implicating Iraq's direct involvement in 9/11. As Chilton notes, "if hearers do indeed make mental representations that involve such [implied] meanings, then it is on the basis of minimal cues, which, incidentally, the speaker could disavow on the grounds that 'he never *actually said* that' [explicitly]" (122). When pressed, administration officials have expressly denied any Iraqi collaboration in 9/11, even while maintaining the idea of a significant connection (see, for example, Hodges 2007a). For example, in a White House press conference on August 21, 2006, President Bush found himself in this position when asked by a reporter what Iraq had to do with the attack on the World Trade Center on 9/11. "Nothing," Bush immediately replied, "except for it's part of—"; and Bush went on to reiterate key elements of the Narrative.

The power of political narrative to structure experience and define sociopolitical reality plays an important role in shaping actions and events on a global scale. Importantly, effective political speech couches partisan interests and actions inside "the claim that these actions are within the general moral order, and hence not justified only by partisan, self-serving grounds" (van Dijk 1998: 258). Thus, the characterization of America's response to terrorism as a war and the imposed adequation of disparate actors, such as Iraq and Al Qaeda, may become naturalized in public under-standings as unquestionable knowledge. In this way, any successful narra-tive erases the interpretive act that it is. In the next three chapters, I move to examine the social circulation of the Narrative in American society.

5

Intertextual Series:
Reproduction and Resistance
in the Media

Third time I've said that. ((laughter)) I'll probably
say it three more times. See, in my line of work you
got to keep repeating things over and over and over
again for the truth to sink in, to kind of catapult the
propaganda.

— George W. Bush (2005, May 22)

INTRODUCTION

Discourse, as Bakhtin emphasizes, "cannot fail to be oriented toward the
'already uttered,' the 'already known,' the 'common opinion' and so forth"
(Bakhtin 1981: 279). Agha (2003) discusses these inevitable connections
across discursive settings in terms of a *speech chain*, which he defines as "a
historical series of speech events linked together by the permutation of individuals across speech-act roles" (247). Importantly, the connections across discursive events help "yield social formations" (Agha 2005a: 4). In Agha's (2003,
2004, 2005b) work on enregisterment (i.e., the formation of speech registers[1]),

---

1. A *register* is "a variety of language defined according to its use in social situations"
(Crystal 1990: 327). Examples include a scientific register, a religious register, a formal
register, an informal register, etc.

he shows how intertextual connections effectively imbue speech registers with their cultural value. In a similar manner, the accrual of situated narratives into shared cultural understandings operates through speech chains. What Bruner (1991) calls *narrative accrual* or what Foucault (1972) discusses as a *discursive formation* can only emerge through multiple, overlapping discursive encounters. Thus, the recontextualization of language from presidential speeches is requisite for the existence of the Narrative as a macro-level discourse.

The media play an important role in the circulation of the Narrative laid out in presidential speeches. In this chapter, I examine the uptake of key phrases in media discourse. As these key phrases enter into social circulation, they form the basis of an intertextual series, i.e., a text that reoccurs across multiple, overlapping contexts. Importantly, as these sound bites and talking points enter into subsequent contexts, they index the prior contexts from which they came and carry with them previously established social meanings.

Indexicality—as developed by Charles Peirce and further refined by Silverstein (1976, 1985, inter alia), Ochs (1992) and others—can be summarized as "the semiotic operation of juxtaposition" (Bucholtz and Hall 2004: 378) whereby contiguity is established between a sign and its meaning. As Bauman (2005) reminds us, "Bakhtin's abiding concern was with dimensions and dynamics of speech indexicality—ways that the now-said reaches back to and somehow incorporates or resonates with the already-said and reaches ahead to, anticipates, and somehow incorporates the to-be-said" (145). Whether prior discourse is overtly marked or implicitly embedded as background knowledge, a particular context is connected to other contexts through some type of intertextual series (Hanks 1986) or speech chain (Agha 2003). Although the indexical associations between a key phrase and its contextual significance may draw on already established meanings—what Silverstein (2003a) terms *presupposed indexicality*—new indexical links may also be created—what Silverstein terms *creative or entailed indexicality*. In other words, the social meanings associated with an indexical sign are both partly pre-established and partly recalibrated when that sign is brought into a new context.[2]

Thus, as key phrases associated with the Narrative enter into new contexts, they effectively point to and remind listeners of the larger narrative

---

2. Put another way, meanings emerge from interaction: the meanings that emerge may simply reaffirm established ones or may involve significant modifications made within the current context. They are never fixed once and for all, but are subject to continual renewal through microlevel discursive encounters.

of which they are a part. When this language is reiterated across contexts, one effect is to further solidify the Narrative as a macrolevel discourse. As Kristeva (1980) describes, repetition may take "what is imitated (repeated) seriously, claiming and appropriating it without relativizing it" (73). However, repetition may also introduce "a signification opposed to that of the other's word" (73). Challenge and resistance may occur through metapragmatic comments that overtly evaluate prior text (Buttny 1997) or through the simple refraction of meaning that takes place anytime prior text is introduced into a new context (Voloshinov 1971). In this chapter, I examine both of these dimensions in turn. In the first part of the chapter, I focus on how intertextual series are established and reinforced in media discourse. In the second part, I explore how intertextual series are reshaped and resignified in ways that challenge the Narrative.

ESTABLISHING AND REINFORCING AN INTERTEXTUAL SERIES

Strategies of entextualization

As Bakhtin (1986) notes, "the utterance is related not only to preceding, but also to subsequent links in the chain of speech communication" (94). Intertextual relations are implicated in a speech chain that not only draws from the past but also anticipates the future. Social actors often recognize that others will take up their words in different contexts, and this knowledge can play into the way they formulate their words. Wilce (2005) includes this sort of anticipation of recontextualization as one of four dimensions of intertextuality that he highlights through examples of laments from several cultures. As he describes, "Through strategies of entextualization, performers make later quotation of their lament a particularly likely response" (Wilce 2005: 62). Similarly, Briggs (1992) provides an examination of how women in Warao society (a subculture of indigenous people in Venezuela) perform their laments called *sana*. He notes that these performers "are well aware that their *sana* will be heard by the entire settlement or, in a large community such as Murako, by everyone who has gathered on the docks and surrounding houses. [. . .] Since audience members will recontextualize *sana* as narratives, (*dehe hido*), lamenters often attempt to shape the ways in which their laments will be retold" (Briggs 1992: 353).

In political discourse, strategies of entextualization forward catchy sound bites or talking points that allow political figures to insert their words into the "circular circulation" (Bourdieu 1996: 22) of the news cycle. A *sound bite* refers to "a short extract taken from a recorded interview or speech" that is recontextualized within media reportage (Talbot, Atkinson and Atkinson 2003: 22). In the major media's coverage of politics, a preference has developed for pithy statements over in-depth arguments. As a result, many politicians have geared their interactions with the media accordingly. If a politician can articulate a point in a concise, clearly worded sound bite, they have a greater chance of having their perspective played over and over again in subsequent media coverage of the issue.

Talking points often help politicians boil down their position into catchy sound bites and ensure that their position is consistently articulated across interactions. Talking points, which consist of a summary of ideas, make use of key phrases and are designed to help politicians and their supporters articulate a particular perspective when talking to others. For example, talking points distributed among administration officials ensure that those officials articulate the same message when talking with the press. In a revelation by Scott McClellan, who served as the White House Press Secretary from 2003 to 2006, the Bush administration even provided daily talking points to sympathetic commentators at Fox News in an attempt to, as McClellan described to Chris Matthews on MSNBC, "shape the narrative to their advantage" (Matthews 2008, July 28; McClellan 2008). At bottom, the reiteration of sound bites and talking points works to give traction to a particular representation of an issue. The idea is that when a particular representation is repeated sufficiently, it may come to be accepted as fact.

The importance of sound bites in conveying a political message is underscored by the fact that presidential speeches are not always broadcast in their entirety across the nation. What most of the public hears from these speeches are selected pieces of quotable segments that are repeated over and over again in news reports. For example, in many speeches President Bush has used the catchy phrase "terrorists and tyrants" to describe the dangers facing America. As discussed in chapter 4, this phrase is part of his adequation (Bucholtz and Hall 2004) of Saddam Hussein with the "war on terror." The alliteration in this collocation makes it particularly appealing as a sound bite. Notably, Bush used this phrase in his 2003 State of the Union address, and a search of the Google News Archive shows a spike in the use of this phrase in the media during that year.

The following excerpt from NPR's *Morning Edition* with host Bob Edwards illustrates the simple incorporation of this sound bite into the news cycle. These transcripts come directly from NPR's web site. In this and the other examples in this chapter, I highlight the key phrase in italics.

Excerpt 1. (NPR.org 2003, February 13)

DON GONYEA reporting: Make no mistake, while the Bush administration downplays the role of polling in the White House, this administration does very much want to have the public's backing for a war to topple Saddam Hussein. The president has made speech after speech in Washington and around the country, relentlessly driving home the point that the Iraqi leader is a threat who must be dealt with. And the topic has dominated high-profile appearances when the president knows his audience is especially large, like the annual State of the Union address.

Soundbite of State of the Union Address

President GEORGE W. BUSH: Some have said we must not act until the threat is imminent. Since when have *terrorists and tyrants* announced their intentions, politely putting us on notice before they strike?

As seen in excerpt 1, Bush's words are incorporated directly into the broadcast with attribution to him as the speaker of those words and the naming of the context from which they came (i.e., "the annual State of the Union address"). Such uses of sound bites are forms of reported speech that insert the politician's words into a subsequent context. In print reportage, such as excerpt 2 from a Reuters report posted on CBSNews.com, the use of quotation marks attributes the phrase "terrorists and tyrants" to Bush.

Excerpt 2. (CBSNews.com [Reuters] 2002, June 10)

President Bush spoke of where the United States was headed strategically in a commencement address at the United States Military Academy at West Point on June 1
    Mr. Bush told the graduates that future U.S. military leaders must be ready to launch a preemptive strike in the war on terrorism, warning of an unprecedented threat of chemical, biological or nuclear attack from *"terrorists and tyrants."*
    Administration officials drafting the new policy said the United States has been forced to move beyond deterrence since Sept. 11 because of the threat posed by terrorist groups and hostile states supporting them, the Post reported.

In excerpt 2, the gist of Bush's speech at West Point a week earlier is retold in the journalist's own words. The exception, however, is the phrase "terrorists and tyrants." This catchy sound bite acts as an anchor to the context of the West Point speech where Bush conveyed the Narrative. The key phrase helps maintain continuity between that context and the subsequent recontextualization of the speech in the journalist's words. Overall, the journalist provides a reading of the West Point speech that remains more or less faithful to the Narrative. In doing so, the phrase "terrorist and tyrants" is further associated with it. That is, it is further established as an index of the Narrative.

The repetition of prior words through reported speech frames works to reinscribe those words into subsequent contexts. Therefore, reported speech frames help to further establish a key phrase as an intertextual series. However, a key phrase that is repeated across different settings may not always be attributed to another source. In this way, a speaker repeats a key phrase without overt attention drawn to the phrase as a repetition (i.e., without directly quoting it), as seen in excerpt 3.

Excerpt 3. (New York Times 2003, January 13)

WASHINGTON, Jan. 13—Senator Joseph I. Lieberman of Connecticut declared today that he was running for president to "make the American dream real again."

Mr. Lieberman, a Democrat who was Al Gore's running mate in 2000, opened his campaign in his home state with sharp criticism of President Bush's performance on both domestic and foreign issues.

"The American Dream is in jeopardy," he [Lieberman] said, "threatened by hateful *terrorists and tyrants* from abroad and a weak economy that makes it harder for Americans to live a better life." President Bush promised a better America when he took office two years ago, but, Mr. Lieberman said, "that promise has not been kept."

In excerpt 3, Senator Lieberman incorporates the slogan "terrorists and tyrants" into his own discourse (which is itself directly quoted within the article). Although he criticizes Bush on economic issues, he nevertheless reinforces the linkage between "terrorists and tyrants" that is endemic in the Narrative. That is, despite his criticisms of Bush, he furthers an important intertextual series that is connected with the idea that the war in Iraq is integrally linked to America's struggle against terrorism. In fact, Lieberman has been a vocal supporter of the war in Iraq and the neoconservative foreign policy spelled out in the Narrative. When running for reelection to his senate seat in 2006, his support of the Iraq war led to his loss in his state's Democratic primary. He then left the Democratic party and won reelection to the senate as an independent candidate. Arguably, he has since become a more vocal supporter of the "war on terror" as well as an ally of Bush in articulating that policy despite their differences on social issues.

Whether attributed to another speaker or taken up as one's own words, the reiteration of a key phrase in a manner that maintains fidelity to a previously established social meaning works to bolster the accrual of that meaning in society. In the next sections, I provide further illustration and discussion of these two types of diachronic repetition: (1) repetition through reported speech, and (2) repetition outside of reported speech frames.

Repetition in reported speech

Previously uttered discourse commonly enters into new contexts as reported speech. The importance of reported speech in the Bakhtinian perspective is underscored by the significant discussion of the phenomenon by Voloshinov (1973), who characterizes reported speech as "speech within speech, utterance within utterance, and at the same time also *speech about speech, utterance about utterance*" (115; italics in original). Voloshinov's comments highlight the capacity of reported speech to not just represent pieces of previously uttered discourse, but to *re-present* what has been said elsewhere by others—that is, to effectively recontextualize a prior utterance with different shades of meaning. Voloshinov (1973) explains that the use of reported speech "imposes upon the reported utterance its own accents, which collide and interfere with the accents in the reported utterance" (154). Bakhtin (1981) articulates this idea in his concept of *double-voiced discourse*, which "serves two speakers at the same time and expresses simultaneously two different intentions: the direct intention of the character who is speaking, and the refracted intention of the author" (324; Irvine 1996: 135–136).

The Narrative is filled with many key phrases that make catchy sound bites or repeatable talking points. Notable, of course, is the "war on terror" moniker itself. Others that I have pulled out of the corpus of presidential speeches include "weapons of terror," "weapons of mass destruction," "[Iraq is the] central front in the war on terror," "stay on the offense," "either you're with us or the terrorists" (and variations), and "we are fighting the terrorists in Iraq so we do not have to face them here at home" (and variations).

The following examples illustrate the direct quotation of such phrases in media coverage of Bush's speeches. In particular, the phrase "weapons of terror" associated with the adequation of Saddam Hussein and al Qaeda, seen in excerpts 4 and 5, appeared most frequently in the Google News Archive at the beginning of 2003 when the Bush administration was working hard to make its case for war against Iraq. The characterization of Iraq as the "central front in the war on terror" (excerpt 6) began to appear in the Google News Archive during the middle of 2003, as the Bush administration attempted to solidify the linkage between Iraq and the "war on terror." The catchiness of this key phrase as a potent sound bite is evidenced by its staying power; it showed a steady presence in media coverage through 2008. Finally, the phrase "stay on the offense" (excerpt 7) began appearing in the latter part of 2003 as the President repeatedly made use of this catchy sound bite in speeches that tied the ongoing war effort in Iraq to the fight against terrorism. Like the "central front" sound bite, it also demonstrated staying power in media coverage through 2008.

Excerpt 4. (FoxNews.com 2002, October 8)

Billed as an "important speech" about Iraq, President Bush told the nation Monday night that Saddam poses a unique threat that must be addressed now rather than later.

"The threat comes from Iraq. It arises directly from the Iraqi regime's own actions, its history of aggression and its drive for *weapons of terror*," Bush said. "The threat from Iraq stands alone because it gathers the most serious dangers of our age in one place."

Excerpt 5. (Post 2003, March 27)

President Bush pledged again yesterday to rid Iraq of *"weapons of terror,"* but coalition forces have so far failed to find proof of Iraqi biological or chemical weapons a week after the start of the U.S.-led invasion.

Excerpt 6. (FoxNews.com [AP] 2005, October 5)

Addressing the nation as the second anniversary of Sept. 11 approached, the president asked Congress for $87 billion for the efforts in Iraq and Afghanistan and declared Iraq the *"central front" in the war on terror*.

Excerpt 7. (CBSNews.com 2003, September 11)

WASHINGTON—President Bush promised Wednesday to *"stay on the offense"* in Iraq to prevent insurgents from disrupting next week's referendum on a new constitution.

The quotations of these key phrases are all contextualized within reportage about the "war on terror" so that each reiteration of the key phrase reinforces its association with the larger Narrative of which they are a part. Excerpts 4 and 5 attribute the phrase "weapons of terror" to Bush, directly quoting his speeches. Interestingly, in excerpt 6 the quotation marks are placed around "central front" rather than the entire phrase "central front in the war on terror." This seems to indicate that the only novel contribution made here by Bush to public discourse consists of the "central front" collocation. The phrase "war on terror" is merely presented as a common label for America's struggle against terrorism and is not included as part of the larger quotation attributed to Bush. After the declaration of the "war against terrorism" by Bush in his speech on September 11, 2001 (recall excerpt 3 in chapter 2), the very idea of a "war" against terrorism and the shortened collocation itself, "war on terror," became widely accepted in American discourse as a label for the effort against terrorism. Naturalized as such, it does not figure into the words that are marked off as a direct quotation here. In fact, it is difficult to find many uses in the mainstream media where this label is marked off with quotation marks, which is indicative of its widespread acceptance. (I take up this topic in more detail later in the chapter.) Finally, excerpt 7 recontextualizes a rendition of the Narrative where Bush talks about the need to "'stay on the offense' in Iraq." This catchy sound bite helps anchor the news report's paraphrase of Bush's argument to the prior context of the speech where Bush made that argument. Thus, the connection between this phrase and the Narrative is further strengthened. Moreover, as key phrases such as this one continue to circulate, they act as potent reminders and reinforcements of the Narrative even when the entire Narrative is not told in elaborate detail.

Elsewhere, key phrases are reiterated through reportage that directly quotes official government statements, as seen in the following example.

Excerpt 8. (CNN.com 2004, May 6)

"We are seeing indications that Al Qaeda continues to prepare to strike U.S. interests abroad," the State Department said in its worldwide caution.

"Al Qaeda attacks could possibly involve nonconventional weapons such as chemical or biological agents as well as conventional *weapons of terror*. We also cannot rule out that Al Qaeda will attempt a catastrophic attack within the U.S."

The reliance of the mainstream media on official government sources is widely recognized among media scholars. A large reason for this is that such sources are seen as authoritative and credible. The effect, however, is to give primacy to the government's preferred way of representing an issue. In excerpt 8, the key phrase "weapons of terror" is embedded within a longer statement of caution issued by the State Department and quoted at length in an article on CNN.com. Here, this catchy phrase appears rather inconspicuously. It occurs within the longer State Department quotation as a naturalized term used in conjunction with its discussion of Al Qaeda. The result is to further bolster the intertextual series and the Narrative with which it is associated. The official story about the "war on terror" is therefore reinforced. Cultural knowledge and what Foucault (1980) terms *regimes of truth* are formed and sustained through the reiteration of officially ratified representations of the world.

In excerpts 9 and 10, indirect reported speech frames are used to reiterate key phrases.

Excerpt 9. (New York Times 2004, October 8)

President Bush has said that Iraq is the *central front in the war on terror*. He is right. Mr. Zarqawi's stated goal is to kill Americans, set off a sectarian war in Iraq and defeat democracy there. He is our enemy.

Excerpt 10. (CBSNews.com [CBS/AP] 2006, September 24)

The president has said the United States is safer since the Sept. 11 attacks and that *fighting the terrorists in Iraq keeps them from attacking America*.

Excerpt 9 is from a piece written by Paul Bremer, the administrator appointed by Bush in 2003 to oversee reconstruction in Iraq. Bremer's piece appears in the *New York Times*. In it, he cites Bush's proclamation that "Iraq is the central front in the war on terror" and reaffirms this notion. As Bremer matter-of-factly states, "He is right." Bremer's authority as an official with experience in Iraq adds weight to this assessment. Excerpt 10 comes from an article on CBSNews.com, compiled with the help of AP wire reports. The article reports on claims made by U.S. intelligence officials that the war in Iraq has worsened the problem of terrorism worldwide. At the end, the article reiterates one of Bush's key talking points in the Narrative: "fighting the terrorists in Iraq keeps them from attacking America." This talking point began to appear in the Google News Archive at the end of 2003, picked up significantly in 2004, and continued to be seen in coverage through 2008. In both excerpts, reported speech frames recontextualize previously uttered words and reinforce the meaning given to those words in their prior context. They reinforce the association of these key phrases with the Narrative so that even if the entire Narrative is not spelled out in elaborate detail, it is nevertheless invoked and affirmed.

The next excerpt comes from an interview on Fox News where journalist Laurie Dhue talks with James Woolsey, the former CIA director and a prominent figure associated with neoconservative foreign policy.

Excerpt 11. (FoxNews.com 2001, November 27)

DHUE: OK. Dick Cheney and Colin Powell have said that they do
           not believe there is any evidence linking Saddam Hussein to
           what happened on 911. What do you think?

WOOLSEY: Well, I don't think 911 is the only issue, or 911 and the
           anthrax. But I must say I think those statements date back
           some weeks to shortly after September 11. I don't know that
           they've said that real recently. But nonetheless, I think the
           issue is terrorism as a whole. And I think one very important
           thing the president said today was that for all practical pur-
           poses, weapons such as nuclear and biological in the hands of
           Saddam Hussein are essentially *weapons of terror*, to terrorize
           other countries. So I think the issue really is terror against us
           and others, including developing *weapons of mass destruction*
           and including, for example, such things as Saddam's attempt
           to assassinate former president Bush in the spring of 1993.

Excerpt 11 further illustrates the way the larger significance of the phrase "weapons of terror," attributed to Bush through an indirect reported speech frame, is reaffirmed by a supporter. In addition, we see the interchangeability between "weapons of terror" and "weapons of mass destruction." The phrase "weapons of mass destruction" is ubiquitous in Bush's speeches prior to and after the invasion of Iraq in 2003. That ubiquity is matched in media coverage; the Google News Archive returns the most results for this phrase from the end of 2002 through the middle of 2003.

Although the phrase "weapons of mass destruction" is associated with Bush and the Narrative, it is not directly attributed to Bush by Woolsey in excerpt 11. The reinforcement of intertextual series in this manner—that is, outside of reported speech frames—is the topic of the next section.

Iterability in others' discourse and chains of authentication

Derrida's (1977) notion of *iterability* accounts for the repetition of intertextual series across speaker roles when the direct attribution of those words to another speaker is lacking. In many ways, for a key phrase to be taken up in this manner is to mark its widespread social acceptance. As briefly noted earlier, the "war on terror" collocation has become the label Americans use for discussing the response to terrorism. It is not just President Bush's term for this struggle, but it is America's term (more on this later). Similarly, key phrases such as "weapons of terror" can be taken up by the media as they formulate reportage in their own words, as seen in excerpt 12.

Excerpt 12. (New York Times 2002, December 9)

Destroying Weapons of Terror
The threat of terrorists' getting hold of nuclear, biological or chemical weapons used to be the stuff of Hollywood melodramas. Now it is a daily nightmare for national security and law enforcement officials around the world.

In excerpt 12, "weapons of terror" becomes part of the headline for the story itself, which appears in the *New York Times*. Just as such phrases make for good sound bites within political speeches they make for catchy titles for newspaper articles. Although using this phrase as a headline is a type of linguistic innovation, it still furthers the intertextual series and reinforces the idea of "weapons of terror" with the "war on terror" in post-9/11 public discourse.

Excerpt 13 comes from an interview on Fox News Sunday. Journalist Chris Wallace interviews the former Spanish Prime Minister Jose Maria Aznar who was a key Bush ally until Aznar's term ended in 2004. Featured in this excerpt is the phrase, "either you're with us, or you're with them [the terrorists]." My search for this talking point in the Google News Archive returned a steady stream of results from the end of 2001 through 2008.

Excerpt 13. (FoxNews.com 2004, April 18)

WALLACE: What will the message be that is sent to the terrorists if Spain drops out of the coalition, pulls its troops out of Iraq?

AZNAR (THROUGH TRANSLATOR):   It will be a very bad message. It would be a message of having managed to achieve their objectives. The only message that terrorists need to get is that they're going to be beaten.

WALLACE: Some people are comparing it to the appeasement of Adolf Hitler before World War II.

AZNAR (THROUGH TRANSLATOR):   There are countries that prefer to think that they're buying comfort at the cost of others, but I don't think that's the way you can act in this world. There are no neutral groups. *Either you're with us, or you're with them.* And those who try to be neutral, I think, are the ones who are going to be paying the highest price. The terrorists are not going to forgive them, and they will have no understanding from those who are fighting against terrorism.

In excerpt 13, Aznar incorporates this key talking point—"Either you're with us, or you're with them [the terrorists]"—into his response to Wallace's question. It should be noted that the actual wording of Aznar's response is co-constructed with his translator; nevertheless, this articulation is a close formulation of the talking point frequently forwarded in the Narrative (recall, for example, excerpt 7 of chapter 3). Importantly, however, Aznar does not attribute this statement to Bush, but takes it up as his own articulation about the war in Iraq and terrorism. Such talking points allow social actors to forward a common message and reinforce a particular narrative. Moreover, the reiteration of such points, especially by a powerful figure like the former Spanish Prime Minister, works to forward a *chain of authentication* (Irvine 1989).

In her examination of language and political economy, Irvine (1989) draws from Putnam (1975) to discuss the way language participates in an economy of value for material commodities. To borrow and expand upon an example from Irvine (1989) and Putnam (1975), imagine a piece of gold. An ordinary person with no training is hard pressed to distinguish between a piece of authentic gold and fool's gold when stumbling upon a golden rock. Moreover, an ordinary person may also be hard pressed to distinguish between a real gold ring and an imitation one on display in a store window. As Putnam (1975) explains, the ordinary person relies "on a special subclass of speakers" whose job is to determine whether something is truly gold or not (228). Such "experts" render the "usage of the term *gold* authoritative" (Irvine 1989: 257). As Irvine (1989) further explains, "The economic and symbolic value of gold for the wider community depends on this. Any gold object circulating in the community must be accompanied by some convincing testimonial to its being authentically gold, if it is to command its full value" (257).

Irvine (1989) then adds an important twist to Putnam's (1975) example. The value of that gold ring is dependent not just on a single reliable testimonial or stamp of an expert's approval, but is generally implicated in what she calls a *chain of authentication*: "a historical sequence by which the expert's attestation—and the label (expression) that conventionally goes along with it—is relayed to other people" (Irvine 1989: 258).[3] A chain of authentication[4] can be thought of as a special type of speech chain where the intertextual relations involved in the chain reaffirm the value of an object.

Importantly, it's not just language that gives an object value in this chain but the use of language by someone who is deemed to be an "expert" (i.e., an authority on the subject) and by others who are trusted to relay that information along the way. Here, Bourdieu's (1977, 1991) ideas on the different forms of capital are helpful: *symbolic capital* in the form of accumulated prestige and honor, *social capital* in the form of relationships and acquaintances, and *cultural capital* in the form of educational credentials and technical qualifications. These forms of capital imbue a speaker, such as the gold expert, with the needed authority to authenticate that gold ring. Symbolic power also plays an important role as others involved in the chain of authentication vouch for the credibility of the gold ring's authenticity. The connections of social actors across discursive encounters form the social system responsible for ratifying and reaffirming the value of the gold. While Irvine (1989) introduces the concept of a chain of authentication in relation to material commodities, it is equally applicable to nonmaterial, verbal commodities—that is, key phrases and narratives that enter into social circulation. Aznar's reiteration of the talking point associated with the Narrative in excerpt 13 lends further credence to the Narrative. He uses his position as a powerful figure in world affairs to forward a

---

3. In a similar vein, see Silverstein's (2005: 12) discussion of Kripke (1972) and Putnam's (1975: 246) notion of a "proper name chain."

4. Note also Bucholtz and Hall's (2004, 2005) use of the term *authentication* in their model of identity formation. They choose the term *authentication* in a deliberate contrast with the term *authenticity*, which often carries an essentialist connotation. Authentication, instead, "highlights the agentive processes whereby claims to realness are asserted" (Bucholtz and Hall 2004: 385). Importantly, such claims are made and not found (Bourdieu 1984).

chain of authentication that bolsters it. As Bourdieu (1991) states, "What creates the power of words and slogans, a power capable of maintaining or subverting the social order, is the belief in the legitimacy of words and of those who utter them" (170). Words are legitimized through chains of authentication where the value assigned to them depends on the symbolic capital of those in the network. There is nothing magical about, say, a given political speech or talking point. The words themselves do not hold sufficient power. For those words or stories to be accepted, they require the right "social conditions in which [the] words are employed" (Bourdieu 1991:107). As Bourdieu explains, "The power of words is nothing other than the *delegated power* of the spokesperson, and his speech—that is, the substance of his discourse and, inseparably, his way of speaking—is no more than a testimony, and one among others, of the *guarantee of delegation* which is vested in him" (Bourdieu 1991: 107; italics in original). The "guarantee of delegation" of which Bourdieu speaks refers to the social conditions that imbue certain social actors with sufficient capital to authenticate claims. Political claims depend upon this recognition of who is allowed to speak with authority. Words, once authenticated, carry that value with them. With the help of chains of authentication, key phrases enter into media circulation and provide inertia for the accrual of a shared cultural narrative. Excerpts 14 and 15 illustrate the incorporation of the key phrase "central front in the war on terror" and concomitant elements of the Narrative into media reportage.

Excerpt 14. (FoxNews.com 2004, January 2)

With Iraq designated as the *central front in the war on terror*, coalition troops are now attempting to secure the country and make way for an Iraqi-led democratic government.

In the original front of the war on terror, Afghanistan, 11,000 U.S. troops continue the fight against Taliban and Al Qaeda remnants, engaging in several operations aimed at pounding mountain hideaways where fighters are believed to be taking refuge.

Excerpt 15. (FoxNews.com 2005, July 12)

Yet, however one comes down on that judgment; it cannot be denied that the current war in Iraq is part of the global war on terror. Indeed, it is that war's *central front*. Not only because there are so many terrorists in Iraq, but because, as Abu Zarqawi has acknowledged, creating a successful democracy in Iraq will be the beginning of the end for jihadist terrorists worldwide.

Excerpt 14 is from an article on FoxNews.com that provides a look back at the previous year. The journalist uses the key phrase "central front in the war on terror" with a very weak attribution. The agent (i.e., the Bush administration) who "designated" Iraq as the "central front in the war on terror" is absent. Moreover, the historical viewpoint adopted in the article (i.e., as an article looking back on the past year) conveys the designation as a widely accepted fact. Thus, it appears as though a specific attribution would be superfluous. The widespread acceptance of the phrase along with the larger narrative it bolsters is further reinforced by the contrast made to the "original front of the war on terror" in the second paragraph. The journalist effectively reiterates the claim found in the Narrative that Iraq and Afghanistan are but different "fronts" in the larger "war on terror." Importantly, the key phrase "central front in the war on terror" acts as a foundation upon which that larger narrative is recapitulated. Excerpt 15, from an article written by prominent neoconservative William Kristol and appearing on FoxNews.com, uses the "central front" talking point to achieve the same result. However, whereas Kristol's piece is an editorial, excerpt 14 is taken from an article ostensibly written as an objective overview of the previous year's events. Particularly in regular reportage (i.e., noneditorial pieces), the incorporation of key phrases plays an important role in further reifying dominant discourses.

CHALLENGING AN ESTABLISHED NARRATIVE

Whereas the last section explored the reiteration of prior text in a way that reinforces a previously established social meaning, here I examine the way recontextualization may introduce "a signification opposed to that of the other's word" (Kristeva 1980: 73). As Bakhtin (1986) notes, "Others' utterances can be repeated with varying degrees of reinterpretation" (91).

Contesting key phrases

As noted earlier, the label "war on terror" has entered into common parlance to characterize and discuss America's response to terrorism after 9/11. FoxNews.com, which provides a decidedly pro-Republican perspective on world events, even began capitalizing the label (i.e., War on Terror) in its own reportage in 2004. Capitalization first begins to appear in my corpus of media discourse in September of that year while other major media outlets spell the term with lower case letters throughout the corpus. This capitalization represents the "war on terror" as more than a convenient metaphor, and instead as a proper noun for referring to a real military war. The turning of the "war on terror" into a proper name through the stylistics of capitalization imbues it with historical cachet. Moreover, as evidenced by much of the reportage on Fox News, the capitalized War on Terror carries with it the notion that it is a global military war fought on different "fronts" in Iraq and Afghanistan, consonant with the Narrative. Thus, the capitalization emphasizes both the authenticity of the "war on terror" qua war and its nature as a discrete and inclusive campaign.

The widespread acceptance of the "war on terror" label in American society makes it difficult to escape. Nevertheless, social actors who oppose the policies it entails use several tactics to contest it as a label even when they must use it. One such tactic is to mark the phrase with the adjective *so-called* so that it becomes the "so-called war on terror." This is the equivalent of using scare quotes to indicate the speaker's (or writer's) ideological distance from the term. In mainstream media reportage, the appearance of "so-called war on terror" generally only appears in direct quotations, in op-ed pieces, and in reader responses on web sites. Excerpt 16, for example, comes from an article in the *New York Times*.

Excerpt 16. (New York Times 2005, December 9)

UNITED NATIONS, Dec. 8 - Secretary General Kofi Annan on Thursday vigorously defended Louise Arbour, the United Nations high commissioner for human rights, after comments she made about detention and torture came under criticism from John R. Bolton, the United States ambassador. [. . .]

The dispute arose Wednesday when Ms. Arbour made a statement and gave a briefing in which she said that secret detention of terror suspects and sending suspects to foreign countries without guaranteed safeguards meant that the international ban on torture "is becoming a casualty of the *so-called war on terror*." She said it was "particularly insidious" that "governments are watering down the definition of torture, claiming that terrorism means established rules do not apply anymore." In comments that appeared directed at the current American effort led by Secretary of State Condoleezza Rice to justify American treatment of prisoners, Ms. Arbour said, "An illegal interrogation technique remains illegal whatever new description a government might wish to give it."

In this excerpt, the phrase "so-called war on terror" appears within a quotation in the article. Louise Arbour, the United Nations high commissioner for human rights, is reported to have used this phrase as she discussed the Bush administration's use of torture in its response to terrorism.

Generally speaking, outside of direct quotations and op-ed pieces (where writers have leeway to indicate their ideological stance), regular reportage from the major media I examined avoids the "so-called" marker. However, I did find a few exceptions. Notably, six articles from the *Wall Street Journal* appearing at the end of 2003 and beginning of 2004 contain reference to the "so-called war on terror" within the body of a news report. The common element of these six articles is the journalist. They are all written by Zahid Hussain, writing from Islamabad, Pakistan. Excerpt 17 is taken from one of these articles.

Excerpt 17. (Wall Street Journal 2004, February 24)

Lt. Gen. David Barno, the top U.S. military commander in Afghanistan, said last week that the two-pronged "hammer and anvil approach" would trap Al Qaeda forces between American and Pakistani soldiers. Pakistan's moves Tuesday come days ahead of a visit to Islamabad by U.S. Defense Secretary Donald Rumsfeld.

Pakistan, a key ally in the Bush administration's *so-called war on terror*, has handed over more than 500 Al Qaeda suspects to the U.S. since the September 11, 2001, attacks on New York and Washington. A statement from the Pakistani military Tuesday said the operation showed Islamabad's "continued resolve" to support the U.S. campaign.

Without speculating on the intention of this particular writer, examples such as these underscore the role of individual agency in resisting the uncritical acceptance of contested labels. In major media television shows, popular personalities may also have more leeway in contesting labels such as the "war on terror." Notably, I found instances where Anderson Cooper uses the phrase "so-called war on terror" on his CNN news show, *Anderson Cooper 360 Degrees*. Excerpt 18 is taken from the transcripts of one of his shows.

Excerpt 18. (CNN.com 2007, November 9)

COOPER: Imagine that. Now a closer look at a key U.S. ally's descent into chaos. [. . .] Now, here's why you should probably care about Pakistan. It has nuclear weapons, for one, and it's a major player in the *so-called war on terror*. Earlier, I spoke with Fareed Zakaria, editor of "Newsweek International" and, we are now happy to say, a CNN contributor.

(BEGIN VIDEOTAPE)

COOPER: The fact that Musharraf successfully thwarted this potentially explosive march on the military capital, Rawalpindi, was today a victory for Musharraf?

FAREED ZAKARIA, CNN CONTRIBUTOR: It suggests two things: one, that he still has control over the military. [. . .]

COOPER: What does this mean for, you know, the *so-called war on terror*? I mean, if—if—if Pakistani troops are supposed to be focused on battling insurgents, *The Washington Post* talking about this—this new counterinsurgency strategy that the Pentagon had planned to be a five-to-seven year effort of really sustained training of Pakistani troops, that seems to be in jeopardy.

In excerpt 18, Cooper indicates a critical stance toward the "war on terror" label. A further check of additional transcripts of his show indicates that his use of the "so-called" qualifier is not necessarily a steady rule. However, as a personality on CNN, his use of the "so-called" qualifier even in a handful of instances bucks the trend adopted by most in the major media. It, therefore, does not go without notice by those who have accepted the label and the idea of a "war on terror," such as some commentators from Fox News. Excerpt 19 is taken from an editorial column by Mike Baker on FoxNews.com.

Excerpt 19. (FoxNews.com 2007, November 13)

Obviously I've veered off course from today's topic, which was to be the domestic side of the *war on terror*. Or as Anderson Cooper calls it, *". . . the so-called war on terror."* That apparently is his patented phrase. Much like "What a load of crap" is the patented phrase here at the Peoples Weekly Brief.

The response to Cooper by the Fox News columnist in excerpt 19 illustrates the dialogic nature of media discourse in the Bakhtinian sense of dialogism. Even though excerpts 18 and 19 are spoken (or written) in different contexts by people at different media outlets, they are connected in a *dialogical network* whereby "media events, such as television and radio programs, press conferences and newspaper articles are networked: connected interactively, thematically and argumentatively" (Leudar, Marsland and Nekvapil 2004: 245; see also Nekvapil and Leudar 2002). Importantly, the jab Baker takes at Cooper in excerpt 19 works to police the boundaries of mainstream discourse. Through his jocular commentary, Baker effectively reinforces the acceptance of the "war on terror" as an uncontested term and mocks Cooper's deviation from this supposedly common-sense idea (compare to Herman and Chomsky 1988 on "flak").

Outside of the major media, independent media figures more commonly incorporate the use of the "so-called" qualifier into regular reportage. Excerpt 20 comes from the transcripts of a broadcast of *Democracy Now*, an independent radio/television news program that provides investigative reporting and a critical perspective on world events. The host, Amy Goodman, is an outspoken critic of the Bush administration.

Excerpt 20. (Democracy Now 2002, January 10)

Since the Bush administration began its *so-called war on terror*, we have reported extensively on the scores of people in detention. The identity of many of these people remains unknown. Largely they are held incommunicado without charges. Today we are going to look at some of the methods the government used in determining what people they would arrest and hold in the aftermath of September 11th.

In excerpt 20, the phrase "so-called war on terror" is found in the spoken remarks that introduce this segment of the show. It also appears in the title given to the segment on the *Democracy Now* web site. Although this particular example is dated to early 2002, a further search found that "so-called" is used consistently on *Democracy Now* broadcasts through the time of my writing. Whereas the capitalization of the War on Terror on FoxNews.com represents one end of an ideological spectrum, the use of the phrase "so-called war on terror" by independent media organizations like *Democracy Now* represents the other end.

Reshaping sound bites

In his discussion of strategies of entextualization, Wilce (2005) notes that although speakers may anticipate the uptake of their words in subsequent contexts, they cannot always control subsequent interpretations of those words. He provides an example of a Bangladeshi woman, Latifa, engaged in two weeks of lamenting while visiting the home of her uncle and cousins. In her laments, she complained of the treatment she had been receiving from her brothers. The lament drew upon reported speech frames to position voices in support of her situation. In addition, the choice of the genre provided a recognized format for legitimizing her problems in the eyes of community members. However, as Wilce (2005) explains, these strategies failed as her laments were recontextualized by witnessing family members not as *bilāp*, the traditionally recognized lament genre, but as *ai purān kāndā*, which translates as "that same old crying." In other words, her relatives recontextualized her laments as inconsequential personal complaints.

Such negative recontextualizations work against speakers' goals and undercut the intent of the original discourse. As discussed earlier in this chapter, strategies of entextualization may aid social actors in positioning their words; however, speakers have no control over their words once they enter into social circulation. As Bush administration critics draw from the Narrative's reservoir of sound bites and talking points, they "assimilate, rework, and re-accentuate" those words in line with their own ideological perspectives and interactional aims (Bakhtin 1986: 89). In short, they reshape the prior text and provide new interpretations and meanings to key phrases. Excerpt 21 is taken from an article in the *New York Times* that quotes a Syrian official who cites and reshapes a popular talking point of the Narrative.

Excerpt 21. (New York Times 2001, October 9)

"The Americans say *either you are with us or you are with the terrorists*," said Adnan Omran, the information minister. "That is something God should say."

This article gives voice to the Syrian official's reading of Bush's sound bite "either you are with us or you are with the terrorists." The official, Adnan Omran, cites this doctrine within a reported speech frame where attribution is given, not just to Bush, but to "the Americans" more generally. As Sacks (1992) points out, the reported speech frame works to convey to listeners "how to read what they're being told" (274). Through accompanying metapragmatic comments, Omran provides this reading: "That is something God should say." Instead of conveying the image of a firm stance against terrorism, Omran characterizes the sound bite as being overly presumptuous and even arrogant. The reinterpretation of these words by Omran does not treat them in a favorable light. Although the incorporation of the sound bite into this context does further the intertextual series, it refracts the larger social meaning it carried with it from the previous contexts where it faithfully represented the Narrative. Excerpt 22, taken from an article in the *Washington Post*, further illustrates this reshaping of a sound bite from the Narrative.

Excerpt 22. (Washington Post 2006, December 7)

Both Baker and Hamilton also questioned one of the Bush administration's original premises for the 2003 invasion—that going into Iraq was necessary to defeat al-Qaeda and other terrorist groups following the Sept. 11, 2001, attacks in New York and Washington.

Asked directly by Sen. Lindsey O. Graham (R-S.C.) whether Iraq was central to the war on terror, Baker said "it may not have been when we first went in," even though he felt "it certainly is now."

Since the invasion, Iraq has attracted foreign fighters who have launched attacks on Americans and helped stir sectarian violence between Iraq's Shiite Muslim majority and its Sunni Muslim Arab minority.

Hamilton said Iraq is *one central front in the war on terror*, "but to put it *the central front* overstates it."

Excerpt 22 features reportage on the testimony before Congress of Lee Hamilton. Along with James Baker, Hamilton was chair of the Iraq Study Group, a bipartisan panel formed by Congress in 2006 to assess the situation in Iraq. Here, we see Hamilton's response to Bush's assertion that "Iraq is the central front in the war on terror." Through a reported speech frame that mixes indirect and direct quotations of Hamilton's statement to Congress, we learn that he views Iraq as "one" but not "the" central front. Although Hamilton still acknowledges the importance of Iraq in the "war on terror," the qualification of the phrase "central front in the war on terror" with the quantifier "one" instead of the definite article "the" lessens the significance of the sound bite, even though it fails to overturn the underlying assumption that the war in Iraq is part and parcel of America's response to terrorism.

Once a macrolevel discourse becomes established, it is difficult to overturn outright. As critics attempt to challenge the Narrative, they reshape its sound bites and talking points in incremental steps. Excerpt 23 further illustrates the redefining of prior text associated with the Narrative. Again, the key phrase involved is the "central front in the war on terror." The excerpt comes from a statement released by Democratic Senator Joseph Biden as reported on FoxNews.com. (Note also how, as discussed earlier, the representation of the label "war on terror" in this excerpt is capitalized by Fox News.)

Excerpt 23. (FoxNews.com 2006, September 6)

U.S. Senator Joseph R. Biden, Jr., D-Del., issued the following statement in reaction to President Bush's speech Tuesday on terrorism:

"By releasing a new strategy to fight terror, the administration acknowledges that its previous strategy has failed to make America safer. The president has squandered the opportunity to unite the country and the world, instead he has divided both.

"The administration's most profound strategic mistake was not finishing the job in Afghanistan—which everyone agreed was the *central front in the War on Terror*—and rushing to war in Iraq, which was not. Today, Afghanistan is on the brink of collapse and Iraq on the verge of chaos. In addition, five years after 9/11, each member of the so-called 'Axis of Evil' is more dangerous; terrorist attacks around the world have nearly quadrupled; the administration's simplistic equation of democracy with elections has helped empower extremist groups like Hezbollah and Hamas; and Katrina and the 9/11 Commission have made it clear we are not prepared for an attack here at home.

"The administration's new strategy seems to adopt many of the critiques Democrats made about the old one. I hope today's change in rhetoric represents a real change in course."

In excerpt 23, Biden contests the notion that Iraq is a "central front in the war on terror" more directly than does Hamilton in excerpt 22. However, Biden is still working with the "war on terror" discourse. Instead of Iraq as the central front, he shifts the referent in the sound bite to Afghanistan. In his statement, there still is a "war on terror" and there still is a "central front." The only difference is the location of that central front. Importantly, he forwards this redefinition of the "central front in the war on terror" inside the claim that his redefinition represents a common-sense understanding of the situation. That is, he presents his redefinition as one "which everyone agreed" upon. This supposedly widely agreed upon definition is juxtaposed with what is implied to be an ideologically tainted representation of the situation by the Bush administration. In this way, Biden illustrates the way political actors represent their own positions as falling within the realm of common interests while they represent their opponents' positions as motivated by partisan interests (van Dijk 1998: 258).

The shifting of the focus in the "war on terror" from Iraq to Afghanistan has been common among Democrats at least since Senator John Kerry's rhetoric to this effect before the 2004 presidential elections in the United

States. During the lead up to the 2008 presidential elections, Senator Barack Obama also redefined the "war on terror" in this manner. This redefinition of the "war on terror" has become prevalent enough so that it has entered into American public discourse as a significant counter narrative to that of the Bush administration. In excerpt 24, taken from transcripts of *Fox News Sunday*, the journalist Chris Wallace uses this counter definition as a foil in his interview with Republican Senator Kit Bond.

Excerpt 24. (FoxNews.com 2007, July 22)

WALLACE: Senator Bond, all this raises the question, "Is the war in Iraq the *central front* in the War on Terror, or have we taken our focus off the central front, which is Al Qaeda in Pakistan?"

BOND: Well, it's both, because Al Qaeda is the number one enemy. This is the greatest threat to the United States. The intelligence community has said that Al Qaeda's top priority is attacking America, the homeland, the United States, attacking U.S. interests and allies abroad.

The either-or frame presented by Wallace in his question echoes the discourse seen in Biden's statement in excerpt 23 (and the discourse of other Democratic figures as noted earlier). That is, he gives credence to the idea that the "central front in the war on terror" may be in the region between Afghanistan and Pakistan as opposed to Iraq (even though his question doesn't preclude the notion that Iraq is still another front). In response, Senator Bond, a Bush administration supporter, upholds the assumptions and explanations inherent in the Narrative, namely, that both Iraq and Afghanistan are critical "fronts" in the "war on terror." As he says in response to Wallace, "it's both." In other words, by implication both Iraq and Afghanistan are "central fronts in the war on terror." These excerpts illustrate the discursive competition that takes place as sound bites enter into the dialogical network of media discourse and are resisted and reshaped by subsequent speakers in an ongoing chain of communication.

Parody as a tool of subversion

Perhaps the most interesting aspect of intertextual connections is the way previously uttered phrases can be reanimated through parodic representations. As Bakhtin (1981) notes, "By manipulating the effects of context

[. . .] it is, for instance, very easy to make even the most serious utterance comical" (340). Moreover, parody can be an effective tool of subversion as it can be used to seriously challenge a dominant discourse and work to establish a counterperspective.

The phrase "weapons of mass destruction," ubiquitous in the Narrative along with "weapons of terror," has provided an easily parodied sound bite for administration critics to exploit. As discussed earlier, this phrase is used within the Narrative in conjunction with terrorism and Saddam Hussein to convey the danger of both within the rubric of the "war on terror." As this phrase is reshaped by administration critics, its association with the Narrative is used to parody the erroneous basis for war in Iraq and the perceived incompetence of the administration's foreign policy. Variations on the phrase "weapons of mass destruction" include phrases such as "weapons of mass distraction," "weapons of mass deception," and "weapons of misdirection."

A search of the Google News Archive between September 11, 2001 and March 11, 2008 returned 231,000 occurrences of the phrase "weapons of mass destruction" in media coverage. The timeline shows the phrase entering into heavy media circulation in the months prior to and after the invasion of Iraq in March of 2003. Likewise, as this sound bite entered into the media's dialogical network in 2003, the parodic responses ("weapons of mass deception" and "weapons of mass distraction") also began to appear, although their overall prevalence is miniscule compared to that of the phrase they parody. Compare the 231,000 occurrences of the phrase "weapons of mass destruction" to the 659 results for the phrase "weapons of mass distraction" and the 765 results for the phrase "weapons of mass deception" over the same time period. The dominance of the Narrative in the major media is notable in this comparison. Nevertheless, parody can be an effective tactic in resisting that imposing narrative. For example, "weapons of mass deception" is a title of a book published by the Center for Media and Democracy (Rampton and Stauber 2003). Appropriate to the title, the book details the way the Bush administration used the threat of weapons of mass destruction in the hands of Saddam Hussein along with his supposed links to terrorists to lead the nation into war. As may be expected, puns like these feature more prominently in blogs and alternative media sources than major media reportage.

Notably, the pun "weapons of misdirection" was used by the Rev. Joseph Lowery in an address he gave at the Coretta Scott King funeral in February 2006. With the current and past living presidents sitting behind him on the dais, Lowery reshaped the "weapons of mass destruction" sound bite into an excoriation of the Bush administration. Part of the power of this example comes from the genre Lowery chose: speaking in poetic verse (represented by the lines and stanzas in my transcription in excerpt 25).

Excerpt 25. (Lowery 2006, February 7)

She extended Martin's message against poverty, racism and war.
    She deplored the terror inflicted by our smart bombs on missions way afar.

    We know now there were no *weapons of mass destruction* over there
        ((cheers for 23 sec))
    but Coretta knew,
    and we knew,
    that there are *weapons of misdirection*
    right down here.

    Millions without health insurance,
    poverty abounds,
    for war billions more,
    but no more for the poor.

In this excerpt, the phrase "weapons of mass destruction" indexes the prior contexts where it has been used by Bush to justify the invasion of Iraq. In this way, it carries with it presupposed knowledge about the truth claims espoused by the Bush administration in these prior contexts. However, even though Lowery draws upon this presupposed understanding, his reiteration of this phrase in the current context works to recalibrate the social meaning associated with it. Instead of simply indexing the truth claims about Iraq's supposed possession of "weapons of mass destruction" forwarded by the White House, it now takes on a new meaning centered on the Bush administration's failures and negligence. In other words, the phrase "weapons of mass destruction," which in Silverstein's (2003a) terms is a "socially conventional indexical" sign, is "dialectically balanced between" *indexical presupposition* and *indexical entailment* (195). The broader social meaning associated with the phrase draws upon the already established meaning it has been given in Bush's prior speeches, but now that meaning is creatively reworked in the context of Lowery's speech.

Of even greater importance is how Lowery's words were themselves subsequently recontextualized as a sound bite in the major media and discussed in the weeks that followed. Excerpt 26 demonstrates the recontextualization of his words on *Fox News Sunday* where Lowery makes an appearance to talk with host Chris Wallace about the remarks. The excerpt begins with a video clip of Lowery's remarks at the King funeral as Wallace introduces Lowery to the show.

Excerpt 26. (FoxNews.com 2006, February 13)

(BEGIN VIDEO CLIP)

REV. JOSEPH LOWERY: We know now there were no *weapons of mass destruction* over there, that there are *weapons of misdirection* right down here. Millions without health insurance, poverty abounds, for war billions more, but no more for the poor.

(END VIDEO CLIP)

CHRIS WALLACE, HOST: That was Reverend Joseph Lowery with sharp words for President Bush during the funeral service Tuesday for civil rights leader Coretta Scott King. Was that the proper time to go after the president? We're going to hear from both sides, starting with Reverend Lowery, who led the Southern Christian Leadership Conference for 20 years. He joins us today from Baltimore. And, Reverend, welcome to *FOX News Sunday*. Thanks for joining us, sir.

LOWERY: Thank you.

The appeal of this parodic reshaping of "weapons of mass destruction" into another sound bite taken up by the major media, "weapons of misdirection," comes both from the stylistics of the remarks and their utterance by a well-known civil rights leader in the immediate presence of President Bush. This example demonstrates how parodic expression can be effective at inserting alternative perspectives to the Narrative into mainstream media coverage, even into the coverage of Fox News which is generally faithful to the Bush administration's perspective. Here, instead of bolstering the Narrative, Lowery uses the phrase and his pun on the phrase to undermine it. The re-accentuation of this phrase seriously challenges the previously established social meanings associated with it.

FROM REPRODUCTION TO RESISTANCE

As key phrases such as sound bites and talking points enter into social circulation in the media, they form intertextual series that provide a common reservoir from which political actors must draw as they engage with each other. The intertextual connections that result play an important role in the establishment and reproduction of dominant discourses; but they also hold the key to reshaping those discourses in ways that resist established meanings and forward new ones. Even in challenging the Narrative, political actors do not create utterances completely from scratch, but rather construct their utterances out of previously spoken words that they "assimilate, rework, and re-accentuate" (Bakhtin 1986: 89). Creativity in discourse is not an unfettered process unconstrained by prior interactions. Rather, creativity exists in the myriad ways prior text can be reworked and given new meanings.

Talking Politics: The Narrative's Reception among College Students

The war on terror is not a figure of speech. It is an
inescapable calling of our generation.

— George W. Bush (2004, March 19)

INTRODUCTION

As van Leeuwen (2005) states, "The texts which discourse analysts analyze form part of social practices—but only part. They realize all or some
of the *actions* that constitute the social practices—but they tell us nothing
about the agents and patients of the actions, or about their place and time"
(13; italics in original). Notably, we learn little about how those texts are
taken up by users and how those users interpret and reinterpret their
meanings. In particular, ideology plays an important role in the interpretive process. Critical linguists have traditionally focused on the ideological dimensions of the text itself or as Voloshinov (1973) points out, the
way in which "every utterance is above all an *evaluative orientation*"
(Voloshinov 1973: 105; italics in original). That is, language conveys
particular ideological perspectives on the world and those perspectives
may be unpacked through close textual analysis. Of equal importance,
however, is the ideology of the text's recipient, since that ideological

predisposition provides an important lens through which those texts are received and interpreted.

Moreover, Spitulnik (1996) points out that media discourse cannot simply be viewed as a vertical mode of communication, "a one-way directionality from a mass communication form to the masses, who supposedly receive it and consume it" (164; see also Spitulnik 1993, Hall 1980). Instead, Spitulnik (1996) argues, "We need also to factor in what is happening at the levels of reception and lateral communication" (164). She further suggests that "the repeating, recycling, and recontextualizing of media discourse" works to form a community "because it establishes an indirect connectivity or intertextuality across media consumers and across instances of media consumption" (Spitulnik 1996: 164).

In short, the Narrative takes on a life of its own outside presidential speeches. Whereas the previous chapter examined the uptake of the Narrative in the media, this chapter focuses on how citizens who are not on the media stage understand America's struggle against terrorism and recontextualize the language of the Narrative as they interact with each other. I examine focus group data from discussions I held with politically involved college students who attended school in the western United States. The aim is to understand how these students, who all care very deeply about the issues facing the nation, receive and reshape the discourse of the "war on terror" that is in social circulation.

As Americans, these students all experienced 9/11 one way or another. Only about half of these students lived in the western United States on September 11, 2001. The others grew up in eastern or southern states before going away to college. Given the different time zones in which they lived and the different activities in which they were involved when the events of 9/11 took place, some were at home and some were at school when they learned of the happenings. Many became aware of the events when they turned on the television. Some first received word from classmates, teachers, or parents. All of them, however, quickly entered into discussions about the events with those around them as they digested the images and explanations they received through the media. In short, they began taking part in the national discourse about 9/11 and terrorism.

As a nation, Americans share significant common ground as they talk about 9/11 and the nation's response to terrorism. Even as they start from that common ground—from the "war on terror" discourse—where they take it varies according to their ideological predispositions. Not surprisingly, the views of these students broke along party lines with Republicans supportive of the Bush administration's policies and Democrats—as well as the two Ron Paul[1] supporters—critical of those policies. (Recall the discussion on bridging assumptions at the end of chapter 4 that cited the partisan differences found in the PIPA 2004b study.) The Narrative is anything but a static text. Rather, it is open to interpretation and reinterpretation as partisans adopt and rework its language.

THE "WAR ON TERROR" AS METAPHOR AND MILITARY CONFLICT

In my discussions with these college students, we spent considerable time discussing the very idea of the "war on terror." I wanted to gain a sense of how they defined it, and what it meant to them when they used the phrase in their own conversations. The "war on terror" meant very different things for the supporters versus the critics—for example, whether it encompassed the war in Iraq. Although the critics were more likely to problematize the idea of a war against terrorism in a way that significantly reshaped the phrase "war on terror," even supporters acknowledged the inadequacy of the metaphor for fully describing the struggle against terrorism. Both Democrats and Republicans frequently likened the "war on terror" to the "war on drugs." They often pointed out that the "war on terror" declared war on a problem, an idea, a concept, or a method rather than a nation-state as did literal wars. Excerpt 1 comes from my discussion with a group of Republicans, all of whom are supporters of President Bush's actions in the "war on terror" and in Iraq. Ethan, however, takes issue with the "war on terror" as a name for those operations. (Transcription conventions are provided in appendix C.)

> Excerpt 1. (Republicans 14-22:00)
>
> *Adam*:   And of course um (.) you know the war on terror has been sort of a label that we've been using to talk about terrorism. Um and President Bush has defined that in many different ways. Um I just want to get your sense of how you guys would define that. What would-what does the war on terror mean? What does it encompass?

1. Ron Paul, a Republican congress member from Texas, used his campaign to advocate a conservative libertarian perspective that included a noninterventionist foreign policy. Although the more mainstream Republican presidential candidates generally supported the Bush administration's "war on terror," Ron Paul provided a dissenting voice within the party. He received a great deal of support from younger voters who identified as libertarians and opposed the war in Iraq.

Ethan: I don't like the name war on terror. I mean because it's just like the
            war on drugs. I mean it's just like=

John: =the war on [happiness.]

Ethan: [Yeah.] ((laughing)) So- so should we have had like during
            World War II should we have named it (.) war on (.) Nazi or fascism? I
            mean it's like fa- like terrorism is going to take place (.) everywhere.

In excerpt 1, the vagueness of the concept of terrorism is highlighted
by John when he jumps in to provide a follow up to Ethan's "war on drugs"
comparison. He jokes about the idea of a "war on happiness." Like terror,
happiness is also an abstract emotion incongruent with a "war" frame. As
Ethan expresses, "terrorism is going to take place everywhere." Others
echoed this sentiment in highlighting the vagueness of terrorism as something against which to fight. In excerpt 2, Steve, a Democrat, humorously
likens the "war on terror" to "a war on people beating each other up."

Excerpt 2. (Democrats 8-5:03)

Adam: So I just want to start off by asking you what you see as some of
           the key issues that Americans face today.

Steve: Uh I'd say that health care is the biggest one. Aside from that (.)
           Yeah health care is the biggest one. Aside from that probably the
           whole war on terror thing. And I'm putting that in quote marks
           [Okay. ((laughs))] since the audio can't pick that up. Uh whatever
           you might call that, that's a pretty big issue. [. . .]

Adam: So (.) when you say- when you put the war on terror in quotes,
           what do you mean- how do you define the war on terror? (.) What
           do you mean by that? What do think that-

Steve: Well I think it's inappropriate to phrase it as a war (.) on terror.
           Because terror is simply a method of conducting (.) violence or
           warfare. I mean like that would be like saying declare a war on (.)
           I don't know, a war on people beating each other up. Who can beat
           each other up [((laughs))] at anytime, anytime you like and so you're
           not really going to be able to stop that. [Mm-hmm.] Whereas wars,
           implicitly at least, even if they take like a hundred years to fight out,
           there should be a definite (.) uh I suppose you could say (.) falsifiable
           way to tell if it's ended (.) or not. [Mm-hmm.] But even if we kept on
           fighting the war on terror, once again, in quote marks, for a thousand
           years, we still wouldn't win it because it would still be possible at
           any time for someone to just go ahead and do (.) terrorist stuff again.

In his dissection of the "war on terror" metaphor in excerpt 2, Steve points out that "terror is simply a method of conducting violence or warfare." He not only objects to the phrase itself but to the entire notion of, as he says, "the whole war on terror thing." He indicates his ideological distance from it by verbally "putting that in quote marks." Elsewhere, another Democrat, Ted, also used, in his words, "the little finger quotes thing" to qualify his use of the phrase. These verbal scare quotes achieve the same effect as the *so-called* marker examined in chapter 5. Since the phrase "war on terror" has become the ubiquitous label for discussing America's response to terrorism, it is difficult for social actors to engage with the topic without using the phrase. Critics indicate the contested nature of the term through tactics such as these. Steve repeats this tactic at the end of excerpt 2 where he must mention the phrase again: "the war on terror, once again, in quote marks."

The problem with the metaphor, as Steve points out in excerpt 2, is that there is no definable endpoint to a "war on terror." Steve explains, "Whereas wars, implicitly at least, even if they take like a hundred years to fight out, there should be a definite, I suppose you could say falsifiable way to tell if it's ended or not." In his comments, Steve highlights where the metaphorical entailments break down. Another Democrat, Philip, invoked the notion of a traditional "battlefield" where armies fight; this is followed by an "armistice" and "everyone goes home." These notions of a traditional war, along with their lexical entailments, are clearly at odds with a "war on terror" fought against nonstate actors.

In contesting the policy of the "war on terror," Democrats sometimes followed these metaphorical entailments to an imagined endpoint, as seen in excerpts 3 and 4.

Excerpt 3. (Democrats 11-43:46)

Adam: What do you think would- How would you define- I mean what would the end of the war on terror look like? (.) And you know what do you think George Bush has in mind when he's talking about winning the war on terror? [Um.] What is- How is he measuring that?

Mike: That is my sole problem with George W. Bush. ((laughing and crosstalk)) Because when he says that (.) certain people- ehh- What the hell does that suppose to mean? How do you end a (.) a war on terror? Hmm-

Lyle: Well we have to kill Darth Vader.

Mike: Okay what does it- I'll answer your question though. What does it look like? (.) Um. (.) What does it look like. (.) It looks a lot like a fascist state where someone's telling us everything to do. ((45 seconds elided))

Lyle: It's Oceania in *1984*. [Yeah.] It's (.) the Orwellian society. It's not a pretty picture. (.) At all. It's (.) the (.) endless war against an unknown enemy (.) that (.) is unwinnable. Simultaneously that war has required the stripping of our freedoms, and (.) the slow reorganization of our society to be purely dedicated towards (.) the continuation of that society and the continuation of the abstract threat, keeps everybody living in fear. [Mm-hmm. Yeah] So the war on terror (.) is causing terror?

Excerpt 4. (Democrats 9-31:10)

Adam: Would- would that ((i.e., killing Bin Laden)) effectively end the war on terror, the struggle against terrorism? Or what do you think would (.) define success in that- in that- uh-

Ted: The problem with that- It's just like the war on drugs. There's no end point. There's no end game for the whole thing. So you can't end the war on terror because there's no discernible- If you invented mind control for all people, then I guess you end the war on terror or something like that, but- (.) Uh you can't just have a war on a concept.

Both of these examples make use of a reductio ad absurdum argument and follow the metaphorical "war on terror" to different possible conclusions. In excerpt 3, Lyle notes that to end the war "we have to kill Darth Vader." The parodic response mocks the Bush administration's Manichean vision of the world, equating it with the clear dichotomy between good and evil seen in the popular Star Wars movies. In epic wars between good and evil, evil is typically embodied in a personage such as Darth Vader in Star Wars. In the "war on terror," Osama Bin Laden fulfills that role in many ways. In excerpt 4, the hypothetical killing of Bin Laden had just figured into the discussion when I asked Ted and Will whether they thought his death would effectively end the "war on terror." Ted responds to the idea of an endpoint by imagining a very different conclusion: "If you invented mind control for all people, then I guess you end the war on terror." Ted's response echoes Lyle's explanation in excerpt 3 where he conveys concern over the Bush administration's repressive domestic policies that have become part of the "war on terror." In particular, Lyle elsewhere expressed concern about the erosion of civil liberties through legislation such as the USA PATRIOT Act and the President's authorization of domestic spying by the National Security Agency. At the end of excerpt 3, Lyle flips the idea of the "war on terror" on its head and rhetorically asks, "So the war on terror is causing terror?" Through his remarks in this example, he effectively works to redefine the "war on terror" as a war *of* terror conducted by the Bush administration. Mike concurs in his point that the end of the Bush administration's war "looks a lot like a fascist state."

Not surprisingly, the Republicans I spoke with saw very different aims for the "war on terror" than these Democratic critics of the administration. As supporters of the President, they firmly embraced the policy behind the name. Although, like Ethan in excerpt 1, they may acknowledge the inadequacy of the phrase for describing the policy, they more easily looked beyond the metaphor and viewed the "war on terror" as a very real war waged on numerous "fronts" such as Afghanistan and Iraq. In a follow-up to Ethan's problematization of the metaphor (seen earlier in excerpt 1), Kyle, a fellow Republican, explains in excerpt 5 why the term "war on terror" is better than other names, such as a "war on Al Qaeda."

Excerpt 5. (Republicans 14-23:23)

Kyle: I don't know if it's a great term because um you know like Ethan said, terrorism is (.) always going to happen but- On the other hand (.) you know (.) to define what we're doing right now as- Especially if you were to define it by country, the war in Iraq, the war in Afghanistan really doesn't capture it. I really don't think the war on Al Qaeda would capture it either because I think there are also terrorist interests uh that are (.) real threats to us that are not encapsulated by Al Qaeda. Uh the biggest one at the moment being um (.) the Iranian sphere and particularly Hezbollah. They're a terrorist organization which is not an Al Qaeda affiliated organization at all. Uh=

Adam: =So you would consider that a part of the war on terror?

Kyle: That and- and to some degree terrorist supporting states like uh (.) Iraq and potentially even North Korea if they are selling to these people. So the war on terror might be too broad of a term, but I don't know how you'd narrow it down without um really misdefining the aim.

((John and Ethan talk about the definition of *terror* for 2 minutes 10 seconds))

Kyle: Yeah uh. Yeah if you want to pick on the term war on terror~terror might not even be the term to pick on, it would be the term war~because a war might be something with a defined end point. Whereas I don't see a defined end point here. I mean obviously you have goals you know (.) get rid of Saddam Hussein, establish a functioning democracy in Iraq, uh capture Osama Bin Laden, uh fall of the Iranian regime. Those are all goals in- in a larger fight against terror. Uh but (.) when they fall down other people are going to pop up and there are always going to be threats. And uh in the- in the you know kind of postmodern world we live in (.) uh you know (.) a lot of those are going to come from nongovernmental organizations rather than states so- I don't see a defined end point. I think we can define missions within that end point. Like Iraq, Afghanistan, um potentially in the future Iran. You have to hope not, but potentially. We can define missions and we can define those wars as having defined end points but I (.) don't think you can define an end point to the war on terror even if you do like the term.

In excerpt 5, Kyle acknowledges the problem of defining a clear end-point to the "war on terror." However, unlike the endpoints imagined by the Democrats in excerpts 3 and 4, Kyle breaks down the aims of the "war on terror" into a list of more concrete military goals or missions. Although he says it is difficult to give a clear endpoint to the "war on terror" itself, "We can define missions and we can define those wars as having defined end points." As Kyle explains, defining the overarching campaign "by country, the war in Iraq, the war in Afghanistan really doesn't capture it." For Kyle, these do not represent separate wars, but merely different "missions" within a bigger "war on terror." Also, that bigger campaign is not just a "war on Al Qaeda," as he notes. It involves, as he describes, "terrorist interests" that include Hezbollah as well as "terrorist supporting states like Iraq and potentially even North Korea if they are selling to these people." The states Kyle names as threats in the struggle against terrorism are in accord with the "axis of evil" named by Bush in his 2003 State of the Union address. Moreover, his listing of the different military "missions" within the broader war—"Iraq, Afghanistan, potentially in the future Iran"—echo the list of nation-states described by neoconservative foreign policy figures as national security threats. As Bush does in the Narrative, Kyle discusses the "war on terror" as an open-ended campaign that subsumes these disparate nations and terrorist groups under one umbrella. As a partisan supporter of the neoconservative foreign policy objectives, Kyle recapitulates the key elements of the Narrative in a favorable light as he makes his case for how to more accurately characterize the "war on terror."

Whereas Kyle defines the "war on terror" in a manner that maintains fidelity to its use within the Narrative, students who are critical of the Bush administration, like Philip in excerpt 6, attempt to redefine the war in Iraq as a separate conflict.

Excerpt 6. (Democrats 7-29:49)

Adam: So do you see- do you see the war in Iraq as part of the war on terror, or something separate?=

Philip: =No. I don't see it as part of the war on terror. What we're dealing with in Iraq has nothing to do with Al Qaeda. I mean it's- it's a civil war. It's a Sunni-Shia conflict. It's an internal conflict. It has nothing to do with Al Qaeda. Um (.) and the insurgents who attack us are just (.) Iraqis who want us out.

If a "war on terror" is a fight against terrorism, how is *terrorism* delimited? Given the vagueness of the "war on terror" label, this question is often answered implicitly by Americans as they filter the phrase through their different ideological frameworks and use it in conversations with each other. Philip's unhesitating response to my question in excerpt 6 implies that the "war on terror" entails a conflict against Al Qaeda. As he explains in distinguishing between the "war on terror" and the war in Iraq, "Iraq has nothing to do with Al Qaeda," which assumes the "war on terror" is effectively a war against Al Qaeda. Philip's notion of the "war on terror" provides a narrow reading of the phrase coined within the Narrative. In contrast, Kyle's definition in excerpt 5 provides a much broader reading. For Kyle, terrorism includes all forms of what he refers to elsewhere as "Islamic terrorism" or "Islamo-fascism" (more on this term later). This broadens the scope of the "war on terror" beyond Al Qaeda to include Hezbollah, as he explains in excerpt 5. Importantly, both readings are plausible as interpretations for the meaning of a "war on terror." Whereas Kyle's reading is more sympathetic and he is willing to read into the phrase a longer list of neoconservative foreign policy objectives, Philip's reading is much less sympathetic and he is unwilling to accept Bush's attempts to link Iraq with the events of 9/11. Nevertheless, both accede to the use of the "war on terror" as a label for a struggle against terrorism, however that is defined.

To refute the notion forwarded by the Bush administration that the war in Iraq is part and parcel of the "war on terror," critics work to redefine the term according to their own preferred reading. In excerpt 6, Philip not only distinguishes the war in Iraq from the war against Al Qaeda, he backs up his claim with a redefinition of the conflict in Iraq. As he says, "It's a civil war. It's a Sunni-Shia conflict. It's an internal conflict." Presumably, the war in Iraq cannot be both a civil war and a war against Al Qaeda. Thus, this counterclaim has been widely used by critics of the war in Iraq to point out the folly of the situation and the way the administration has linked it to 9/11 and the fight against Al Qaeda. Such reformulation provides a clear choice between two different interpretations of the war in Iraq (see chapter 7 for more on these interpretations). The discursive competition over the larger social meanings associated with key phrases such as the "war on terror" plays out in conversations such as these as Americans talk politics with each other.

FURTHERING INTERTEXTUAL SERIES

Chapter 5 examined several examples of key phrases associated with the Narrative that have formed intertextual series in the media. Many of these sound bites and talking points also make their way into the conversations Americans have with each other. In excerpt 7, Colin, a Republican and vocal supporter of the Bush administration's foreign policy, discusses what he sees as the reasons for the U.S. invasion of Iraq.

Excerpt 7. (Republicans 1-14:00)

Colin: I mean because what I saw is that- I saw definitely the links between Al Qaeda and Iraq. I mean everybody- it's a huge- it's huge- It's debatable. Definitely. But (.) um I mean having (.) an unstable leader that (.) is willing to (.) drop a chemical weapon on his own people just to kill a couple of Iranians that up in the- up in the Kurdish area, I mean he didn't like the Kurds anyways but (.) uh (.) definitely.~I mean somebody who's going to do that is not going to hesitate, and who has a history of violence against- (.) Or just radicalism. And not sort of based in Islam but uh (.) but- To just to have somebody like that to have, or be developing or be trying to develop nuclear weapons, weapons of mass destruction, anything like that [Uh-huh.] I think definitely is a threat to America when he's ready to give those to somebody who's ready to fly- or who's willing to fly into the towers- planes into the towers. [Uh-huh.] Uh, into American- on

American soil. And I think (.) a hu:ge part of it *is fighting it there so that we do not fight it in America,* I mean that's a hu:ge-
[on- on-],

Adam: [Meaning the] war on terror?

Colin: Yeah. [Uh-huh.] I mean if we- if that- that's what it takes (.) to- (.) to fight a war in Iraq and to find a- stabilize democracy in the Middle East in order for us not to (.) be hit again and again.~I mean we haven't been hit- Everybody thought we'd be hit. I thought- I thought we'd be hit for sure. I know there were a lot of people in America who thought we'd be hit for sure within the next (.) what has it been? It's been five years, six years, uh-

Excerpt 7 illustrates the effectiveness of the Narrative's adequation (Bucholtz and Hall 2004) of Iraq and Al Qaeda in justifying the war in Iraq. The rationale of "links between Al Qaeda and Iraq" form the basis of Colin's proclaimed support for the war in Iraq, which he sees as part of the "war on terror." The issue of a direct connection between Saddam Hussein and Al Qaeda has been a contentious issue in the American debate over the war. As seen in chapter 4, Bush provides many references to Saddam Hussein and terrorists in general in the Narrative. However, specific references to Al Qaeda in particular appear less often. Listeners must rely upon bridging assumptions (Brown and Yule 1983: 257) to come to a firm conclusion about the presence of such links. Colin's position as a partisan Republican supporter of the administration allows him to bring a favorable set of ideological assumptions to the evidence presented by the administration about Iraq. This allows him to provide a broad reading of the Narrative so that, as he says, "I definitely saw the links between Al Qaeda and Iraq."

As Colin expresses his views about Iraq and the "war on terror," he draws from a talking point examined in chapter 5: *we are fighting the terrorists in Iraq so we don't have to fight them in America.* This key phrase and its variants form part of an intertextual series that helps convey the linkage between the war in Iraq and the "war on terror." Colin notes, "I think a huge part of it is fighting it there so that we do not fight it in America." Colin stresses this point by lengthening the vowel in "huge" and re-iterating, "I mean that's huge." As Colin draws from the reservoir of prior talking points forwarded by Bush, he maintains fidelity to their prior use within the Narrative. This allows him to help further reify the Narrative as a macrolevel discourse.

Later in the same discussion, a fellow Republican, Bill, uses another key phrase to emphasize the importance of using the military in places like Iraq to wage the "war on terror," as seen in excerpt 8.

Excerpt 8. (Republicans 1-15:36)

    Bill: Well it's like Bush says, *"We're taking the fight to them."* Because if we were- you know if we were to just kind of like (.) throw a little offensive here and then back off, they're not going to- they're not going to respond to that at all. They're going to be like, "Well, American military won't- they won't do anything about it. They're all talk." So- (.) and- and Bush's policy which everyone (.) disagrees with~or the liberals anyway with (.) you know they're trying to [go full force take the- the-]

   Colin: [A lot of them (.)]

    Bill: Yeah. Well. (.) Whatever. But uh *taking the fight to them* is- That is really just (.) making them back down. And they actually know okay, that they're not- they're not- they're not fooling around so-

  Adam: Meaning the terrorists right?

    Bill: The terrorists are thinking, "Okay the Americans aren't fooling around." I mean everyone else may be (.) you know, a bunch of spineless jellyfish. So-

In excerpt 8, Bill makes use of a reported speech frame to cite the President's words directly. These words are used to bolster his argument about the importance of an offensive military strategy in the fight against terrorism. Bill states, "Well it's like Bush says, 'We're taking the fight to them.'" The direct quotation adds the weight of the President's authority to Bill's argument. Bill then takes up these words into his own speech later in the excerpt to reiterate them outside a reported speech frame. This excerpt directly builds on the discussion by Colin in excerpt 7 about the importance of fighting the "war on terror" in Iraq. The pronoun "them" not only refers to terrorists, as Bill affirms, but its use with the notion of fighting the war in Iraq ties the two concepts together. Thus, the "terrorists" become synonymous with the "enemy" in Iraq. Between excerpts 7 and 8, Bill and Colin jointly reconstruct key assumptions and arguments forwarded in the Narrative. Moreover, this achievement is aided through the reiteration of key phrases to further intertextual series in a manner that, as Kristeva (1980) describes, takes "what is imitated (repeated) seriously, claiming and appropriating it without relativizing it" (73).

In the public debate about the war in Iraq, President Bush has framed the options as an either-or choice between "staying the course" or "cutting and running." This framing of choices provides ideal sound bites and talking points for supporters of the war. Republicans I talked with made efficient use of these key phrases to articulate their views on continuing the war in Iraq, as seen in excerpts 9 and 10.

Excerpt 9. (Republicans 14-37:25)

Adam: How would uh- What would you suggest for- for going forward from here?

Ethan: *Stay the course.* I mean- I- I honestly think we shouldn't even be talking- There's no reason why we should be talking about bringing troops home right now.

Excerpt 10. (Republicans 2-5:06)

Adam: So what's your current position on (.) the war in Iraq?

Derek: Uh I support the troops and I think that- I understand that we should *stay the course* because right now *cutting and running* is probably not the best thing to do. Um (.) I think- But I really do think that we should have finished it the first time through in the Gulf War in 1991, and not had to go back in a second time.

Excerpt 9 comes amidst discussion about the situation in Iraq. In response to my question about what he would suggest for resolving the problems, Ethan flatly states, "Stay the course." In excerpt 10, in response to my question about his position on the war in the Iraq, Derek formulates his response through the either-or framework laid out by supporters of the war in the larger public debate. He says, "I understand that we should stay the course because right now cutting and running is probably not the best thing to do." Later, Derek discussed his support for the strategy implemented in early 2007 to increase the number of troops in Iraq, and said he felt the numbers should have been increased from the very beginning. Many of the Republican supporters of the war frequently voiced support for a strong flexing of the U.S. military's might and the use of overwhelming force. They often expressed the opinion that many of the troubles in Iraq could be solved through a larger military presence.

MAKING SENSE OF ANALOGIES WITH
HISTORICAL CONFLICTS

As discussed in chapter 2, the Narrative draws upon past conflicts such as World War II and the Cold War to characterize the "war on terror." In any analogy, the mappings between the source and target domains are never perfect; thus, room for interpretation and reinterpretation exists. The Democrats and Republicans I spoke with had very different ideas about how to read and apply historical reference points from the nation's collective memory to the "war on terror" and the war in Iraq.

Although many rejected the use of World War II as a historical comparison, instead favoring Vietnam, World War II did factor into the accounts given by some Republicans. Specifically, in these instances they used World War II as a source to describe the nature of the enemy in the "war on terror" (including Iraq) as well as to understand how best to reconstruct Iraq (as a front in the "war on terror") amidst the difficulties there. In excerpts 11 and 12, Kyle, a Republican, explains the parallels he sees between the ideology of the enemy during World War II and the ideology of the enemy in the "war on terror." Excerpt 11 comes during discussion of the motivations of those who carried out the events of 9/11; Kyle introduces the term "Islamo-fascism" to characterize their ideology. In excerpt 12, he further details this ideology.

Excerpt 11. (Republicans 14-15:52)

Kyle: Yeah, I just want to say- And you know we can talk a lot about- And there is a lot of talk about whether the economic factors, or psychological factors, and maybe you can make a case there's a certain amount of jealousy there. Uh but I don't think you should- And this might- this might be passé to say in some- some leftist circles, but I don't think you can discount the fact that (.) um there is just um a lot of hate (.) um I don't want to- () In- in that sort of ideology, in that sort of uh (.) um Islamo-fascist ideology which is prevalent over there. And it is hate, and it is a dogma of (.) of violence. Not Islam itself, but Islamo-fascism as an ideology. ((several minutes elided))

Adam: And do you- do you see parallels with uh (.) um past wars where we fought fascism? Or-

Kyle: I don't- As far as methodologically, no. But as far as the nature of- of the enemy, I think there is an extreme correlation probably. Between Bin Laden, uh Ahmadinejad, a few of those other (.) uh

individuals of that ilk. Um and- and Hitler because it's a (.) genocid-
ally based form of totalitarian ideology hell bent on taking over the
world~so I see an extreme correlation there between Nazism and (.)
uh the current Islamo-fascist ideology.

Excerpt 12. (Republicans 14-20:12)

Adam: And you mentioned uh Islamo-fascism.

Kyle: Right.

Adam: Um how would you define that ideology, that- that term?

Kyle: Um well I would define that term uh in the sense of a totalitarian
ideology, uh similar to what we would call fascism or Nazism-
Actually I- I use Islamo-fascism because people know what it
means~I actually don't think it is hard enough of a term~personally
I prefer the term Islamo-Nazism? Um because it is a totalitarian
ideology, totalitarian being defined as an ideology which uh (.) is
focused on changing everything about private life uh you know as
far as uh Communism or fascism restructuring the lives of people,
their moral values, the societal structure. So uh and that would be
the fascism end of it~it's a totalitarian thing whereas uh (.) Islamo-
Well obviously it- it's an Islamic based form [Uh-huh.] of- of
fascism. And like I said I don't like the term because I don't think
it's harsh enough and I think if there's- what is being done which
includes, in my opinion, a lot of hatred of (.) particular Jews but
also Americans, I think uh has the genocidal angle to it. So I much
prefer the term Islamo-Nazism.

Wars require an enemy; and the process of *distinction* (Bucholtz and
Hall 2004) that separates "us" from "them" begins by defining that enemy
as representative of values antithetical to "ours." The collective memory
of America's enemy in World War II provides an exploitable source
domain for the process of *othering* that must occur for a "war on terror" to
be waged. As Kyle defines the enemy through the term "Islamo-fascism"
in excerpt 11, he draws on World War II as a source to characterize "the
nature of the enemy" in the current "war on terror." Bush uses the term
himself in several speeches, although it is mainly limited to speeches given
in the fall of 2005. Importantly though, within the larger Narrative,
"Islamo-fascism" is used interchangeably with terms such as "Islamic extremism" among others, which Bush describes as follows in a speech on
October 6, 2005: "Some call this evil Islamic radicalism; others, militant

Jihadism; and still others, Islamo-fascism."[2] These synonyms provide a common reservoir of terms to label the enemy.

Kyle draws from this common reservoir of terms to index the body of ideas about the enemy present in the Narrative. As Kyle notes in excerpt 12, "I use Islamo-fascism because people know what it means." At least for those who share his ideological position, the term carries certain understandings about the enemy. Kyle details his understanding in excerpt 12. He explains, "It is a totalitarian ideology, totalitarian being defined as an ideology which is focused on changing everything about private life." He then names more specific examples of totalitarian ideologies: "Communism and fascism." In the Narrative, Bush refers to these as the "murderous ideologies of the twentieth century" (recall chapter 2). Despite the differences between Communism and fascism, both the Narrative and Kyle's description merge the two together through a focus on their common totalitarian bent. As Kyle sums up, "It's a totalitarian thing." In other words, the antidemocratic nature of these ideologies poses a common threat to American values. This background is then transferred to the ideology of the current enemy, which is "an Islamic based form of fascism." Like Bush in his speeches, in excerpt 11 Kyle emphasizes that he is not talking about "Islam itself, but Islamo-fascism as an ideology."

Even when partisan supporters draw from the Narrative in ways that reproduce it, subtle linguistic innovation may occur. In elaborating on Islamo-fascism in excerpt 12, Kyle takes the term and reworks it into "Islamo-Nazism."[3] This allows him to ground his discussion of the "nature of the enemy" more firmly within historical reference to World War II. In excerpt 11, he draws a correlation between "Bin Laden, Ahmadinejad, a few of those other individuals of that ilk, and Hitler." Not only does this take Hitler as a source to characterize Bin Laden, but the placement of the President of Iran, Ahmadinejad, into the same category as Bin Laden

2. In a White House fact sheet posted along with this speech, the ideology is detailed as follows: "The Terrorists Serve a Clear and Focused Ideology. The ideology known as Islamic radicalism, militant Jihadism, or Islamo-fascism—different from the religion of Islam—exploits Islam to serve a violent political vision that calls for the murder of all those who do not share it. The followers of Islamic radicalism are bound together by their shared ideology, not by any centralized command structure. Although they fight on scattered battlefields, these terrorists share a similar ideology and vision for the world openly stated in videos, audiotapes, letters, declarations, and websites" (White House 2005, October 6).

3. Although Kyle is not the first to use the term Islamo-Nazism, Bush himself does not use it in any of his speeches. The key point here is that others in the broader community involved in reproducing aspects of the macrolevel discourse about the "war on terror" introduce subtle variation into the system.

works to further the notion that Iran could potentially be the next front in the "war on terror." The lumping together of Bin Laden and Ahmadinejad as well as "other individuals of that ilk" contributes to the linkage of the Middle Eastern countries central to the Bush administration's foreign policy: Afghanistan, Iran, Iraq, among others. Moreover, it paints the "us" versus "them" dichotomy in broad strokes. Kyle opposes "our values" with the "Islamo-fascist ideology which is prevalent over there" (excerpt 11). The deictic element "there" in this statement geographically completes the distinction between "us" and "them."

While Kyle conveys the significance of the term Islamo-fascism for many Bush supporters and adeptly reiterates the Narrative's connections between the current and past enemies in the nation's conflicts, critics clearly have a different understanding of the analogy and the term *Islamo-fascism*. Excerpt 13 comes from a discussion with the two Republican supporters of Ron Paul. As vocal critics of the Bush administration's foreign policy, they did not believe the war in Iraq was linked to the "war on terror." We had just finished watching a clip from a speech by Mitt Romney, the Republican presidential candidate, who had announced the suspension of his campaign in February 2008. In the clip, as well as much of his campaign, Romney reiterated many of the tenets of the Narrative. Andy provides his thoughts on Romney's remarks in excerpt 13.

Excerpt 13. (Ron Paul Republicans 10-39:53)

   Andy: And he hammers home those points on war and terror and evil and (.) extre:mism, I think I heard Islamo-fascism or something which (.) I think is probably one of the stupidest terms that's come about from this whole ((laughing)) you know (.) this whole situation.

   Adam: Yeah.

   Andy: And I think it's just typical.

   Adam: What do you think that means, Islamo-fascism? What-

   Andy: I've thought about that and I don't know. ((laughing)) Um (.) talking about- I mean- I kind of thought about- Mussolini kind of defined fascism as (.) um like a marriage between um state and uh- It was like a corporatist state. And (.) I don't see that with Islamism- Islam. I don't see what that has to do with fascism.

   Adam: Yeah.

   Becky: They just scare people. People are scared of that word.

   Andy: Instead of using Communism, it's now fascism.

In summarizing the gist of Romney's remarks, Andy notes in excerpt 13, "I think I heard Islamo-fascism or something." Interestingly, the term never occurred in the clip I played for them. Nevertheless, Andy appears to associate this term—one among several interchangeable labels for the enemy in the Narrative—with the "war on terror" discourse used by Romney in his speech. As Andy says, "I think it's just typical." For Andy, Romney's remarks typify the macrolevel discourse about the "war on terror," which he views as laughable. The term Romney actually used was "evil extremism." Andy also uses "extremism" to characterize Romney's remarks, and does so with a lengthening on the middle vowel in a way that seems to mock Romney. As Andy says more specifically of the term Islamo-fascism, "I think [it] is probably one of the stupidest terms that's come about from this whole situation."

As excerpt 13 continues, I ask Andy what he thinks Islamo-fascism means. Unlike Kyle in excerpts 11 and 12, Andy sees no connection between fascism and Islam. He starts by citing Mussolini and the notion of fascism as a type of "corporatist state," but unlike Kyle he makes no analogy between fascism during World War II and the current nature of the enemy in the "war on terror." "I don't see what that [Islam] has to do with fascism," he concludes. After Becky jumps in to indicate her belief that words such as these are used to "just scare people," Kyle notes that labels for traditional enemies are interchangeable. "Instead of using Communism, it's now fascism." This characterization of Communism and fascism lies in stark contrast to the merging of the two under the umbrella of totalitarianism in Kyle's remarks or as the "murderous ideologies of the twentieth century" in the Narrative, as pointed out earlier. Here, Andy and Becky expose the fungibility of labels used to define enemies in times of war. They resist the Narrative by rejecting these labels as valid reference points.

In addition to drawing from World War II to describe the nature of the enemy in the "war on terror," Bush supporters also echoed the analogy in the Narrative between the reconstruction of Japan and the reconstruction of Iraq. In excerpt 14, Republicans use this analogy to explain how to go about nation-building in Iraq.

Excerpt 14. (Republicans 14-46:35)

> *Zack*: I understand and I- I actually agree uh somewhat with Ethan on
> that one. That we shouldn't be trying to fight a conventional war
> against guerillas. I mean- We saw what happened when we did
> that in Vietnam. We lost way more people. Well I don't want
> to say () way more people. We just- we just lost a lot of people

as compared with other wars. And uh we're kind of seeing that in this one, but thankfully we haven't lost a lot of life. Um but I think what we need to do is find leadership (.) uh that of uh people who uh (.) generals from World War II such as Patton or- or=

Ethan: =Isn't he six feet under the ground? ((laughs))

Zack: He's six feet under the ground. ((laughing)) But we need people <u>like</u> him (.) running this war and actually running the country. I- I think it was kind of a bad move (.) to set up a government that quick. I think we needed to take control of Iraq militarily and then set up a- a military- a military (.) uh authoritarian government to take care of everything and then (.) when as much opposition is crushed, then set up a so-called democracy if you want.

Kyle: Well and- and there is a parallel for that. And- it- it doesn't <u>sound</u> good but it's- But really politics, and especially when you get into war and nation building unfortunately it's a results oriented game not a process oriented game. And I- you know if you compare what we did in Iraq to what we did in Japan and how it's turned out, we've- In Japan, we (.) didn't do anything as far as self-government for years~I mean Douglass MacArthur literally wrote that country's constitution guaranteeing freedom of religion, parliamentary government, uh ownership of property by women, yaddi yaddi yadda. And today Japan is a successful, functioning, thriving democracy, and an ally of the United States, and they are generally happy to be that way.

Ethan: Aren't they some of the happiest people in the world too? Aren't Japanese?

Kyle: Well they also have one of the highest suicide rate-

John: Highest teenage suicide rate.

Kyle: All right, we're not going to get into the minutiae of Japanese culture here. But now contrast that with what we did in Iraq. We went in there and decided we wanted to let them write their own constitution, we'll let you play with Islamic law here, there, and the other- you know, smaller troop presence, and it produced lesser results. If you're going to do a nation building operation, you do it the way MacArthur did it.

Memories about the past are not merely filled with historical figures, but with historical heroes. In the nation's collective memory about triumphs against dangerous enemies, historical figures are elevated to the status of heroes who embody the qualities to which the nation aspires. In the Narrative, Bush often refers to the "war on terror" as the "calling of a new generation." He then urges the current generation to take up the call like the "greatest generation" did before, in the World War II era. In his speeches, Bush sometimes alludes to historical figures from that era. Whether presidents or common soldiers, these figures are presented as embodiments of the qualities of leadership and bravery needed in times of war. In a similar manner, in excerpt 14, Zack draws upon "generals from World War II such as Patton" to exemplify the type of leadership we need today. "We need people like him running this war and actually running the country," Zack says.

In addition to Patton, Kyle names General Douglass MacArthur, who oversaw the occupation of Japan after their surrender at the end World War II. Kyle holds up MacArthur's reconstruction of Japan after the war as an ideal example of what should be done in Iraq. He effectively blames the problems in Iraq on not following this example. "If you're going to do a nation building operation," he says, "you do it the way MacArthur did it." The result of a successful reconstruction effort, like that in Japan, is to turn a former enemy into an ally. As Bush describes of America's efforts in postwar Japan in a speech on August 22, 2007, "the Japanese would transform themselves into one of America's strongest and most steadfast allies." Likewise, Bush expects the same of Iraq, as he states in a speech on August 31, 2006: "Victory in Iraq will result in a democracy that is a friend of America and an ally in the war on terror." Kyle reiterates these talking points as he concludes that "today Japan is a successful, functioning, thriving democracy, and an ally of the United States." Although Kyle and others do not see World War II as a good example of how the war should be fought, it nevertheless holds out lessons on how to build democracy in occupied Iraq.

By far, the most popular analogy among focus group participants was the war in Vietnam. This was true for both administration critics, who saw Iraq as separate from the "war on terror," as well as administration supporters, who saw Iraq as integral to the "war on terror." Although they both used Vietnam as a source domain, they did so for different reasons—with one exception. The one point of similarity included the notion that both Vietnam and Iraq involved the use of guerilla tactics by an insurgency. In this regard, they saw the more traditional warfare used in World War II (i.e., armies fighting on battlefields) as an ill-fitting comparison for the methods of warfare used in the current conflict. In contrast, given the asymmetrical warfare used against the U.S. military in Iraq, both critics and supporters of the war saw Vietnam as a compelling comparison. This was the case regardless of whether they viewed the enemy in Iraq as "terrorists" or as Iraqis defending their homeland from an invading force. I examine the different readings of the Vietnam analogy in more detail in the next chapter as part of a broader look at the discursive competition over the Vietnam analogy in American society.

THE DIALOGIC EMERGENCE OF THE NARRATIVE

As Mannheim and Tedlock (1995) argue, "cultures are continuously produced, reproduced, and revised in dialogues among their members" (2). Dialogues take place in the nation not only in the media, but also in the day-to-day conversations citizens have with each other. As Spitulnik (1996) emphasizes, it is important to not only look at the media as a vertical mode of communication, but also as a lateral one that features "the social circulation of media discourse outside of contexts of direct media consumption" (Spitulnik 1996: 164). Citizens do not simply absorb entextualized political messages filtered through the media and broadcast via a one-way channel into their homes. Rather, in conversations with each other, they discuss and debate the issues presented in political speeches and media discourse. As they draw on a common reservoir of prior discourse, they interpret and reinterpret the meanings of key phrases such as the "war on terror" and the sound bites and talking points found in the Narrative. Larger social meanings about America's struggle against terrorism are ultimately worked out in these multiple sites of overlapping interactions.

7

Whose Vietnam?: Discursive Competition over the Vietnam Analogy

I'm going to try to provide some historical perspective to show there is a precedent for the hard and necessary work we're doing, and why I have such confidence in the fact we'll be successful.

—George W. Bush (2007, August 22)

INTRODUCTION

An important aspect of the Narrative is its ability to subsume disparate foreign policy objectives under the rubric of the "war on terror." For the Bush administration and its supporters, Iraq has become the "central front in the war on terror." However, administration critics reject this conflation of Iraq and the fight against terrorism. In voicing opposition to what they see as a separate and unrelated war in Iraq, critics have frequently adopted the Vietnam War as an analogy. They argue that the administration has plunged the United States into a "quagmire" in Iraq analogous to the way the nation was embroiled in Vietnam. American involvement in Vietnam, which began early in the 1960s and lasted well into the 1970s, cost the lives of nearly 60,000 U.S. soldiers and untold numbers of Vietnamese. It represents a bitter moment in America's collective memory about itself.

There is no dearth of public discourse about the war or debate over its broader meaning. Like World War II, the Vietnam War provides a ripe source of comparison for the current war. However, unlike World War II, the lessons of this historical comparison are less *readerly* (Barthes 1977) and more open to interpretation and contestation.

Political discourse is marked by the struggle over the representation of ambiguous issues, and the larger social meanings about the war in Iraq and the "war on terror" are anything but certain in American public discourse. "This competition over the meaning of ambiguous events, people, and objects in the world has been called the 'politics of representation' (Holquist 1983; Shapiro 1987; Mehan and Wills 1988)" (Mehan 1996: 253). As Americans continue to come to terms with the Bush administration's policies in the "war on terror," the representation over the war in Iraq has arguably become one of the most contested aspects of the Narrative. The ubiquity of the Vietnam analogy in oppositional voices has become hard to ignore even for the President. After rejecting or at least avoiding the Vietnam War as a source of comparison for the war in Iraq, President Bush seemed compelled to answer the critics and provide his own reading of the analogy to bring Iraq back within the fold of the Narrative. This chapter examines the use of this analogy by critics of the war as well as Bush's attempt to appropriate the analogy and weave it into his own narrative. In this chapter, I bring together all three forms of data examined throughout the book. Namely, I draw on media discourse and my discussions with college students opposed to the war to provide a picture of the oppositional discourse about the war in Iraq. I then examine a key speech given by Bush in 2007 where he focuses on the Vietnam analogy, along with the use of this analogy by college students in support of the war.

THE OPPOSITION'S USE OF THE VIETNAM ANALOGY

The politics of representation play out in the media where voices come together to characterize the nature of the conflict in Iraq. The construction of the Vietnam analogy in media discourse relies heavily on reported speech frames to quote and cite recognized political leaders and government officials. In this way, the analogy is ratified through the voices of those who possess "symbolic authority" (Bourdieu 1991: 106). That is, to further use Bourdieu's (1991) terms, they act as spokespersons, or "authorized representatives" (111) for the oppositional perspective within the national debate.

Excerpts 1 and 2 feature three prominent Democratic figures speaking in opposition to the war. All express this opposition through the use of the Vietnam analogy. These excerpts come from news coverage in the first part of 2004, the year of the presidential race between President Bush and Senator John Kerry. Excerpt 1 is from a column in *USA Today* that discusses the inevitability of the Iraq/Vietnam comparison. Excerpt 2 is an article on the CBS News web site that recaps comments Kerry made on a *60 Minutes* show.

Excerpt 1. (USA Today 2004, April 9)

Or does the renewed fighting have the potential to become for Bush what the Tet offensive was for Lyndon Johnson — a moment when U.S. public opinion fundamentally shifts, and with it, history? In contentious testimony before the 9/11 commission, national security adviser Condoleezza Rice said there was no "silver bullet" that could have prevented the terrorist attacks in New York and Washington, D.C. It's looking more and more like there is no silver bullet for Iraq, either.

In an impassioned speech, Sen. Edward Kennedy, D-Mass., declared Iraq "George Bush's Vietnam." Sen. Robert Byrd, D-W.Va., made the same comparison.

Excerpt 2. (CBS.com 2004, January 25)

Kerry, who fought in Vietnam as a Navy lieutenant, junior grade, was wounded in battle three times. He told Bradley he was disillusioned with that war "within weeks, almost," and compared it to the current situation in Iraq.

"[Vietnam] is young people dying for the wrong reasons, because leaders don't do the things that they should to protect them," said Kerry. "Yes I do [see a parallel with Iraq]. This president breached faith with the lesson. . .we learned in Vietnam. You truly should go to war as a matter of last resort. This president rushed to war without a plan to win the peace," he added.

These excerpts demonstrate the furthering of a chain of authentication (Irvine 1989; recall chapter 5) that endorses the Vietnam analogy in public discourse. Not only is the analogy reiterated across multiple media contexts, but the repetitions gain authority by citing Senators Kennedy, Byrd, and Kerry. Bourdieu (1991) emphasizes the importance of the social conditions that not only shape what words are spoken, but also give them power, authority, and legitimacy. He uses the analogy of the Homerian *skeptron* in which the person who holds this staff is invested with the authority to speak and to be heard. Senators are agents who possess sufficient symbolic capital to be given a prominent stage in the national media. They effectively bear the skeptron, and their words are afforded legitimacy. In this way, the citations of these three senators work to authenticate the Vietnam analogy as part of the oppositional discourse about the war in Iraq.

In excerpt 1, Kennedy's endorsement of the Vietnam analogy comes through the citation of a short sound bite that characterizes his criticism of the Bush administration's handling of the war in Iraq. As the journalist writes, "Sen. Edward Kennedy, D-Mass., declared Iraq 'George Bush's Vietnam.'" The reference to Vietnam in this sound bite goes beyond its purely denotational meaning. Here, Vietnam effectively indexes an understanding about the Vietnam War as a messy, tragic, and unnecessary conflict in American history. That is, in Kennedy's speech, the Vietnam analogy works by pointing back to prior contexts in which the Vietnam War has been criticized by opponents. Those contexts anchor the analogy in a set of negative connotations about Vietnam, which are then mapped over to the current war in Iraq. The sound bite effectively encapsulates these dual understandings about Vietnam and Iraq in a single noun phrase (i.e., "George Bush's Vietnam") that becomes recontextualized in the media coverage. The analogy is then seconded through the citation of another senator: "Sen. Robert Byrd, D-W.Va., made the same comparison." In this way, the voices of these two senators enter into the chain of authentication that furthers the Vietnam analogy as part of the oppositional discourse to the war in Iraq.

In excerpt 2, the direct quotation of words spoken by Senator Kerry in a *60 Minutes* program is preceded by a list of his credentials. In addition to being a senator, Kerry's credentials include serving in Vietnam as a "Navy lieutenant" who "was wounded in battle three times." This symbolic capital provides Kerry's words, which are presented in the subsequent quotation, with cachet in the national debate. As an authorized representative of the oppositional discourse in that debate, his words become part of the ongoing speech chain that authenticates the analogy as a valid representation of the issue. Moreover, the framing of these words within the news article facilitates this speech chain. The quotation itself comes from an interview Kerry gave on *60 Minutes*. Whether or not the analogy was central to Kerry's remarks during that interview, it now becomes central to the article that recontextualizes selections of the interview. The journalist's additions, which are found in brackets in the quotation in excerpt 2, do more than simply fill in context to Kerry's reported words; they contextualize Kerry's words within the news article in line with the article's emphasis on the Vietnam analogy. Thus, media recontextualizations may work to amplify a chain of authentication.

Congressional opponents to the President's war in Iraq are not limited to Democratic senators. Senator Chuck Hagel, a Republican, has become a vocal critic of the administration's foreign policy and handling of the war. The next excerpt comes from an article in his home state's paper of record, the *Omaha World Herald*.

Excerpt 3. (Omaha World Herald 2006, July 30)

U.S. Sen. Chuck Hagel's declaration that Iraq has become an "absolute replay of Vietnam" provoked strong reactions from defense experts and the White House on Saturday.

The Nebraska Republican made the comparison in a Friday interview with the *World-Herald*, where he also sharply criticized the Pentagon's plans to boost U.S. forces in Iraq.

"He's absolutely right," Lawrence Korb, a former senior Defense Department official in the Reagan administration, said of the Vietnam comparison. "The signs are all around."

Korb, who works at a centrist think tank, also agreed with Hagel's view that the Pentagon's reversal of plans to reduce troops this year would hurt the Army in the long run.

"Yes, they're ruining the all-volunteer Army," Korb said.

Hagel's voice is another in the speech chain that forwards the Vietnam analogy. Unlike his Democratic counterparts, whose opposition is more or less expected, Hagel represents a dissenting voice from within the President's own party. His voice, therefore, works to authenticate the analogy from a position seemingly untainted by partisan bias. In other words, insofar as a member of the President's own political party is expected to support the President or at least refrain from vocal criticism, such dissent carries extra weight in the chain of authentication. Not surprisingly, in political debates that break along party lines, partisans from one party often highlight dissenting voices from within the other party as proof that their position is unmotivated by partisan interests. If a respected Republican senator agrees "that Iraq has become an 'absolute replay of Vietnam'" (excerpt 3), then this characterization of the situation holds more weight than would be the case if only Democratic partisans were to make this assessment. In his other media appearances, Hagel frequently uses the term "quagmire" along with the words "bogged down" to refer to both

Vietnam and Iraq. This language is firmly in line with the opposition's understandings about the Vietnam War as an analogical source for faulting the war in Iraq.

In addition to the voices of Congressional leaders, the chain of authentication in media reportage also includes other figures recognized as experts, such as former government officials. In excerpt 3, Hagel's characterization of the war is further supported through the citation of "a former senior Defense Department official in the Reagan administration." This official, Lawrence Korb, is quoted as saying of Hagel's assessment, "He's absolutely right." Further direct quotations are introduced by the journalist with accompanying metapragmatic comments that highlight Korb's agreement with Hagel's view. In this way, a supposedly more objective voice (i.e., detached from Congressional politics) is presented to corroborate the perspective of a currently serving politician. This ratification by former government officials is further seen in excerpt 4, from an Associated Press article.

Excerpt 4. (AP 2006, November 17)

"Ironically, we went into Vietnam to fight one war, the Cold War, and found ourselves in the middle of a struggle over nationalism," said P.J. Crowley, a military and national security aide in the Clinton administration. "And we're seeing the same thing in Iraq."

"We may have well thought we were going into Iraq as part of the war on terror, but now we find ourselves in the middle of a civil war," Crowley said.

In excerpt 4, "P.J. Crowley, a military and national security aide in the Clinton administration" is quoted about the parallels he sees between Vietnam and Iraq. The former official's credentials allow him to comment upon the situation with a degree of authority. Through direct quotations in the article, the official conveys an important parallel between Vietnam and Iraq. Namely, both are presented as "a struggle over nationalism." That struggle is removed from the Cold War in the case of Vietnam, and unrelated to the "war on terror" in the case of Iraq. Importantly, the war in Iraq is here redefined as "a civil war." This redefinition of the war in Iraq removes it from the umbra of the "war on terror." Moreover, the Vietnam analogy helps opponents achieve this redefinition. The analogy and this redefinition work hand in hand to define the war in Iraq, like the Vietnam War, as an exercise in failed judgment with little redeeming value.

In my discussions with politically involved college students, opponents of the war in Iraq shared this understanding about the Vietnam analogy. Will, a Democrat, expresses this understanding in excerpt 5, which comes as we discussed whether Iraq shared any parallels with past conflicts in the nation's history.

Excerpt 5. (Democrats 9-18:40)

Adam: What do you think?

Will: I would definitely compare the war in Iraq to Vietnam even though the Bush administration completely denies it. Just because uh- like there wasn't really any real accomplishment in Vietnam, and I think they're really trying to get something accomplished in Iraq but they don't know what it is yet. ((laughs)) And so um (.) yeah like I don't really see it as comparable to World War II (.) because you're not fighting an insurgency, you didn't have a nation that's at civil war, um- World War II was just countries fighting against each other and this is completely different.

As Will represents the oppositional discourse in excerpt 5, he states that "there wasn't really any real accomplishment in Vietnam." Likewise, in Senator Kerry's words seen earlier in excerpt 2, Vietnam represents "young people dying for the wrong reasons." In this oppositional discourse, the war is seen as a tragic mistake. As Will further characterizes the situation in excerpt 5, he discusses it in terms of "a nation that's at civil war." For many critics of the Bush administration's policy and the war in Iraq, this Vietnam analogy, complete with the redefinition of Iraq as a civil war, forms the basis of an oppositional discourse that separates Iraq from the "war on terror."

BUSH'S APPROPRIATION OF THE VIETNAM ANALOGY

During a prime time press conference on April 13, 2004, a reporter asked Bush about his thoughts on the comparison between Iraq and Vietnam. In response, the President flatly replied, "I think the analogy is false." However, the wide play given to the analogy in public discourse made it hard for Bush to continue to deny, especially as it threatened the Narrative's encapsulation of Iraq within the rubric of the "war on terror." On August 22, 2007, Bush addressed the national convention of the Veterans of Foreign Wars (VFW) in Kansas City, Missouri. In his speech, he adopted the Vietnam analogy as a valid comparison for understanding Iraq as part of the "war on terror." In what follows, I examine how Bush brings Vietnam into the fold of the Narrative in this speech. Rather than a separate war viewed as a "quagmire," Bush's Vietnam provides lessons on how to remain steadfast in an ideological struggle against the modern equivalent of the Communists of the Cold War.

As with any rendition of the Narrative, the precipitating event of 9/11 acts as an important reference point. In the speech's opening remarks, Bush includes this obligatory element, as seen in excerpt 6.

Excerpt 6. (Bush 2007, August 22)

I stand before you as a wartime President. I wish I didn't have to say that, but an enemy that attacked us on September the 11th 2001 declared war on the United States of America. And war is what we're engaged in.

The statement in excerpt 6 is embedded within Bush's words of thanks to various members of the VFW, which are standard in any speech given in front of a particular audience. Thus, this explicit reference to "September the 11th 2001" occurs well before the narrative portion of the speech begins. Nevertheless, it provides an important anchor for the narrative that soon follows. True to form, the Narrative proper begins with reference to a precipitating event, as seen in excerpt 7a.

Excerpt 7a. (Bush 2007, August 22)

I want to open today's speech with a story that begins on a sunny morning, when thousands of Americans were murdered in a surprise attack. And our nation was propelled into a conflict that would take us to every corner of the globe. The enemy who attacked us despises freedom, and harbors resentment at the slights he believes America and Western nations have inflicted on his people. He fights to establish his rule over an entire region. And over time he turns to a strategy of suicide attacks destined to create so much carnage, that the American people will tire of the violence and give up the fight.

The description of the precipitating event in excerpt 7a could be from any of Bush's numerous renditions of the Narrative. He talks of "a surprise attack" and an enemy who "despises freedom" and uses "suicide attacks." Through this description, he sets up an allusion to the events of 9/11 and the terrorist enemy he has detailed in speeches to the American public over the prior six years. Moreover, this description parallels the explicit reference to 9/11 provided earlier in excerpt 6. Once he sets up this indirect reference, however, he flaunts the listener's expectations and provides a surprise twist, as seen in excerpt 7b.

Excerpt 7b. (Bush 2007, August 22)

If this story sounds familiar, it is. Except for one thing. The enemy I
have just described is not Al Qaeda, and the attack is not 9/11, and the
empire is not the radical caliphate envisioned by Osama Bin Laden.
Instead what I've described is the war machine of Imperial Japan in the
1940s, its surprise attack on Pearl Harbor, and its attempt to impose its
empire throughout East Asia. Ultimately the United States prevailed in
World War II, and we have fought two more land wars in Asia.

In excerpt 7b, Bush claims to speak not of the events of 9/11 and Al
Qaeda, but rather of "the war machine of Imperial Japan in the 1940s, its
surprise attack on Pearl Harbor, and its attempt to impose its empire
throughout East Asia." In actuality, the allusion set up in excerpts 7a and
7b is to both 9/11 and Pearl Harbor, both Al Qaeda and Japan. Bush draws
upon the parallels he has repeatedly made between 9/11 and Pearl Harbor,
in particular, and the "war on terror" and World War II, in general. Here,
however, he merely transposes the two. He uses 9/11 and Al Qaeda as
sources for describing Pearl Harbor and Japan's role in World War II.
Despite the transposition of source and target, the result is the same as in
any rendition of the Narrative: parallels are set up between the "war on
terror" and World War II.

Crucially, as Bush opens his narrative with an analogy to World War
II, he focuses exclusively on "the war machine of Imperial Japan in the
1940s." That is, rather than drawing upon Nazi Germany or the European theater as a source of comparison as he does in other speeches
(recall chapter 2), here he places sole attention on the Pacific theater of
World War II. He then moves from this exclusive focus on Japan into a
broader geographical focus on the Asian region. In excerpt 7b, he states
that after "the United States prevailed in World War II," the nation
"fought two more land wars in Asia." American involvement in these
wars, the Korean War and the Vietnam War, are then developed in turn
as the speech progresses.

Bakhtin's (1981) notion of the *chronotope* refers to the "intrinsic con-
nectedness of temporal and spatial relationships" in narrative (84; Silverstein 2005). In this rendition of the Narrative, World War II is associated
with the Korean War and the Vietnam War through their spatial (i.e., geographical) relationship with one another. The historical time difference
between these disparate conflicts shrinks as they enter together into a
common temporal position within narrative time (Ricoeur 1984; Bruner
1991: 6). In this way, "spatial and temporal indicators are fused into one

carefully thought-out, concrete whole" (Bakhtin 1981: 84). As a result, through a stepwise progression from Japan to Korea to Vietnam, Bush sets up a geographically linked equivalence class between the wars fought in these three Asian countries. In addition to their common geographical location, Bush ties them together as "ideological struggles," as seen in excerpt 8.

Excerpt 8. (Bush 2007, August 22)

There are many differences between the wars we fought in the Far East and the war on terror we're fighting today. But one important similarity is at their core they're ideological struggles. The militarists of Japan and the Communists in Korea and Vietnam were driven by a merciless vision for the proper ordering of humanity. They killed Americans because we stood in the way of their attempt to force their ideology on others. Today the names and places have changed but the fundamental character of the struggle has not changed.

In excerpt 8, Bush reiterates the linkage between what he terms elsewhere the "murderous ideologies of the twentieth century" (recall chapter 2). Instead of Nazis or fascists, here he references the "militarists of Japan" along with the "Communists in Korea and Vietnam." For Bush, the conflation of these disparate enemies works because they were all involved in "ideological struggles." Insofar as fascism, Japanese imperialism/militarism, and Communism can all be characterized as ideologies, they are interchangeable as different faces of a familiar enemy that America has encountered in the past. To this list can then be added the ideology of, as termed elsewhere in the Narrative, "Islamic radicalism" or "militant Jihadism." Importantly, these ideologies' "similarity is at their core," as Bush describes, so that their differences are merely superficial. Bush states, "Today the names and places have changed but the fundamental character of the struggle has not changed." In this way, he assimilates the Vietnam analogy into this notion of a larger ideological struggle. In particular, Bush's Vietnam is a central front in the Cold War's battle against Communism, just as Bush's Iraq is the "central front in the war on terror." Through Vietnam's link to the Cold War and, in broader terms, the link between the ideologies of the Cold War and World War II, Bush adapts the Vietnam analogy in a manner that is wholly consistent with the Narrative. Bush's Vietnam, therefore, conveys very different historical lessons than the Vietnam of his critics.

Once Bush has discursively established this framework for viewing Vietnam, he develops the lessons of his analogy for the "war on terror." He begins in excerpt 9a by citing the voices of those who opposed the Vietnam War when it was in progress.

Excerpt 9a. (Bush 2007, August 22)

As a matter of fact many argued that if we pulled out, there would be no consequences for the Vietnamese people. In 1972 one anti-war senator put it this way, "What earthly difference does it make to nomadic tribes or uneducated subsistence farmers in Vietnam or Cambodia or Laos whether they have a military dictator, a royal prince, or a socialist commissar, in some distant capital that they've never seen and may never heard of?" A columnist for the *New York Times* wrote in a similar vein in 1975 just as Cambodia and Vietnam were falling to the Communists. "It's difficult to imagine," he said, "how their lives could be anything but better with the Americans gone." A headline on that story dated Phnom Penh summed up the argument, "Indochina without Americans, for most a better life."

As Buttny (1997; see also, Buttny and Williams 2000) points out, reporting the words of others is often done to construct representations of those who are quoted. In excerpt 9a, Bush quotes an unnamed "antiwar senator" and a "columnist for the *New York Times*" to build an image of the antiwar perspective during the Vietnam era. Although these quotes come from Senator William Fulbright and journalist Sydney Schanberg, the reported speech frames do not provide precise attributions. Attributions beyond the anonymous "anti-war senator" and "columnist for the *New York Times*" are in fact unnecessary and perhaps even detrimental to the use of their words in the present context. Their words are not brought into the speech to directly argue against the speakers as individuals. Rather, Bush brings in these words to provide a general characterization of the type of discourse spoken by critics during the Vietnam War. The vague nominal attributions help contextualize the quotations as typical of this discourse. Moreover, the anonymous attributions to "one anti-war senator" and "a columnist for the *New York Times*" backgrounds the social and cultural capital of these speakers and their experience in arriving at their critical stance against the Vietnam War. Little fidelity is maintained to the prior context in which these words were used. Here, they are framed as wholly out of touch with the emphasis in the current context on the "consequences for the Vietnamese people" after America ended its involvement in Vietnam. Although the words of critics are cited, which supposedly presents their stance through their own words, the antiwar perspective presented by Bush is a straw man of his own creation. In this way, it acts as a foil to his view in favor of the war.

With a caricature of the antiwar perspective established, Bush then knocks down this straw man in a dialogical retort, as excerpt 9b continues.

Excerpt 9b. (Bush 2007, August 22)

The world would learn just how costly these misimpressions would be. In Cambodia, the Khmer Rouge began a murderous rule in which hundreds of thousands of Cambodians died by starvation, and torture, and execution. In Vietnam former allies of the United States and government workers, and intellectuals, and businessmen were sent off to prison camps, where tens of thousands perished. Hundreds of thousands more fled the country on rickety boats, many of them going to their graves in the South China Sea. Three decades later, there is a legitimate debate about how we got into the Vietnam War and how we left. There's no debate in my mind that the veterans from Vietnam deserve the high praise of the United States of America. ((applause)) Whatever your position is on that debate, one unmistakable legacy of Vietnam is that the price of America's withdrawal was paid by millions of innocent citizens whose agonies would add to our vocabulary new terms like "boat people," "re-education camps," and "killing fields."

The implicit cues embedded within the reported speech frames discussed earlier are followed in excerpt 9b by explicit metapragmatic comments about the quoted words. Characterized as "misimpressions," this reading crucially applies to the impressions of antiwar critics in general and not just the senator and journalist who are directly quoted in 9a. As Bush enumerates a series of tragic historical events that took place in Southeast Asia in the 1970s ("In Cambodia, the Khmer Rouge began a murderous rule . . . "), he provides a causal explanation for why they took place. Namely, these negative events are presented as resulting from the "misimpressions" of the war's critics. This evaluation is presented as a fact that stands outside the "legitimate debate about how we got into the Vietnam War and how we left." As Bush states, "Whatever your position is on that debate, one unmistakable legacy of Vietnam is that the price of America's withdrawal was paid by millions of innocent citizens. . ." With this rhetorical move, Bush effectively positions one perspective in that debate—the one he is trying to convey—as an objective fact removed from the debate's partisan positions.

At the end of excerpt 9b, Bush further alludes to the historical events in Southeast Asia through the naming of three key phrases associated with those events. He notes that "the price of America's withdrawal was paid by millions of innocent citizens whose agonies would add to our vocabulary new terms like 'boat people,' 're-education camps,' and 'killing fields.'" Basso's (1996) work on how the Western Apache speak with place-names underscores the effectiveness of economical metonyms such as these. As Basso (1996) describes, Apache speakers often invoke a particular place-name in the midst of conversation to conjure up a shared narrative associated with that place. Without reiterating the narrative itself, mentioning the place-name is sufficient to set interlocutors into the proper position from which they can view the scene and recall the events that took place there. In a similar way, Bush's use of these key phrases indexes the historical context in which these terms became known. They conjure up a set of ideas about the devastating events that took place in Southeast Asia in the 1970s. In conjuring up these images of the "boat people," the "re-education camps," and the "killing fields," Bush portrays these scenes as "the price of America's withdrawal" from Vietnam.

Importantly, the lessons from Bush's Vietnam analogy are not merely presented as his own perspective. Rather, as seen in excerpt 9c, Bush directly connects Vietnam and Iraq through the words of the current "enemy" in the "war on terror," which helps corroborate his perspective.

Excerpt 9c. (Bush 2007, August 22)

There was another price to our withdrawal from Vietnam, and we can hear it in the words of the enemy we face in today's struggle. Those who came to our soil and killed thousands of citizens on September the 11th, 2001. In an interview with a Pakistani newspaper after the 9/11 attacks, Osama Bin Laden declared that "the American people had risen against their government's war in Vietnam, and they must do the same today." His number two man, Zawahiri, has also invoked Vietnam. In a letter to Al Qaeda's chief of operations in Iraq, Zawahiri pointed, and I quote, to "the aftermath of the collapse of the American power in Vietnam and how they ran and left their agents." End quote. Zawahiri later returned to this theme declaring that the Americans, quote, "know better than others that there is no hope in victory. The Vietnam specter is closing every outlet." Here at home some can argue our withdrawal from Vietnam carried no price for American credibility, but the terrorists see it differently.

Reported speech frames work to provide evidence and corroborate accounts (Hill and Irvine 1993). In excerpt 9c, the direct quotations of Osama Bin Laden and "his number two man, Zawahiri," provide evidence to back up Bush's account of Vietnam and its meaning for the war in Iraq. Allusions to Vietnam figure into quotes attributed to both men; and their words further a chain of negative consequences said to stem from America's withdrawal from Vietnam. Through these representations of the enemy's words, Bush affirms his perspective on Vietnam and strengthens the links between that understanding and the "war on terror." The belief in the objectivity of quoted words provides much of the power of reported speech frames to provide corroboration. One need not merely believe Bush when he says the price of withdrawal from Vietnam was costly. Here, current enemies of the nation can be heard to confirm that view. This allows Bush to disavow that his claims merely stem from his own interested position in his explanation of history.

Moreover, these quotations convey a subtle adequation (Bucholtz and Hall 2004) of the "enemy" and administration critics. Bush conveys this notion by quoting Bin Laden: "Osama Bin Laden declared that 'the American people had risen against their government's war in Vietnam, and they must do the same today.'" The implication is that to oppose the wars in Vietnam (like the senator and journalist cited in 9a) or Iraq (like current critics) is to side with the enemy, because the enemy is shown in 9c to advocate a similar stance. In Bush's Vietnam and Iraq, there are only two options: victory or defeat. In this binary, withdrawal equates to surrender, which means defeat. The only remaining option is continuation of war until the enemy is utterly defeated. The option of withdrawal and defeat is taken by those who lack the will to persevere. Those who understand the sacrifices required to see the war through to victory opt for continuation. (Recall the discussion in chapter 3 on how the closing episode in the Narrative features this theme of resolve amidst challenges.) The importance of remaining steadfast and resolved is conveyed by Bush through the words of Zawahiri: "Zawahiri pointed, and I quote, to 'the aftermath of the collapse of the American power in Vietnam and how they ran and left their agents.' End quote." Within the framework of Bush's speech, these words provide a stinging rebuke to domestic war critics. Through the reanimation of Zawahiri's words, Bush demonstrates that "another price to our withdrawal from Vietnam" comes through the loss of "credibility" in the world. As he states, "Here at home some can argue our withdrawal from Vietnam carried no price for American credibility, but the terrorists see it differently." Bush's lessons from Vietnam are therefore affirmed through the words of America's current enemy in the "war on terror." Bush summarizes these lessons as the speech continues in excerpt 9d.

Excerpt 9d. (Bush 2007, August 22)

We must listen to the words of the enemy. We must listen to what they say. Bin Laden has declared that "the war in Iraq is for you or us to win. If we win it, it means your disgrace and defeat forever." Iraq is one of several fronts in the war on terror. But it's the central front. It's the central front for the enemy that attacked us and wants to attack us again, and it's the central front for the United States and to withdraw without getting the job done would be devastating. ((applause))

In excerpt 9d, the either-or dichotomy between victory and defeat, between "us" and the "enemy," is again conveyed, not through Bush's own words, but through the words of Bin Laden. Bush states, "Bin Laden has declared that 'the war in Iraq is for you or us to win. If we win it, it means your disgrace and defeat forever.'" Bush uses reported speech to convey his own characterization of the issue. The result of not heeding the enemy's words, as Bush concludes, "would be devastating." He spells out the consequences in more detail in excerpt 9e.

Excerpt 9e. (Bush 2007, August 22)

If we were to abandon the Iraqi people, the terrorists would be emboldened. They would use their victory to gain new recruits. As we saw on September the 11th, a terrorist safe haven on the other side of the world can bring death and destruction to the streets of our own cities. Unlike in Vietnam, if we withdraw before the job is done, this enemy will follow us home. And that is why, for the security of the United States of America, we must defeat them overseas so we dot- do not face them in the United States of America. ((applause))

The encapsulation of Iraq within the "war on terror" is made obvious in excerpt 9e where the enemy in Iraq is denoted as "the terrorists." Moreover, the consequences of withdrawal from Iraq are framed in terms of their effect on the terrorists—presumably, the Al Qaeda terrorists quoted earlier. Bush notes that "the terrorists would be emboldened." The dichotomy between victory and defeat is also framed as a victory either for the United States or the terrorists. Bush states that the terrorists "would use their victory to gain new recruits." Thus, the war in Iraq is unequivocally portrayed as part and parcel of the struggle against terrorism in the "war on terror." In Bush's Vietnam, America left before the job was completed, and this resulted in humiliation and defeat.[1] In Bush's Iraq, "if we withdraw before the job is done, this enemy will follow us home." Bush emphasizes this assessment through the reiteration of a key talking point from the Narrative: "we must defeat them overseas so we do not face them in the United States of America." (Recall, for example, Colin's remarks in excerpt 7 of chapter 6, which also reiterate this talking point.)

As noted at the end of chapter 6, both college Democrats and Republicans favored Vietnam as a source for understanding the current war in Iraq, whether or not they saw Iraq as part of the "war on terror." They both saw parallels between the guerilla tactics used in Vietnam and the asymmetrical warfare in Iraq. Beyond this point, however, their readings of Vietnam as a source of comparison diverged sharply. Not surprisingly, supporters of the Bush administration shared similar ideas to those conveyed by Bush in his Vietnam speech. In particular, these supporters frequently pointed to the loss of public will as a factor in both wars. Excerpts 10 and 11 are from different groups of college Republicans. In both we are discussing the parallels between Vietnam and Iraq.

Excerpt 10. (Republicans 1-33:32)

Adam: So do you see- Do you see any um (.) analogies between Vietnam and Iraq?=

Bill: =It's the same- It's almost- I think it correlates almost (.) very similarly because- ((clears throat)) Vietnam, initially we came in there. It looked good. Looked good. But somehow like (.) you know politicians basically. I you know (.) won't say either way pretty much but- They've just kind of dragged on like, "No we shouldn't send more troops. Okay we'll put them on hold for a little bit." But then you know, slowly it just kind of thins their strategy out. Before long it's like, "Well, in the past we could have sent more troops and it would have been- We would have just got the job done then and there." But. Because it's dragged out, everyone's been worn thin so now we have to pull out.

---

1. The notion, as expressed by Bush, that the military wasn't allowed to "finish the job" in Vietnam has been emphasized in some pop culture portrayals of the Vietnam War and its aftermath, for example, in Sylvester Stallone's Rambo movies and Chuck Norris's Missing in Action movies. Certainly, the idea resonates with a large part of the American public.

Colin: I think=

Bill: =I think that's exactly what's happening. Now- I think- War's been- Now war's been left too much up to the politicians. When it should just be, you know, let our military leaders go out there and do their job.

Colin: I think the only like- I'm pretty sure that the only correl- the biggest correlation I see is basically the deterioration of the public will. And like I said it's a huge thing to me? Like it just is but, I- I think that really is the main thing I can see- that as time goes on it the thing t- to oppose the war. And it- [I mean here we're supporting more our troops]

Adam: [So why do you think- why do you think that is?]

Colin: than we did in Vietnam. [Okay.] But opposing the war and almost even- and undermining the war. I think it's almost the Americans' fault that we're losing. I mean honestly-

Excerpt 11. (Republicans 2-10:30)

Adam: So you mentioned Vietnam. Do you see parallels between Vietnam and what's going on in Iraq? Or are there other um historical lessons (.) uh (.) from different conflicts in the past that we might be able to draw some- some lessons from to-

Derek: I definitely see parallels between Vietnam um- just- Not necessarily even just there between the- So you've got the terrorists as far as the guerillas and the Viet- the Viet Cong and that sort of stuff. But you also have the uh dissati- dissatisfaction of the American people at home. I don't think we've quite reached the level of protests that occurred in the seventies. I wasn't there, so I really can't vouch for that one personally ((laughing)) but from what I've heard- What I've learned- Just- But the dissatisfaction with the (.) running of the war seems to (.) um (.) be concurrent but- I don't think (.) major differences um- The reasons that we are there- [Mmm-hmm.] Um (.) as far as- It's basically containment versus responding to an action that was taken against us. So. [Mmm-hmm.] I think- We are far more justified for being in Iraq than we are- than we were for being in Vietnam.

Bush's exhortation to remain steadfast in the war effort stems from the view that public protests are a sign of weakness and lack of resolve.

The notion of the public's role in supporting the war can be seen in both excerpts 10 and 11. In excerpt 11, Derek talks of the "dissatisfaction of the American people at home." In excerpt 10, Colin speaks of "the deterioration of the public will." Although Derek does not spell out the consequences of this parallel for the war in Iraq, Colin does. As Colin emphasizes the importance of this issue, he notes that "it's a huge thing to me." He explains that "opposing the war" is almost like "undermining the war." As Bush conveys in 9c, through his quotation of Bin Laden, to oppose the war is to effectively share the enemy's stance. In the binary between victory and defeat, to oppose the war is to cause America to lose and the enemy to win. Colin states explicitly, "I think it's almost the Americans' fault that we're losing." Thus, the blame for the problems in Iraq, just as in Vietnam, is placed on the shoulders of domestic dissenters. When Bush speaks in 9b of the "misimpressions" of war critics, he places a heavy burden of guilt upon them just as Colin does here. In another focus group, John, a Republican, noted, "We just lost Vietnam politically because [of] so much unrest at home." In these views, the difficulties of war have nothing to do with an ill-conceived foreign policy or the way that policy has been implemented. Rather, the main difficulties stem from "unrest at home." As Bush conveys in 9d, the only thing preventing victory in Iraq is the public's desire to end the war prematurely "without getting the job done." In excerpt 10, Bill echoes this concern with "getting the job done," which is prevented by the political dissenters. As he notes, "in the past we could have sent more troops" and "just got the job done then and there." Instead, "everyone's been worn thin so now we have to pull out." Bill conveys his distaste for politicians that question the President: "Now war's been left too much up to the politicians. When it should just be, you know, let our military leaders go out there and do their job." At bottom, the main stumbling block to victory in Iraq, according to this view, seems to be the democratic process in the United States.

Whereas opponents of the wars in Vietnam and Iraq see little strategic value in the wars, supporters firmly point to the importance of Vietnam in the containment of Communism during the Cold War. This vision of Vietnam was shared by many college Republicans I spoke with. However, these supporters pointed out that the notion of containment does not map precisely between Vietnam and Iraq. Whereas the reason for fighting in Vietnam was the containment of Communism in the Cold War, the reason for fighting in Iraq, they say, is not merely for the containment of terrorism but as a response to 9/11. As Derek explains in excerpt 11, "It's basically containment [in Vietnam] versus responding to an action that was taken against us." Although Derek does not explicitly mention 9/11 as that "action taken against us," he uses the language of the "war on terror" to describe the enemy in Iraq. Notably, as he lays out the parallels between Vietnam and Iraq, he maps "the terrorists" in Iraq onto the Viet Cong in Vietnam: "So you've got the terrorists as far as the guerillas and the Viet Cong." Through the descriptor "the terrorists in Iraq," Derek effectively conveys the notion that Iraq is an integral part of the "war on terror." Later in our discussion, he confirmed this view. In another focus group, Ethan, a Republican, was more explicit in stating that "9/11 was the reason" for the war in Iraq (recall the discussion of 9/11 as precipitating event in chapter 3 and the discussion of historical-causal entailment in chapter 4). Although these supporters of the administration do not go so far as to directly implicate Saddam Hussein in the events of 9/11, they nevertheless view 9/11 as the precipitating event for the "war on terror" inclusive of the "front" in Iraq. Due to 9/11, Derek notes, "We are far more justified for being in Iraq than we were for being in Vietnam." The effectiveness of the Narrative in justifying the war in Iraq can be seen in statements such as these. For supporters of the war, the enemy in Iraq is not comprised of insurgents involved in a civil war, as the war's critics maintain. Rather, the enemy in Iraq is comprised of Islamic terrorists involved in a campaign of terror against the United States. Although Iraq and the "war on terror" may be akin to Vietnam and the Cold War, Iraq is far more justified because, as Derek states, in Iraq the United States is "responding to an action that was taken against us."

THE DIALOGIC REVISION OF THE NARRATIVE

The use of a historical analogy is not only about interpreting the present. It is also about interpreting the past conflict that acts as a source domain in the comparison. Ultimately, Bush's Vietnam is about the Cold War's struggle against Communism. This reading contrasts with his critics' portrayal of Vietnam as a struggle against Vietnamese nationalists attempting to repel an invading force. The different readings of the present war in Iraq rest on these different readings of the past. Bush's Iraq is the "central front in the war on terror." The difficulties there stem from America's ideological struggle against terrorist enemies akin to those of the Cold War. For opponents of the war, the only connections between Iraq and terrorism are the ones manufactured by the Bush administration's policy. The conflict in Iraq is seen primarily as a civil war, which America's involvement can only make worse.

The discursive competition over the representation of the Vietnam analogy in public debate is open to challenge and re-presentations. At stake in the politics of representation is whose Vietnam should be used for understanding the war in Iraq. Given the popularity of the Vietnam analogy in the opposition's discourse about Iraq, even dominate macrolevel narratives such as the Narrative must be dialogically revised in response to competing pressure. The appropriation of the Vietnam analogy by Bush in his August 22, 2007 speech illustrates this process. As Bush incorporates Vietnam as a source domain for understanding the war in Iraq and the "war on terror," he merges it with the focus in the Narrative on an ideological struggle akin to the Cold War. In doing so, he attempts to replace the critics' vision of Vietnam as an internal conflict in which America's continued involvement only accomplishes more death and misery.

8

Conclusion

Our speech, that is, all our utterances (including
creative works), is filled with others' words, varying
degrees of otherness or varying degrees of "our-
own-ness," varying degrees of awareness and
detachment. These words of others carry with them
their own expression, their own evaluative tone,
which we assimilate, rework, and re-accentuate.

—Mikhail Bakhtin (1986: 89)

DISCOURSE AND SOCIAL TRANSFORMATION

As noted in the introductory chapter, a powerful narrative such as the Bush
"War on Terror" Narrative is a discursive formation that sustains a regime of
truth (Foucault 1972, 1980). It forwards assumptions and explanations that
regulate how the issue of 9/11 and terrorism can be meaningfully discussed
in American society. To speak about America's response to terrorism after
9/11 is to speak of the "war on terror" and to speak within the "war on terror"
discourse. This discourse provides a common language that allows social
actors to discuss and debate the topic. Even as social actors resist the discourse they must appropriate its language to be listened to and understood.

One problem with the notion of a master narrative, or a dominant macrolevel discourse, is that the concept leaves "no room for tensions, contradictions, or oppositional actions on the part of individuals and collectivities" (Ahearn 2001: 110). Although my goal in this book has been to illuminate the Narrative as a macrolevel discourse that profoundly shapes and regulates sociopolitical reality, I have also endeavored to illustrate that the Narrative is not static, unbending or all-dominating so that resistance is impossible. On one hand, intertextual connections across discursive events are the foundation for the accrual of a situated narrative into a macrolevel discourse. Reiteration of discourse in a manner that maintains fidelity from one context to the next works to reproduce and strengthen the Narrative. Yet strict fidelity rarely exists in practice. As Inoue (2006) suggests, all discourse exists "on moving discursive ground" (32). As discourse enters into subsequent contexts, it is inevitably reshaped to some degree. Thus, recontextualization always leaves open the possibility for the introduction of new meanings and transformations of the text; and therein rests the potential for resistance and social transformation.

Williams (1977) notes, "The reality of any hegemony, in the extended political and cultural sense, is that, while by definition it is always dominant, it is never either total or exclusive" (113). Certeau (1984) provides a useful construct to understand the limits of the hegemonic influence of dominant discourses. He speaks of the diversionary practice that he calls *la perruque* (literally in French, "the wig"), an idiom for "the worker's own work disguised as work for his employer" (Certeau 1984: 25). This trope represents the idea that while workers are constrained by the rules and regulations imposed upon them by their employers, they often come up with ways to subvert these constraints to "borrow" some of their work time for their own personal aims. Certeau explains, "Without leaving the place where he has no choice but to live and which lays down its law for him, he establishes within it a degree of *plurality* and creativity" (Certeau 1984: 30; italics in original). The modern office worker, for example, might use "company time" to send personal e-mails to friends. The worker is officially "on the job," but appropriates that time for his/her own aims.

In more general terms, those subjected to the constraints of a dominating force often find ways to carve out their own creative expression within those constraints. Certeau provides the example of the indigenous communities in the Americas that were subjected to the laws of the Spanish colonizers. In adopting the laws imposed upon them, they reinterpreted those laws in ways that differed from the Spaniards' original intent. "They metaphorized the dominant order: they made it function in another register"

(Certeau 1984: 32). In other words, although the indigenous communities adopted and worked within the dominant, Spanish imposed system, they adapted to the system on their own terms, using their own cultural backgrounds to give meaning to the rules of that system in line with their own experiences and customs. Likewise, as emphasized in the book, those engaged in public discourse about war and terrorism do not simply absorb the explanations of the "war on terror" presented in the Bush administration's discourse, but rather receive it on their own terms.

Certeau's construct provides a way for understanding how an imposing regime of language, such as the Bush "War on Terror" Narrative, can be subtly transformed through the everyday discursive interactions in which people are engaged. Both critics and supporters of the Bush administration's policy are well versed in the "war on terror" discourse. As Americans, they operate within its bounds as they discuss and debate 9/11 and America's response to terrorism. After all, the Narrative does not belong solely to Bush or his partisan supporters, but to all Americans. Nevertheless, like Certeau's worker engaged in *la perruque*, speakers have their own aims and intentions in using the language of the "war on terror." Inevitably, such pressures serve to shape and reshape the Narrative over time.

All this underscores the idea that the creativity introduced into an established system arises from within that system itself. A "big D" discourse such as the Bush "War on Terror" Narrative constrains social actors who draw from its reservoir of prior words in formulating their own (re)articulations. This, however, does not preclude creativity. Social actors are not automatons that simply mimic the discourse imposed upon them from a position of power, relegated to immutably reproduce it. After all, change is perhaps the only constant in life, and history is filled with discursive shifts (Foucault 1970). The stability of a macrolevel discourse from within the position of a particular socio-historical moment is but an illusion. Variation occurs as the discourse moves across contexts; and creativity exists in the reanimation and re-accentuation of prior statements in ways that reshape and resignify the dominant discourse. Like Certeau's workers engaged in the practice of *la perruque*, Americans engaged in public discourse about 9/11 and terrorism may operate within the bounds of the Narrative but what they do with that discourse can never be predetermined.

This idea is well represented in the work of Derrida, Butler, and other poststructuralist theorists. Inoue (2006) summarizes as follows: "Citation produces copies in difference. As Derrida (1977) says of signature, it must be identical from one instance to another, but each instance is also different. Butler (1997: 10–11) sees this in the performativity of the speaking body" (23) where gender identity is re-inscribed in each new interaction. Each context in which that identity is re-inscribed, however, opens the potential to subvert the dominant categories. Inoue (2006) notes, "It is precisely in such repetition in difference, in the unforeseen context, that we can look for the dislocation of the regime of power and, perhaps, the articulation of what we could call 'agency'" (23).

Any act of recontextualization within the bounds of a larger discourse is the exercise of agency. As Duranti (2004) discusses, "any act of speaking involves some kind of agency, often regardless of the speaker's intentions and the hearer's interest or collaboration" (451). Thus, as Duranti (2004) cautions, although intentionality is often closely associated with agency, it is not identical. Nor should agency, as Ahearn (2001) warns, be equated with free will or reduced to resistance. The notion of an autonomous individual engaged in intentional actions does little to explain "the social nature of agency and the pervasive influence of culture on human intentions, beliefs, and actions" (Ahearn 2001: 114). For sociocultural linguists involved in investigations of discourse as social action, agency is better defined as "the socioculturally mediated capacity to act" (Ahearn 2001: 112). When agents act, they accomplish a variety of social goals. Resistance is but one of many possibilities in the "multiplicity of motivations behind all human actions" (Ahearn 2001: 116). As Butler (1990) summarizes, "In a sense, all signification takes place within the orbit of the compulsion to repeat; 'agency,' then, is to be located within the possibility of a variation on that repetition" (145). Moreover, as Butler (1990) emphasizes, "it is only *within* the practices of repetitive signifying" that subversion can take place (145). Likewise for Certeau, individuals operating within a dominant order exert pressure on that order from within as they pursue their own aims.

At bottom, the recontextualization of the Narrative does not come down to a simple choice of acceptance versus denial. The reproduction of key phrases in ways that work to reproduce the Narrative is not the rote action of "cultural dupes" (Hall 1981) that lack agency to critically assess or respond. Nor is resistance of the Narrative the attentive action of cultural subjects that somehow possess agency where others lack it. Moreover, in recognizing that both types of actions are agentive, the issue cannot be simplified by stating that the Bush administration's supporters work to conserve whereas the critics work to resist the Narrative. In reanimating the language of the Narrative, the supporter may help undermine it and the critic may help reify it. Even the supporter may sometimes parody the "war on terror" metaphor and the critic may use the "war on terror" label in an uncontested manner. As both supporter and critic discuss and debate politics, their motivations are multiple and derive from the interactional context in which they find themselves. Their agency comes from orienting to the interactional demands of the situation and engaging in discursive practice, which is socio-culturally mediated by the constraints established by the "war on terror" discourse. Certeau (1984) notes that "the speech act is at the same time a use *of* language and an operation performed *on* it" (33; italics in original). Through the agentive act of speaking, social actors make a discourse "vulnerable to unpredictable futures" and open to "the possibility of resignification" (Inoue 2006: 21). As they speak within the "war on terror" discourse, the possibilities for reshaping it are not always foreseen or consciously pursued. Nevertheless, the possibilities are there.

REGIME (OF LANGUAGE) CHANGE IN WASHINGTON

On November 4, 2008, Americans elected Barack Obama as the forty-fourth president of the United States; and on January 20, 2009, the nation turned the page from the Bush administration and started a new chapter with the Obama administration. Along with the change of administrative regimes in Washington came a shift in the regime of language, as well. Although the wars in Afghanistan and Iraq remained, the ubiquitous label for referencing these wars—and linking them together as one global "war on terror"—is simply absent in Obama's discourse. What Obama does reference instead, as seen in his victory speech in Chicago on election night, are the "two wars" in which the United States is involved.

Excerpt 1. (Obama 2008, November 4 – Election Night Victory Speech)

For even as we celebrate tonight, we know the challenges that tomorrow will bring are the greatest of our lifetime – *two wars*, a planet in peril, the worst financial crisis in a century. Even as we stand here tonight, we know there are brave Americans waking up in the deserts of *Iraq* and the mountains of *Afghanistan* to risk their lives for us.

With the Obama administration, the phrase "war on terror" has subtly slipped out of presidential discourse, replaced by the simple reference to the two wars (and not "fronts" of a single war) in which America is engaged. Excerpt 2, taken from Obama's address to Congress a month into his presidency, further illustrates this discursive shift as he references Iraq and Afghanistan—"both wars"—as separate conflicts.

Excerpt 2. (Obama 2009, February 24 – Address to Joint Session of Congress)

Finally, because we're also suffering from a deficit of trust, I am committed to restoring a sense of honesty and accountability to our budget. That is why this budget looks ahead ten years and accounts for spending that was left out under the old rules; and for the first time, that includes the full cost of fighting in Iraq and Afghanistan. For seven years, we have been a nation at war. No longer will we hide its price. We are now carefully reviewing our policies in *both wars*, and I will soon announce a way forward in Iraq that leaves Iraq to its people and responsibly ends this war. And with our friends and allies, we will forge a new and comprehensive strategy for Afghanistan and Pakistan to defeat al Qaeda and combat extremism. Because I will not allow terrorists to plot against the American people from safe havens half a world away.

Echoes of the Bush "War on Terror" Narrative can be heard in Obama's discourse about combating extremism and defeating al Qaeda; and Obama, as evidenced by his rhetoric as well as his policy of escalating the number of troops sent to the region, certainly views the war in Afghanistan as an important element in an unfinished fight against the Al Qaeda terrorists responsible for 9/11. Nevertheless, he now speaks of the "war in Afghanistan" and not the "war on terror." Even when he draws from the reservoir of catchy sound bites that accumulated during the Bush era, as seen in excerpt 3 from a speech he gave at the State Department a few days after his inauguration, he no longer speaks of a "war on terror."

Excerpt 3. (Obama 2009, January 22 – Address to State Department Employees)

Another urgent threat to global security is the deteriorating situation in Afghanistan and Pakistan. This is the *central front* in our enduring *struggle against terrorism and extremism*. There, as in the Middle East, we must understand that we cannot deal with our problems in isolation. There is no answer in Afghanistan that does not confront the Al Qaeda and Taliban bases along the border, and there will be no lasting peace unless we expand spheres of opportunity for the people of Afghanistan and Pakistan. This is truly an international challenge of the highest order.

In this example, Obama recycles the "central front" sound bite as he describes "the deteriorating situation in Afghanistan and Pakistan." However, he no longer uses it in conjunction with the "war on terror" label, as candidate Obama often did during his campaign and as we saw critics doing in chapter 5 (recall, for example, then-Senator Biden doing this in excerpt 23 of chapter 5). Here, instead of talking about the "central front in the war on terror," Obama talks of "our enduring struggle against terrorism and extremism." Instead of a "war on terror" per the Bush narrative, Obama, as well as Clinton before Bush, talks of a "struggle against terrorism." Through this descriptor, Obama conveys the notion that the nation is engaged with a resolute problem, and is contending with an adversary. Although a "struggle against terrorism" may involve fighting, as evidenced by the war in Afghanistan, the militarization of the struggle is contingent rather than necessary. This differs substantially from the notion of the "war on terror" where the problem is fundamentally conceptualized in military terms. A "war on terror," as we have seen throughout the book and in the Bush administration's policy, necessitates a military response. Notably, for President Obama, the war in Afghanistan is just that, the "war in Afghanistan." It is not, per Bush, the "war on terror."

What is fascinating in this discursive shift is that the language of both President-elect and President Obama (as opposed to candidate Obama) represents a significant departure from the "war on terror" frame. There is no longer an attempt to simply redefine the "war on terror," as seen earlier in the tactics of Bush administration opponents while Bush was in office. As president of the United States, Obama now holds the Homerian *skeptron*, to use Bourdieu's (1991) analogy, and is now vested with the authority to speak and to be heard *on his own terms*. Instead of responding to the agenda set by Bush, which required working within the Bush "War on Terror" Narrative to be heard, Obama now holds, as Bourdieu (1991) describes, "the *delegated power* of the spokesperson" (107; italics in original). He holds the symbolic authority needed to set a new agenda, both discursively and politically. The tactic of redefinition is no longer needed, and the "war on terror" simply fades from presidential discourse.

Two months after Obama's inauguration, the mostly inconspicuous absence of the phrase "war on terror" from American political discourse briefly became a topic of conversation in the press. An article in the *Washington Post* reported on a memo e-mailed to Pentagon staff members. The memo reportedly noted that "this administration prefers to avoid using the term 'Long War' or 'Global War on Terror' [GWOT]. Please use 'Overseas Contingency Operation'" (Wilson and Kamen 2009, March 25). Follow-up coverage a few days later quoted Secretary of State Hillary

Clinton as saying, "The (Obama) administration has stopped using the phrase and I think that speaks for itself" (Reuters 2009, March 31). As to whether the earlier reported memo represented official policy or an official directive from the White House, the article quoted Clinton as saying, "I have not heard it used. I have not gotten any directive about using it or not using it. It is just not being used" (Reuters 2009, March 31).

The effects of the discursive shift can already be seen when searching for the phrase in American press coverage before and after Obama took office. Searches of the Google News Archive and Lexis Nexis database show a drop in the circulation of the phrase in 2009. As the phrase fades from presidential discourse, it also fades from media discourse as it falls out of the "circular circulation" (Bourdieu 1996: 22) of the news cycle. The Bush "War on Terror" Narrative is being replaced by a new regime of language in Washington, and only time will tell how the presidential discourse of the Obama administration (and reactions to it) will shape the new cultural narratives that Americans come to embrace and resist.

As emphasized at the outset, meaning making is never complete after one speech event, but consists of an ongoing process that spans multiple, overlapping encounters. In short, sociopolitical reality requires more than a single authoritative pronouncement to be established. Meanings are both constructed and contested across intertwined contexts where cultural understandings are produced, reproduced, and potentially subverted. As shown in this book, the Bush "War on Terror" Narrative has organized America's experience of 9/11 and formulated its response to terrorism throughout the last seven years of the Bush administration. As America closes the book on the Bush administration, it is important to recognize that language not only holds the capacity for justifying violence and leading a nation into war, but it also holds the capacity to build tolerance and sow peace.

APPENDIX A

Corpus of Presidential Speeches

2001, September 11	Prime Time Address to the Nation from the White House, Washington, DC
2001, September 12	Remarks to the Press from the Cabinet Room of the White House, Washington, DC
2001, September 14	Remarks at the National Day of Prayer and Remembrance at the National Cathedral, Washington, DC
2001, September 20	Address to a Joint Session of Congress, Washington, DC
2001, November 8	Prime Time Address to the Nation from the World Congress Center, Atlanta, GA
2001, November 10	Address to the United Nations General Assembly, New York, NY
2001, November 28	Remarks at the Farmer Journal Corporation Convention at the J.W. Marriott, Washington, DC
2001, December 7	Remarks on Pearl Harbor Day at the USS Enterprise Naval Station, Norfolk, VA
2002, January 29	State of the Union Address, Washington, DC
2002, February 16	Remarks to Military Personnel and Families, Anchorage, AK
2002, April 17	Remarks at Virginia Military Institute, Lexington, Virginia
2002, June 6	Prime Time Address to the Nation from the White House, Washington, DC
2002, September 5	Remarks at the Kentucky Fair and Exposition Center, Louisville, Kentucky

2002, September 11	Prime Time Address to the Nation from Ellis Island, New York, NY
2002, September 12	Address to the United Nations General Assembly, New York, NY
2002, October 2	Remarks from the Rose Garden, Washington, DC
2002, October 7	Remarks at the Cincinnati Museum Center, Cincinnati, OH
2002, October 16	Remarks at the Signing of the Iraq War Resolution, White House, Washington, DC
2002, December 31	Remarks to the Press in Crawford, TX
2003, January 3	Remarks at Fort Hood, TX
2003, January 28	State of the Union Address, Washington, DC
2003, February 6	Remarks from the White on Colin Powell's UN Briefing, Washington, DC
2003, February 9	Remarks at the 2003 Congress of Tomorrow Republican Retreat Reception, White Sulphur Springs, WV
2003, February 26	Remarks to the American Enterprise Institute, Washington, DC
2004, April 16	Remarks at Boeing Integrated Defense Systems Headquarters, Saint Louis, MO
2003, May 1	Announcement of the End of Major Combat Operations in Iraq from the USS Abraham Lincoln off the Coast of San Diego, CA
2003, May 2	Remarks at United Defense Industries, Santa Clara, CA
2003, July 1	Remarks at the Reenlistment of Military Service Members, White House, Washington, DC
2003, September 7	Prime Time Address to the Nation from the White House, Washington, DC
2003, September 12	Remarks to Military Personnel and Families at Fort Stewart, GA
2003, October 9	Remarks to Military Reservists and Families at Pease Air National Guard Base, Portsmouth, NH
2003, November 6	Remarks at the 20th Anniversary of the National Endowment for Democracy, Washington, DC
2004, January 20	State of the Union Address, Washington, DC
2004, January 22	Remarks at the Roswell Convention and Civic Center, Roswell, NM
2004, March 18	Remarks to Military Personnel at Fort Campbell, KY
2004, March 19	Remarks from the White House on the Anniversary of the Invasion of Iraq, Washington, DC
2004, May 24	Remarks at the US Army War College, Carlisle, PA
2004, June 2	Remarks at the US Air Force Academy Graduation Ceremony, Colorado Springs, CO
2005, February 2	State of the Union Address, Washington, DC
2005, March 8	Remarks at the National Defense University, Washington, DC
2005, June 28	Prime Time Address to the Nation from Fort Bragg, NC
2005, August 24	Remarks to Military Personnel and Families in Nampa, ID

2005, October 6	Remarks at the National Endowment for Democracy, Washington, DC
2005, October 25	Remarks at the Joint Armed Forces Officers' Wives' Luncheon at Bolling Air Force Base, Washington, DC
2005, December 7	Remarks at the Omni Shoreham Hotel, Washington, DC
2005, December 18	Prime Time Address to the Nation from the White House, Washington, DC
2006, January 10	Remarks to the Veterans of Foreign Wars, Washington, DC
2006, February 9	Remarks at the National Guard Building, Washington, DC
2006, March 22	Remarks at Capitol Music Hall, Wheeling, WV
2006, April 6	Remarks at Central Piedmont Community College, Charlotte, NC
2006, August 31	Remarks at the American Legion National Convention, Salt Lake City, UT
2006, September 5	Remarks at the Capital Hilton Hotel, Washington, DC
2006, September 6	Remarks from the White House on the Creation of Military Commissions, Washington, DC
2006, September 7	Remarks at the Cobb Galleria Centre, Atlanta,
2006, September 11	Prime Time Address to the Nation from the White House, Washington, DC
2006, September 29	Remarks at the Wardman Park Marriott Hotel, Washington, DC
2007, January 23	State of the Union Address, Washington, DC
2007, February 15	Remarks at the Mayflower Hotel, Washington, DC
2007, April 4	Remarks to Military Personnel at Fort Irwin, CA
2007, April 10	Remarks at the American Legion Post 177, Fairfax, VA
2007, June 12	Remarks at the Victims of Communism Memorial, Washington, DC
2007, July 4	Remarks to the West Virginia Air National Guard, Martinsburg, WV
2007, July 24	Remarks at Charleston Air Force Base, Charleston, SC
2007, July 26	Remarks to the American Legislative Exchange Council, Philadelphia, PA
2007, August 22	Remarks at the Veterans of Foreign Wars National Convention, Kansas City, MO
2007, August 28	Remarks to the 89th Annual National Convention of the American Legion, Reno, NV
2007, November 1	Remarks at the Heritage Foundation, Washington, DC
2008, January 28	State of the Union Address, Washington, DC
2008, January 31	Remarks from Las Vega, NV
2008, March 19	Remarks from the Pentagon, Arlington, VA

Transcription Conventions for Presidential Speeches

.	(period)	Falling intonation
?	(question mark)	Rising intonation
,	(comma)	Continuing intonation
-	(hyphen)	Marks an abrupt cut-off
()	(empty parentheses)	Unintelligible speech
((laughs))	(double parentheses)	Transcriber's comments / description of non-speech activity
italics	(words in *italics*)	Salient features discussed in the analysis

N.B. The following conventions, based on Gee (1986), may also be used:

- Line breaks represent rhetorical pauses
- Stanza breaks represent new idea units

Transcription Conventions for Focus Group Interviews

.	(period)	Falling intonation
?	(question mark)	Rising intonation
,	(comma)	Continuing intonation
-	(hyphen)	Marks an abrupt cut-off
~	(tilda)	Rapid speech, words run together
:	(colon)	Length
<u>word</u>	(underlining)	Indicates stress/emphasis placed on word
[ ]	(brackets)	Simultaneous or overlapping speech
=	(equal sign)	Latching, or contiguous utterances
(.)	(period in parentheses)	Pause in flow of speech
()	(empty parentheses)	Unintelligible speech
((laughs))	(double parentheses)	Transcriber's comments / description of non-speech activity
italics	(words in italics)	Salient features discussed in the analysis

Media Discourse Data

AP 2006, November 17. "Analysis: Bush Echoes Familiar Refrain," by Tom Raun.

CBSNews.com [Reuters] 2002, June 10. "First-Strike Military Policy for U.S.?"

CBSNews.com, 2003, September 11. "The Legacy of Sept. 11."

CBS.com 2004, January 25. "Kerry Fires Back at Clark."

CBSNews.com [CBS/AP] 2006, September 24. "Report: Iraq War Made Terrorism Worse."

CNN.com 2004, May 6. "U.S. warns of continued Al Qaeda threat."

CNN.com 2007, November 9. "Anderson Cooper 360 Degrees."

Democracy Now 2002, January 10. "The National Security Agency and the So-Called War on Terror."

FoxNews.com 2001, November 27. "Iraq in the Crosshairs?"

FoxNews.com 2002, October 8. "Bush Makes Case against Iraq."

FoxNews.com 2004, January 2. "Year in Review: Big Wins in War on Terror in 2003," by Dan Gallo.

FoxNews.com 2004, April 18. "Transcript: Jose Maria Aznar on 'Fox News Sunday.'"

FoxNews.com 2005, July 12. "Victory in Spite of All Terror," by William Kristol.

FoxNews.com [AP] 2005, October 5. "Bush: Troops Prepare for Iraq Elections."

FoxNews.com 2006, February 13. "Transcript: Rev. Joseph Lowery, Author Ron Christie on 'FNS.'"

FoxNews.com 2006, September 6. "Biden Responds to Revised War on Terror Plan."

FoxNews.com 2007, July 22. "Transcript: Sens. Bond, Bayh on 'FOX News Sunday.'"

FoxNews.com 2007, November 13. "Will 'Endless War on Terror' End in Global Soccer Game?" by Mike Baker.

New York Times 2001, October 9. "United in Cause, Syria Allows Foes of Israel in Its Midst," by Douglas Jehl.

New York Times 2002, December 9. "Destroying Weapons of Terror."

New York Times 2003, January 13. "Lieberman Announces Presidential Run," by David Stout.

New York Times 2004, October 8. "What I Really Said About Iraq," by L. Paul Bremer III.

New York Times 2005, December 9. "Annan Defends U.N. Official Who Chided U.S.," by Warren Hoge.

NPR.org 2003, February 13. "Analysis: How the Bush Administration Is Going About Preparing the Nation for War."

Omaha World Herald 2006, July 30. "Hagel's Iraq-Vietnam parallel draws mixed reaction in D.C.," by Jake Thompson.

USA Today 2004, April 9. "Escalating Violence Makes Iraq/Vietnam Comparison Inevitable," by Chuck Raasch.

Wall Street Journal 2004, February 24. "Pakistani Troops Grab Fighters in Raid along Afghan Border," by Zahid Hussain.

Washington Post 2003, March 27. "Banned Weapons Remain Unseen," by Joby Warrick.

Washington Post 2006, December 7. "Chairmen Urge Bush to Follow Recommendations," by Howard Schneider.

References

Adams, Peter; Towns, Alison; and Gavey, Nicola. 1995. "Dominance and Entitlement: The Rhetoric Men Use to Discuss their Violence Towards Women." *Discourse & Society* 6(3): 387–406.

Agha, Asif. 2003. "The Social Life of Cultural Value." *Language and Communication* 23: 231–273.

Agha, Asif. 2004. "Registers of Language." In *A Companion to Linguistic Anthropology*, Alessandro Duranti (ed.), 23–45. Malden, MA: Blackwell.

Agha, Asif. 2005a. "Introduction: Semiosis across Encounters." *Journal of Linguistic Anthropology* 15(1): 1–5.

Agha, Asif. 2005b. "Voice, Footing, Enregisterment." *Journal of Linguistic Anthropology* 15(1): 38–59.

Agha, Asif and Wortham, Stanton (eds.). 2005. Special Issue: Discourse across Speech Events: Intertextuality and Interdiscursivity in Social Life. *Journal of Linguistic Anthropology* 15(1).

Ahearn, Laura. 2001. "Language and Agency." *Annual Review of Anthropology* 30: 109–137.

Allen, Graham. 2000. *Intertextuality.* London and New York: Routledge.

Álvarez-Cáccamo, Celso. 1996. "The Power of Reflexive Language(s): Code Displacement in Reported Speech." *Journal of Pragmatics* 25: 33–59.

Anderson, Benedict. 1983. *Imagined Communities.* New York: Verso.

Authier-Révuz, Jacqueline. 1982. "Hétéreogenéité montrée et hétérogenéité constitutive: éléments pour une approche de l'autre dans le discourse." *DRLAV* 32.

Bakhtin, Mikhail. 1981. *The Dialogic Imagination: Four Essays.* Michael Holquist (ed.) and Caryl Emerson and Michael Holquist (trans.). Austin: University of Texas Press.

Bakhtin, Mikhail. 1986. *Speech Genres and Other Late Essays*, Vern W. McGee (trans.), Caryl Emerson and Michael Holquist (eds.). Austin: University of Austin Press.

Barthes, Roland. 1967. *Elements of Semiology*, Annette Lavers and Colin Smith (trans.). New York: Hill and Wang.

Barthes, Roland. 1974. *S/Z*, Richard Miller (trans.). New York: Hill and Wang.

Barthes, Roland. 1975. *The Pleasure of the Text*, Richard Miller (trans.). New York: Hill and Wang.

Barthes, Roland. 1977. *Image – Music – Text*, Stephen Heath (trans.). New York: Hill and Wang.

Basso, Keith. 1996. *Wisdom Sits in Places: Landscape and Language among the Western Apache*. Albuquerque: University of New Mexico Press.

Bauman, Richard. 1986. *Story, Performance, and Event: Contextual Studies of Oral Narrative*. Cambridge: Cambridge University Press.

Bauman, Richard. 2005. "Commentary: Indirect Indexicality, Identity, Performance: Dialogic Observations." *Journal of Linguistic Anthropology* 15(1): 145–150.

Bauman, Richard and Briggs, Charles L. 1990. "Poetics and Performance as Critical Perspectives on Language and Social Life." *Annual Review of Anthropology* 19: 59–88.

Baxter, Judith. 2003. *Positioning Gender in Discourse: A Feminist Methodology*. New York: Palgrave MacMillan.

Becker, A.L. 1995. *Beyond Translation: Essays Towards a Modern Philology*. Ann Arbor: University of Michigan Press.

Bell, Allan. 1991. *The Language of News Media*. Oxford: Blackwell.

Bin Laden, Osama. 2003, February 12. Text of Osama bin Laden tape played on Aljazeera television (translated into English by the BBC). Available: http://news.bbc.co.uk/1/hi/world/middle_east/2751019.stm.

Blommaert, Jan. 2005. *Discourse: A Critical Introduction*. Cambridge: Cambridge University Press.

Bourdieu, Pierre. 1977. "The Economics of Linguistic Exchanges." *Social Science Information* 16: 645–668.

Bourdieu, Pierre. 1984. *Distinction: A Social Critique of the Judgment of Taste*. Cambridge, MA: Harvard University Press.

Bourdieu, Pierre. 1986. "The forms of capital." In *Handbook of Theory and Research for the Sociology of Education*, J.G. Richarson (ed.), 241–258. Westport, CT: Greenwood Press.

Bourdieu, Pierre. 1987a. *Choses Dites*. Paris: Editions de Minuit.

Bourdieu, Pierre. 1987b. "What makes a social class? On the theoretical and practical existence of groups." *Berkeley Journal of Sociology* 32:1–18.

Bourdieu, Pierre. 1991. *Language and Symbolic Power*, Gino Raymond and Matthew Adamson (trans.), John B. Thompson (ed.). Cambridge, MA: Harvard University Press.

Bourdieu, Pierre. 1996. *Sur la Télévision*. Paris: Liber – Raisons d'Agir.

Briggs, Charles. 1992. "'Since I Am a Woman, I Will Chastise My Relatives': Gender, Reported Speech, and the (Re)Production of Social Relations in Warao Ritual Wailing." *American Ethnologist* 19(2): 337–361.

Briggs, Charles and Bauman, Richard. 1992. "Genre, Intertextuality, and Social Power." *Journal of Linguistic Anthropology* 2(2): 131–172.

Brokaw, Tom. 1998. *The Greatest Generation*. New York: Random House.

Brown, Gillian and Yule, George. 1983. *Discourse Analysis*. Cambridge: Cambridge University Press.

Bruner, Jerome. 1991. "The Narrative Construction of Reality." *Critical Inquiry* 18: 1–24.

Bucholtz, Mary and Hall, Kira. 2004. "Language and identity." In *A Companion to Linguistic Anthropology*, Alessandro Duranti (ed.), 369–394. Malden, MA: Blackwell.

Bucholtz, Mary and Hall, Kira. 2005. "Identity and Interaction: A Sociocultural Linguistic Approach." *Discourse Studies* 7(4–5): 585–614.

Bucholtz, Mary and Hall, Kira. 2008. "All of the Above: New Coalitions in Sociocultural Linguistics." *Journal of Sociolinguistics* 12(4): 401–431.

Bumiller, Elisabeth. 2002, September 7. "Traces of Terror: The Strategy; Bush Aides Set Strategy to Sell Policy on Iraq." *New York Times*. Available: http://web.lexis–nexis.com/universe/document?_m=2eea1df8f484a5d5dff401c82a523496&_docnum=1&wchp=dGLbVtz–zSkVA&_md5=d2508c766b785e5ddb5fe507bf9523f3.

Butler, Judith. 1990. *Gender Trouble*. New York: Routledge.

Butler, Judith. 1997. *Excitable Speech: A Politics of the Performative.* New York: Routledge.

Buttny, Richard. 1997. "Reported Speech in Talking Race on Campus." *Human Communication Research* 23(4): 477–506.

Buttny, Richard. 1998. "Putting Prior Talk into Context: Reported Speech and the Reporting Context." *Research on Language and Social Interaction* 31(1): 45–58.

Buttny, Richard and Williams, Princess L. 2000. "Demanding Respect: The Uses of Reported Speech in Discursive Constructions of Interracial Contact." *Discourse & Society* 11(1): 109–133.

Cameron, Lynne and Stelma, Juurd. 2004. "Metaphor Clusters in Discourse." *Journal of Applied Linguistics* 1(2): 107–136.

Certeau, Michel de. 1984. *The Practice of Everyday Life*, S. Rendall (trans.). Berkeley: University of California Press.

Chang, Gordon C. and Mehan, Hugh B. 2006. "Discourse in a Religious Mode: The Bush Administration's Discourse in the War on Terrorism and its Challenges." *Pragmatics* 16(1): 1–23.

Chernus, Ira. 2006. *Monsters to Destroy: The Neoconservative War on Terror and Sin.* Boulder, CO: Paradigm Publishers.

Chilton, Paul. 2004. *Analysing Political Discourse.* London: Routledge.

Chilton, Paul and Lakoff, George. 1995. "Foreign policy by metaphor." In *Language and Peace*, C. Schäffner and A. Wenden (eds.), 37–60. Aldershot, England: Dartmouth.

Chilton, Paul and Schäffner, Christina. 2002. "Themes and principles in the analysis of political discourse." In *Politics as Text and Talk: Analytic Approaches to Political Discourse*, Paul Chilton and Christina Schäffner (eds.), 1–41. Amsterdam and Philadelphia: John Benjamins.

Chomsky, Noam. 2003, August 11. "Preventive war: 'The supreme crime.'" *Z Magazine.* Available: www.zmag.org/content/showarticle.cfm?ItemID=4030.

Cirincione, Joseph. 2003, March 19. "Origins of Regime Change in Iraq." *Carnegie Endowment for International Peace Proliferation Brief* (6)5. Available: http://www.ceip.org/files/nonprolif/templates/Publications.asp?p=8&PublicationID=1214.

Coupland, Nikolas. 2007. *Style: Language Variation and Identity.* Cambridge, UK: Cambridge University Press.

Corts, Daniel P. and Pollio, Howard R. 1999. "Spontaneous Production of Figurative Language and Gesture in College Lectures." *Metaphor and Symbol* 14(2): 81–100.

Crystal, David. (1990). *A Dictionary of Linguistics and Phonetics.* Malden, MA: Blackwell.

Derrida, Jacques. 1976. *Of Grammatology.* Baltimore: Johns Hopkins University Press.

Derrida, Jacques. 1977. *Limited Inc.: abc.* Baltimore: Johns Hopkins University Press.

Derrida, Jacques. 1978. *Writing and Difference.* London: RKP.

Dunmire, Patricia. 2007. "'Emerging Threats' and 'Coming Dangers': Claiming the Future for Preventive War." In *Discourse, War and Terrorism*, Adam Hodges and Chad Nilep (eds.), 19–43. Amsterdam: John Benjamins.

Dunmire, Patricia. 2009. "'9/11 Changed Everything': An Interxtextual Analysis of the Bush Doctrine." *Discourse & Society* 20(2): 195–222.

Duranti, Alessandro. 2004. "Agency in Language." In *A Companion to Linguistic Anthropology*, Alessandro Duranti (ed.), 451–473. Malden, MA: Blackwell.

Entman, Robert. 1993. "Framing toward clarification of a fractured paradigm." *Journal of Communication,* 43(4), 51–58.

Fairclough, Norman. 1989. *Language and Power.* London: Longman.

Fairclough, Norman. 1992a. *Discourse and Social Change.* Cambridge: Polity Press.

Fairclough, Norman. 1992b. "Discourse and Text: Linguistic and Intertextual Analysis within Discourse Analysis." *Discourse & Society* 3(2): 193–217.

Fairclough, Norman. 1995a. *Critical Discourse Analysis.* London: Longman.

Fairclough, Norman. 1995b. *Media Discourse.* London: Edward Arnold.

Fairclough, Norman. 2000. *New Labour, New Language.* London: Routledge.

Fillmore, Charles J. 1982. "Frame semantics." In *Linguistics in the Morning Calm*, 111–137. Seoul, South Korea: Hanshin Publishing.

Fillmore, Charles J. 1985. "Frames and the Semantics of Understanding." *Quaderni di Semantica*, 6(2): 222–254.

Foucault, Michel. 1970. *The Order of Things: An Archeology of the Human Sciences.* New York: Random House.

Foucault, Michel. 1972. *The Archaeology of Knowledge.* London: Tavistock.

Foucault, Michel. 1978. *The History of Sexuality.* New York: Pantheon Books.

Foucault, Michel. 1980. *Power / Knowledge: Selected Interviews and Writings.* New York: Pantheon Books.

Foucault, Michel and Kritzman, Lawrence D. 1988. *Politics, Philosophy, Culture: Interviews and Other Writings, 1977–1984.* New York: Routledge.

Fowler, Roger, Gunther Kress, Robert Hodge, and Tony Trew. 1979. *Language and Control.* London: Routledge.

Gal, Susan. 1991. "Between Speech and Silence: The Problematics of Research on Language and Gender." In *Gender at the Crossroads of Knowledge: Feminist Anthropology in the Post-Modern Era*, M. di Leonardo (ed.), 175–203. Berkeley: University of California Press.

Gal, Susan. 2005. "Language Ideologies Compared: Metaphors of Public/Private." *Journal of Linguistic Anthropology* 15(1): 23–37.

Gal, Susan. 2006. "Linguistic Anthropology." In *Encyclopedia of Language and Linguistics*, Keith Brown (ed.), 171–185. London: Elsevier.

Gee, James Paul. 1986. "Units in the Production of Narrative Discourse." *Discourse Processes* 9: 391–422.

Gee, James Paul. 1996. *Social Linguistics and Literacies.: Ideology in Discourse* (2nd ed.). London: Taylor and Francis.

Gee, James Paul. 2005. *An Introduction to Discourse Analysis: Theory and Method.* New York: Routledge.

Geertz, Clifford. 1973. *The Interpretations of Cultures.* New York: Basic Books.

Goffman, Erving. 1974. *Frame Analysis.* Cambridge, MA: Harvard University Press.

Goffman, Erving. 1981. *Forms of Talk.* Philadelphia: University of Pennsylvania Press.

Gordon, Cynthia. 2006. "Reshaping Prior Text, Reshaping Identities." *Text & Talk* 26(4–5): 545–571.

Gramsci, Antonio. 1971. *Prison Notebooks.* New York: International Publishers.

Halbwachs, Maurice. 1980 [1951]. *The Collective Memory.* New York and London: Harper and Row.

Hall, Stuart. 1980. "Encoding and Decoding." In *Culture, Media, Language*, Stuart Hall et al. (eds.). London: Hutchinson.

Hall, Stuart. 1981. "Notes on Deconstructing the Popular." In *People's History and Socialist Theory*, R. Samuel (ed.), 227–239. London: Routledge & Kegan Paul.

Hall, Stuart. 1996. "The Problem of Ideology: Marxism without Guarantees." In *Stuart Hall: Critical Dialogues in Cultural Studies*, D. Morley and K.H. Chen (eds.), 25–46. London: Routledge.

Hall, Stuart. 1997. "The Work of Representation." In *Representation: Cultural Representations and Signifying Practices*, Stuart Hall (ed.), 13–74. London: Sage.

Halliday, M.A.K. 1973. *Explorations in the Function of Language.* London: Edward Arnold.

Hanks, William F. 1986. "Authenticity and Ambivalence in the Text: A Colonial Maya Case." *American* Ethnologist 13(4): 721–744.

Hanks, William F. 1987. "Discourse Genres in a Theory of Practice." *American Ethnologist* 14(4): 668–692.

Hanks, William F. 1989. "Text and Textuality." *Annual Review of Anthropology* 18: 95–127.

Heintzelman, Lori. 2009. *The Re-education of Desire: The Role of Narrative in Religious-based Sexual Identity Transformation.* Unpublished PhD dissertation, University of Colorado at Boulder.

Herman, Edward S. and Chomsky, Noam. 1988. *Manufacturing Consent: The Political Economy of the Mass Media.* New York: Pantheon Books.

Hill, Jane. 2005. "Intertextuality as Source and Evidence for Indirect Indexical Meanings." *Journal of Linguistic Anthropology* 15(1): 113–124.

Hill, Jane and Irvine, Judith. 1993. *Responsibility and Evidence in Oral Discourse.* Cambridge: Cambridge University Press.

Hodges, Adam. 2004. "'The Battle of Iraq': The Adequation of Saddam Hussein and Osama bin Laden in the Bush War on Terror Narrative." Paper presented at the Society for Linguistic Anthropology Conference, November 19, 2004. University of California, Berkeley, CA.

Hodges, Adam. 2007a. "The Political Economy of Truth in the 'War on Terror' Discourse: Competing Visions of an Iraq/al Qaeda Connection." *Social Semiotics* 17(1): 5–20.

Hodges, Adam. 2007b. "The Narrative Construction of Identity: The Adequation of Saddam Hussein and Osama bin Laden in the 'War on Terror.'" In *Discourse, War and Terrorism*, Adam Hodges and Chad Nilep (eds.), 67–87. Amsterdam: John Benjamins.

Hodges, Adam. 2008. "The Politics of Recontextualization: Discursive Competition over Claims of Iranian Involvement in Iraq." *Discourse & Society* 19(4): 479–501.

Hodges, Adam. 2010. "Discursive Constructions of Global War and Terror." In *The Handbook of Language and Globalization*, Nikolas Coupland (eds.), 305–322. Malden, MA: Wiley-Blackwell.

Holquist, Michael. 1983. "The Politics of Representation." *The Quarterly Newsletter of the Laboratory of Comparative Human Cognition* 5(1): 2–9.

Inoue, Miyako. 2006. *Vicarious Language: Gender and Linguistic Modernity in Japan.* Berkeley: University of California Press.

Irvine, Judith. 1989. "When Talk Isn't Cheap." *American Ethnologist* 16(2): 248–267.

Irvine, Judith. 1996. "Shadow Conversations: The Indeterminacy of Participant Roles." In *Natural Histories of Discourse*, Michael Silverstein and Greg Urban (eds.), 131–159. Chicago: University of Chicago Press.

Irvine, Judith and Gal, Susan. 2000. "Language Ideology and Linguistic Differentiation." In *Regimes of Language*, Paul Kroskrity (ed.), 35–84. Santa Fe: School of American Research.

Jakobson, Roman. 1953. "Discussion in Claude Lévi-Strauss, Roman Jakobson, Carl F. Voeglin and Thomas A. Sebeok," Results of the Conference of Anthropologists and Linguists. *International Journal of American Linguistics Memoir* 8: 11–21.

Jhally, Sutt and Earp, Jeremy. 2004. *Hijacking Catastrophe: 9/11, Fear and the Selling of American Empire.* Northampton, MA: Olive Branch Press.

Klocke, Brian. 2004. *Framing the World: Elite Ideologies in U.S. Media Discourse of the War on Terrorism Campaign.* Unpublished PhD dissertation, University of Colorado.

Koller, Veronika. 2003. "Metaphor Clusters, Metaphor Chains: Analyzing the Multifunctionality of Metaphor in Text." *Metaphorik.de* (5): 115–134.

Kripke, Saul. 1972. "Naming and Necessity." In *Semantics of Natural Language*, Donald Davidson and Gilbert Harman (eds.), 253–366. Dordrecht, Netherlands: D. Reidel Publishing Co.

Kristeva, Julia. 1980. *Desire in Language: A Semiotic Approach to Literature and Art*, Thomas Gora, Alice Jardine and Leon S. Roudiez (trans.), Leon S. Roudiez (ed.). New York: Columbia University Press.

Kroskrity, Paul. (ed.). 2000. *Regimes of Language.* Santa Fe: School of American Research.

Labov, William. 1972. "The transformation of experience in narrative syntax." In *Language in the Inner City: Studies in the Black English Vernacular*, William Labov (ed.), 354–396. Philadelphia: University of Pennsylvania Press.

Labov, William. and Waletzky, Joshua. 1967. "Narrative analysis: Oral versions of personal experience." In *Essays on the Verbal and Visual Arts*, J. Helm (ed.), 12–44. Seattle: University of Washington Press.

Lakoff, George. 1987. *Women, Fire, and Dangerous Things: What Categories Reveal about the Mind.* Chicago: University of Chicago Press.

Lakoff, George. 1993. The Contemporary Theory of Metaphor. In *Metaphor and Thought* (second edition), A. Ortony (ed.), 202–251. Cambridge: Cambridge University Press.

Lakoff, George. 2001. "Metaphors of Terror." In *The Days After*. Chicago: University of Chicago Press. Available: http://www.press.uchicago.edu/News/911lakoff.html.

Lakoff, George and Johnson, Mark. 1980. *Metaphors We Live By*. Chicago: University of Chicago Press.

Lakoff, George and Johnson, Mark. 1999. *Philosophy in the Flesh: The Embodied Mind and its Challenge to Western Thought.* New York: Basic Books.

Lakoff, George and Turner, Mark. 1989. *More Than Cool Reason: A Field Guide to Poetic Metaphor*. Chicago: University of Chicago Press.

Leudar, Ivan; Marsland, Victoria; and Nekvapil, Jirí. 2004. "On Membership Categorization: 'Us', 'Them' and 'Doing Violence' in Political Discourse." *Discourse & Society* 15(2–3): 243–266.

Lewis, David. 1979. "Scorekeeping in a language game." In *Semantics from Different Points of View*, R. Bauerle, U. Egli and A. von Stechow (eds.). Berlin: Springer–Verlag.

Linde, Charlotte. 1993. *Life Stories: The Creation of Coherence*. New York: Oxford University Press.

Maingueneau, Dominique. 1987. *Nouvelles Tendances en Analyse du Discours.* Paris: Hachette.

Mannheim, Bruce and Tedlock, Dennis. 1995. "Introduction." In *The Dialogic Emergence of Culture*, Dennis Tedlock and Bruce Mannheim (eds.), 1–32. Urbana and Chicago: University of Illinois Press.

Martin, J.R. and Ruth Wodak. 2003. "Introduction." In Martin and Wodak (eds.) *Re/reading the Past,* 1–16. Amsterdam: Benjamins.

Matthews, Chris. 2008, July 25. "Transcripts: Hardball with Chris Matthews." MSNBC. Available: http://www.msnbc.msn.com/id/25885493/.

Maybin, Janet. 2001. "Language, struggle and voice: The Bakhtin/Volosinov writings." In *Discourse Theory and Practice: A Reader*, M. Wetherell, S. Taylor and S.J. Yates (eds.), 64–71. London: Sage.

McClellan, Scott. 2008. *What Happened: Inside the Bush White House and Culture of Deception.* New York: Public Affairs.

Mehan, Hugh. 1996. "The Construction of an LD Student: A Case Study in the Politics of Representation." In *Natural Histories of Discourse*, M. Silverstein and G. Urban (eds.), 253–276. Chicago: University of Chicago Press.

Mehan, Hugh and Wills, J. 1988. "MEND: A Nurturing Voice in the Nuclear Arms Debate." *Social Problems* 35(4): 363–383.

Musolff, Andreas. 2004. *Metaphor and Political Discourse: Analogical Reasoning in Debates about Europe*. New York: Palgrave Macmillan.

Musolff, Andreas. 2006. "Metaphor Scenarios in Public Discourse." *Metaphor and Symbol* 21(1): 23–38.

National Commission on Terrorist Attacks upon the United States. 2004a. *Executive Summary of the 9/11 Commission Report.* Available at http://www.gpoaccess.gov/911/pdf/execsummary.pdf.

National Commission on Terrorist Attacks upon the United States. 2004b. *The 9/11 Commission Report: Final Report of the National Commission on Terrorist Attacks upon the United States.* New York: W.W. Norton.

National Intelligence Council. 2005. *Mapping the Global Future*. Report of the National Intelligence Council's 2020 Project. Available: http://www.dni.gov/nic/NIC_ globaltrend2020.html.

NC – see National Commission on Terrorist Attacks upon the United States.

Nekvapil, Jirí and Leudar, Ivan. 2002. "On Dialogical Networks: Arguments about the Migration Law in Czech Mass Media in 1993." In *Language, Interaction and National Identity*, S. Hester and W. Housley (eds.), 60–101. Aldershot: Ashgate.

Nelson, Daniel N. 2003. "Conclusion: Word peace." In *At War With Words*, M.N. Dedaić, and D.N. Nelson, (eds.), 449–468. New York: Mouton de Gruyter.

NIC – see National Intelligence Council.

Ochs, Elinor. 1992. "Indexing Gender." In *Rethinking Context: Language as Interactive Phenomenon*, Alessandro Duranti and Charles Goodwin (eds.), 335–358. Cambridge: Cambridge University Press.

Ochs, Elinor and Capps, Lisa. 2001. *Living Narrative: Creating Lives in Everyday Storytelling*. Cambridge, MA: Harvard University Press.

Ortony, Andrew (ed.). 1993. *Metaphor and Thought* (second edition). Cambridge: Cambridge University Press.

Pew Research Center for the People and the Press. 2002, October 10. "Americans Thinking About Iraq, But Focused on the Economy: Midterm Election Preview." Available: http://people–press.org/reports/display.php3?ReportID=162.

Phillips, Louise. 1996. "Rhetoric and the Spread of the Discourse of Thatcherism." *Discourse & Society* 7(2): 209–241.

PIPA – see Program for International Policy Attitudes.

Potter, Jonathan. 1996. *Representing Reality: Discourse, Rhetoric and Social Construction*. London: Sage.

Priest, Dana. 2005, January 14. "Iraq new terror breeding ground: War created haven, CIA advisers report." *Washington Post*, A01.

Program for International Policy Attitudes. 2004a, April 22. "US Public Beliefs on Iraq and the Presidential Election." University of Maryland. Available: http://www.pipa.org/OnlineReports/Iraq/IraqReport4_22_04.pdf.

Program for International Policy Attitudes. 2004b, October 21. "The Separate Realities of Bush and Kerry Supporters." University of Maryland. Available: http://www.pipa.org/OnlineReports/Pres_Election_04/Report10_21_04.pdf.

Putnam, Hilary. 1975. "The Meaning of Meaning." In *Mind, Language and Reality: Philosophical Papers 2*, H. Putnam (ed.), 215–271. Cambridge: Cambridge University Press.

Rampton, Sheldon and Stauber, John. 2003. *Weapons of Mass Deception: The Uses of Propaganda in Bush's War on Iraq*. New York: Center for Media and Democracy.

Reuters. 2009, March 31. "Obama team drops "war on terror" rhetoric." Available: http://uk.reuters.com/article/worldNews/idUKTRE52T7N920090330.

Ricoeur, Paul. 1984. *Time and Narrative*. Chicago: University of Chicago Press.

Riessman, Catherine Kohler. 1993. *Narrative Analysis*. London: Sage Publications.

Sacks, Harvey. 1992. *Lectures on Conversation*. Cambridge: Blackwell.

Semino, Elena. 2008. *Metaphor in Discourse*. Cambridge: Cambridge University Press.

Senate Intelligence Committee. 2006, September 8. Report of the Select Committee on Intelligence on Postwar Findings about Iraq's WMD Programs and Links to Terrorism and How They Compare with Prewar Assessments together with Additional Views. Available: http://intelligence.senate.gov/phaseiiaccuracy.pdf.

Shapiro, Michael. 1987. *The Politics of Representation*. Madison: University of Wisconsin Press.

Silberstein, Sandra. 2002. *War of Words: Language, Politics, and 9/11*. London: Routledge.

Silverstein, Michael. 1976. "Shifters, Linguistic Categories, and Cultural Description." In *Meaning in Anthropology*, Keith Basso and Henry Selby (eds.), 11–55. Albuquerque: University of New Mexico Press.

Silverstein, Michael. 1985. "Language and the Culture of Gender: At the Intersection of Structure, Usage, and Ideology." In *Semiotic Mediation: Sociocultural and Psychological Perspectives*, Elizabeth Mertz and Richard J. Parmentier (eds.), 219–259.

Silverstein, Michael. 2003a. "Indexical Order and the Dialectics of Sociolinguistic Life." *Language and Communication* 23: 193–229.

Silverstein, Michael. 2003b. *Talking Politics: The Substance of Style from Abe to 'W'*. Chicago: Prickly Paradigm Press.

Silverstein, Michael. 2005. "Axes of Evals: Token versus Type Interdiscursivity." *Journal of Linguistic Anthropology* 15(1): 6–22.

Spitulnik, Debra. 1993. "Anthropology and Mass Media." *Annual Review of Anthropology* 22: 293–315.

Spitulnik, Debra. 1996. "The Social Circulation of Media Discourse and the Mediation of Communities." *Journal of Linguistic Anthropology* 6(2): 161–187.

Stevenson, Seth. 2001, December 6. "Pipe Dreams." *Slate*. Available: http://www.slate.com/id/2059487/.

Talbot, Mary; Atkinson, Karen; and Atkinson, David. 2003. *Language and Power in the Modern World.* Edinburgh: Edinburgh University Press.

Tannen, Deborah. 1989. *Talking Voices: Repetition, Dialogue, and Imagery in Conversational Discourse*. New York: Cambridge University Press.

Tannen, Deborah. 2006. "Intertextuality in Interaction: Reframing Family Arguments in Public and Private." *Text & Talk* 26(4–5): 597–617.

Tannen, Deborah and Wallat, Cynthia. 1987. "Interactive Frames and Knowledge Schemas in Interaction: Examples from a Medical Examination/Interview." *Social Psychology Quarterly* 50(2): 205–216.

Taylor, Charles. 1979. "Interpretation and the Sciences of Man." In *Interpretive Social Science: A Reader,* Paul Rabinow and William M. Sullivan (eds.). Berkeley: University of California Press.

Taylor, Charles. 1985. *Human Agency and Language: Philosophical Papers 1.* Cambridge: Cambridge University Press.

Terkel, Studs. 1984. *"The Good War": An Oral History of World War II*. New York: Pantheon.

Tovares, Alla V. 2005. *Intertextuality in Family Interaction: Repetition of Public Texts in Private Settings.* Unpublished PhD dissertation, Georgetown University.

Van Dijk, Teun A. 1991. *Racism and the Press.* London: Routledge.

Van Dijk, Teun A. 1998. *Ideology.* London: Sage.

Van Leeuwen, Theo. 2005. "Three models of interdisciplinarity." In *A New Agenda in (Critical) Discourse Analysis*, R. Wodak and P. Chilton (eds.), 3–18. Amsterdam: John Benjamins.

Voloshinov, V.N. 1971. "Reported Speech." In *Readings in Russian Poetics: Formalist and Structuralist Views*, Ladislav Matejka and Krystyna Promorska (eds.), 149–175. Cambridge, MA: MIT Press.

Voloshinov, V.N. 1973. *Marxism and the Philosophy of Language*, Ladislav Matejka and I.R. Titunik (trans.). New York: Seminar Press.

Vygotsky, Lev S. 1987. "Thinking and Speech." In *The Collected Works of L.S. Vygotsky*, Robert W. Rieber and Aaron S. Carton (eds.), Norris Minick (trans.), 39–285. New York: Plenum Press.

Werth, Paul. 1999. *Text Worlds: Representing Conceptual Space in Discourse.* London: Longman.

White House. 2005, October 6. "Fact Sheet: President Bush's Remarks on the War on Terror." Available: http://www.whitehouse.gov/news/releases/2005/10/20051006–2.html.

Wilce, James M. 2005. "Traditional Laments and Postmodern Regrets: The Circulation of Discourse in Metacultural Context." *Journal of Linguistic Anthropology* 15(1): 60–71.

Williams, Raymond. 1977. *Marxism and Literature.* Oxford: Oxford University Press.

Wilson, Scott and Kamen, Al. 2009, March 25. "'Global War On Terror' Is Given New Name: Bush's Phrase Is Out, Pentagon Says." *Washington Post*, A04.

Wittgenstein, Ludwig. 1969. *On Certainty.* Dennis Paul and G.E.M. Anscombe (trans.), G.E.M. Anscombe and G.H. von Wright (eds.). New York: Harper and Row.

Wittgenstein, Ludwig. 2001. *Philosophical Investigation,* trans. G.E.M. Anscombe, 3rd ed. Oxford: Blackwell.

Wodak, Ruth and van Dijk, Teun A. (eds.). 2000. *Racism at the Top: Parliamentary Discourses on Ethnic Issues in Six European States.* Klagenfurt, Austria: Drava Verlag.

Young, Katharine. 1989. "Narrative Embodiments: Enclaves of the Self in the Realm of Medicine." In *Texts of Identity*, John Schotter and Kenneth J. Gergen (eds.), 152–165. London: Sage.

Zinken, Jörg. 2003. "Ideological Imagination: Intertextual and Correlational Metaphors in Political Discourse." *Discourse & Society* 14(4): 507–523.

Index

9/11 Commission, 3, 5, 64, 106, 135
  See also National Commission on
    Terrorist Attacks upon the United States
ABC News, 13
accommodation, 75
act of war, 7, 19, 20, 23, 28, 31, 43
Adams, Peter, 59
adequation (tactic of), 66, 67, 71, 78, 81, 83, 87,
    91, 122, 146
Afghanistan
  "Battle" of Afghanistan, 42, 48–51, 60
  referenced in Bush's speeches, 47, 48, 50, 51, 53,
    54, 60, 68–70, 76, 78
  referenced in focus groups, 118, 119
  referenced in media discourse, 91, 98, 101, 106
  referenced in Obama's speeches, 157, 158
agency, 33, 66, 101, 118, 156, 157
Agha, Asif, 9, 10, 84, 85
Ahearn, Laura, 154, 156
Allen, Graham, 11, 36
Álvarez-Cáccamo, Celso, 11
analogy
  analogy and metaphor, 20, 31
  Cold War, 34, 39, 125, 142
  Vietnam, 17, 125, 131, 133
  World War II, 32, 34, 125, 128, 129, 131, 140
Anderson, Benedict, 39
Arbour, Louise, 100, 101
Associated Press, 13, 138
Atkinson, David, 87

Atkinson, Karen, 87
authentication (tactic of), 66
  See also chain of authentication
Authier-Révuz, Jacqueline, 9
authorization (tactic of), 66
Authorization for Use of Military Force against
    Iraq, 81
  See also Iraq War Resolution
Authorization for Use of Military Force against
    Terrorists, 81
axis of evil, 106, 119
Aznar, Jose Maria, 95, 96

Baker, James, 105
Baker, Mike, 102, 103
Bakhtin, Mikhail, 8, 9, 11, 12, 29, 35, 57, 84–86,
    90, 99, 102, 104, 107, 111, 142, 153
Barthes, Roland, 9, 11, 30, 36, 40, 134
Basso, Keith, 145
Bauman, Richard, 8, 9, 19, 20, 40, 85,
Baxter, Judith, 6
Becker, A.L., 10
Bell, Allan, 12
Biden, Joseph, 105, 106, 159
Bin Laden, Osama
  referenced in Bush's speeches, 33, 57, 141, 145,
    147
  referenced in focus groups, 117, 119, 125
Blommaert, Jan, 5
Bond, Kit, 107

Bourdieu, Pierre, 66, 67, 87, 97, 98, 134, 135, 159, 160
Bremer, Paul, 93,
bridging assumptions, 82, 114, 122
Briggs, Charles, 8, 19, 20, 40, 86,
Brokaw, Tom, 35
Brown, Gillian, 6, 62, 122
Bruner, Jerome, 4, 5, 19–21, 39–43, 45, 52, 57, 58, 63, 69, 70, 78, 82, 85, 142
Bucholtz, Mary, 9, 16, 47, 65, 67–71, 85, 87, 97, 122, 126, 146
Bumiller, Elisabeth, 65
Butler, Judith, 155, 156
Buttny, Richard, 16, 86, 143
Byrd, Robert, 135, 136

Cameron, Lynne, 20
capital
    cultural capital, 97, 144
    forms of capital, 97
    political capital, 67
    social capital, 97
    symbolic capital, 67, 97, 98, 136
capitalization, 14, 99, 100, 103
Capps, Lisa, 4, 70, 76
Card, Andrew, 65
CBS News, 13, 93, 135
Center for Media and Democracy, 108
central front in the war on terror, 13, 14, 16, 17, 41, 42, 56–58, 90–93, 98, 99, 105–107, 133, 142, 151, 159
Certeau, Michel de, 66, 154, 155–157
chain-complex, 35
chain of authentication, 95–98, 135–138
Chang, Gordon C., 29, 35
Cheney, Dick, 94
Chernus, Ira, 5, 35
Chilton, Paul, 20–22, 28, 75, 82
Chomsky, Noam, 48, 103
chronotope, 141
circumstantial evidence, 76, 77
Cirincione, Joseph, 65
citationality, 10
civil war, 60, 120, 121, 138, 139, 151
Clinton, Bill, 25, 138, 159
Clinton, Hillary, 159, 160
CNN News, 13, 92, 93, 101, 102
coherence by contemporaneity, 71
collective memory, 30, 32, 36, 39, 125, 126, 130, 133
common sense, 7, 28, 29, 39, 103, 106
Communism, 17, 36, 38, 39, 126, 127–129, 142, 150, 151
    Communist ideology, see ideology
    Communist revolution, 33
    Communists, 35, 140, 142

complicating action, 44, 50, 52
Cooper, Anderson, 101–103
context sensitivity and negotiability, 57, 82
Corts, Daniel, 20
Coupland, Nikolas, 11
creativity, 111, 154, 155
criminal act, 20, 23, 28
Critical Discourse Analysis, 7, 9
critical linguists, 22, 44, 112
Crowley, P.J., 138
Crystal, David, 85

Darth Vader, 116, 117
deictic, 49, 128
delegated power of the spokesperson, 98, 159
democracy
    referenced in Bush's speeches, 25, 131
    referenced in focus groups, 119, 122, 130
    referenced in media discourse, 93, 99, 106
Democracy Now, 103
denaturalization (tactic of), 66
Derrida, Jacques, 10, 11, 95, 155
dialogism, 8, 9, 12, 102
    dialogic, 17, 102, 132, 144, 151, 152
    dialogical network, 29, 102, 107, 108
discourse, described, 6–8
    "big D" discourse, 6, 7, 42, 155
    "little d" discourse, 6, 7
    discursive formation, 5, 6, 85, 153
    dominant discourse, 108, 155
    Foucauldian discourse, 6, 7, 63
    macrolevel discourse, 4, 63, 86, 105, 122, 127, 129, 154, 155
    microlevel discourse, 4, 7, 85
    political discourse, 5, 8, 10, 17, 74, 81, 82, 86, 134, 159
    public discourse, 4, 8, 14, 92, 95, 107, 134, 135, 136, 139, 155
distinction (tactic of), 47, 66, 126
doctrine of precedent, 76
double-voiced discourse, 90
Dunmire, Patricia, 48, 74
Duranti, Alessandro, 156
Durkheim, Emile, 63

Earp, Jeremey, 65
either you are with us or with the terrorists, 13
    either you're with us or the terrorists, 90
    either you're with us, or you're with them, 95, 96
enregisterment, 84
Entman, Robert, 22
epic narrative, 36
erasure, 31, 32, 66, 74, 81
Europe, 33, 141
evaluation, 22, 36, 44, 45, 47, 49–52, 54, 57, 70, 71, 78, 145

evaluative accent, 22
evaluative orientation, 22, 112

Fairclough, Norman, 7, 9, 10, 22, 27, 30, 71, 82
fascism, 34, 36, 37, 38, 39, 115, 126, 127, 128, 129, 142
    fascist state, 118
    fascists, 35, 37, 117, 142
    see also Islamo-fascism
Fillmore, Charles J., 21, 22
focalization, 32
focus group data, 11, 14, 15, 17, 113
Foucault, Michel, 5–7, 17, 63, 85, 93, 153, 155
Fowler, Roger, 73
Fox News, 13, 87, 91, 94–96, 98–100, 102, 103, 105–107, 109, 110
frame
    dominant frame, 5
    Goffmanian frame, 19, 22
    semantic frame, 21
France, 78
freedom
    referenced in Bush's speeches, 24, 24–26, 31, 34, 35, 37, 43, 44, 46–48, 56, 58, 61, 66, 140
    referenced in focus groups, 130
Fulbright, William, 143

Gal, Susan, 4, 31, 74,
Gavey, Nicola, 59
Gee, James Paul, 7, 31, 43, 68
Geertz, Clifford, 30
genre, 19, 20, 104, 109
Germany, 33, 78, 141
Goffman, Erving, 11, 12, 22
good war, 36
Goodman, Amy, 103
Google News Archive, 13, 87, 91, 94, 95, 108, 160
Gordon, Cynthia, 11
Gramsci, Antonio, 28
greatest generation, 35

Hagel, Chuck, 137, 138
Halbwachs, Maurice, 30
Hall, Kira, 9, 16, 47, 65–67, 85, 87, 97, 122, 126, 146
Hall, Stuart, 6, 7, 22, 113, 156
Halliday, M.A.K., 22
Hamilton, Lee, 105, 106
Hanks, William, 8, 10, 42, 85
hegemony, 28, 154
Heintzelman, Lori, 4
Herman, Edward S., 103
hermeneutic composability, 41
Hill, Jane, 13, 146
historical-causal entailment, 68–70, 151

history
    history and discourse, 6, 39, 63, 146, 155
    nation's history, 15, 19, 30, 31, 136, 139
    referenced in Bush's speeches, 33–35, 44, 61, 72, 91
Hitler, Adolph, 32–34, 96, 126, 127
Hodge, Robert, 73
Hodges, Adam, 32, 34, 65, 82
Holquist, Michael, 134
Homerian skeptron, 136, 159
Hussain, Zahid, 101
Hussein, Saddam
    referenced in Bush's speeches, 56, 61, 73–75, 77, 78, 80
    referenced in focus groups, 119
    referenced in media discourse, 88, 91, 94

ideational function, 22
identity, 47, 65–68, 71, 97, 103, 156
ideology
    Communist ideology, 32, 38, 39
    ideology and erasure, 31, 66, 74
    ideology and identity, 66
    ideology and interpretation, 82, 112, 113, 120, 122
    ideology and metaphor, 20–22
    ideological bias, 57, 58, 82, 106
    ideological distance, 100, 116
    ideological inspired policy, 71
    ideological perspective/position, 20, 22, 23, 27–29, 33, 39, 101, 104, 127
    ideological spectrum, 103
    ideological struggle, 34, 36, 39, 140, 142, 151, 152
    ideological underpinnings of discourse, 22
    Islamo-fascist ideology, 125–128, 142
    murderous ideology, 34, 36, 38, 127, 129, 142
    terrorist ideology, 37–38
    totalitarian ideology, 127
illegitimation (tactic of), 66
indexicality, 13, 85
    index of the Narrative, 89, 127
    index of precipitating event, 46
    index of prior contexts, 85, 109, 145
    index of "us" vs. "them," 27
    index of understandings about Vietnam, 136
Inoue, Miyako, 7, 29, 154–157
interdiscursivity, 9, 10
    see also intertextuality
intertextuality, 5, 8–10, 17, 86, 113
    constitutive intertextuality, 9
    intertextual connections, 4, 8, 10, 17, 84, 107, 110, 154
    intertextual gap, 19, 20, 28, 40
    intertextual relations, 19, 86, 97
    intertextual series, 10, 13, 14, 16, 84–86, 89, 93, 95, 104, 110, 121–123
    manifest intertextuality, 9

Iraq
   "Battle" of Iraq, 43, 48, 49, 55–58
   referenced in Bush's speeches, 53, 54, 55–57, 61,
      68, 70, 72, 73, 75–77, 79, 145, 147
   referenced in focus groups, 118–124, 130, 139,
      148, 149
   referenced in media discourse, 91–93, 96, 98, 99,
      105–107, 135, 137, 138
Iraq War Resolution, 72, 73, 79, 81
Irvine, Judith, 31, 66, 81, 90, 96, 97, 135, 146
Islam, 121, 125, 127–129
   Islamic extremism, 126
   Islamic fundamentalism, 67
   Islamic law, 130
   Islamic radicals, 38
   Islamic radicalism, 38, 39, 126, 127, 142
   Islamic terrorism, 120
   Islamic terrorists, 151
Islamo-fascism, 38, 120, 125, 126–129
iterability, 10, 95

Jakobson, Roman, 9
Japan, 7, 129, 130, 131, 141, 142
Jhally, Sutt, 65

Kamen, Al, 159
Kennedy, Edward, 135, 136
Kerry, John, 10, 82, 135–137
King, Coretta Scott, 108, 110
King, Martin Luther, 109
Klocke, Brian, 11, 35
Koller, Veronika, 20
Korb, Lawrence, 137, 138
Korea, 118, 119, 142
Kress, Gunther, 73
Kripke, Saul, 97
Kristeva, Julia, 8–11, 16, 86, 99, 123
Kristol, William, 99
Kroskrity, Paul, 5

Labov, William, 43, 44, 46, 58
Lakoff, George, 20–22, 24
Laos, 143
Lenin, Vladimir, 32–34
Leudar, Ivan, 26, 29, 103
Lewis, David, 75
lexical correspondences, 23–25, 27, 29
Lieberman, Joseph, 89
Linde, Charlotte, 4
linguistic anthropology, 7, 8
logic of complementarity, 74, 78, 79
Lowery, Joseph, 108–110

Maingueneau, Dominique, 9
Manichean, 59, 117
Mannheim, Bruce, 9, 132

Marsland, Victoria, 26, 29, 103
Martin, J.R., 4
Matthews, Chris, 87
Maybin, Janet, 23
McClellan, Scott, 87
media discourse data, 13
Mehan, Hugh, 29, 35, 134
metadiscourse, 28
metaphor, 15, 19–24, 27, 30, 100, 114, 116
metapragmatic, 16, 86, 104, 138, 144
metarepresentation, 28
militant Jihadism, 38, 127, 142
murderous ideologies, see ideology
Musolff, Andreas, 20, 28
Mussolini, Benito, 128, 129
MSNBC News, 13, 87

narrative
   narrative accrual, 4, 85
   narrative necessity, 39, 52, 63
   narrative realm, 45, 62
   narrative seduction, 42
   narrative time, 142
National Commission on Terrorist Attacks upon the
      United States, 3, 5, 65
   See also 9/11 Commission
national consciousness, 39
National Intelligence Council, 58, 68
national security team, 23, 25
Nazism, 26, 34, 36, 115, 127
   Islamo-Nazism, 126, 127
   Nazis, 35, 142
   Nazi Germany, 35, 141
   Nazi regime, 33
Nekvapil, Jirí, 26, 29, 103
Nelson, Daniel N., 6
neoconservative, 89, 94, 99, 119, 120
New York Times, 13, 65, 89, 93, 95, 100,
      104, 143
NPR, 13, 88

Obama, Barack, 17, 107, 157–160
Ochs, Elinor, 4, 70, 76, 85
Omran, Adnan, 104
Ortony, Andrew, 20

Pakistan, 52–55, 61, 101, 107, 158, 159
parallelism, 12, 37–38, 74
parody, 11, 107, 108, 110, 117, 156
participation framework, 12
particularity, 19, 20
Paul, Ron, 15, 93, 114, 128
PBS News, 13
Pearl Harbor, 31, 32, 141
Peirce, Charles, 85
Pew Research Center for the People and the Press, 64

Phillips, Louise, 7
politics of representation, 134, 152
Pollio, Howard R., 20
Potter, Jonathan, 33, 34
Powell, Colin, 77, 80, 94
power
    delegated power, 98, 159
    power and authority, 136
    power and discourse, 8, 17, 63, 81, 82
    power and domination, 155
    power and identity, 67, 68
    power and social reality, 4
    regime of power, 156
    symbolic power, 97
precipitating event, 31, 32, 42–46, 49, 52, 56, 60,
    62, 69, 74, 140, 151
preemptive vs. preventive war, 48
presupposition, 29, 57, 70, 75, 109
Priest, Dana, 58, 68
primary framework, 19
Program on International Policy Attitudes, 65,
    82, 114
pun, 108, 110
Putnam, Hilary, 96, 97

quotation marks, 9, 88, 92

Rampton, Sheldon, 108
readerly text, 30, 36, 40
reductio ad absurdum, 117
regime of language, 5, 155, 157, 160
regime of truth, 5, 6, 63, 93, 153
Reuters, 88, 160
Rice, Condoleezza, 100, 135
Ricoeur, Paul, 45, 141
Riessman, Catherine Kohler, 4, 18
Romney, Mitt, 128, 129

Sacks, Harvey, 104
scare quotes, 100, 116
Schäffner, Christina, 21, 22
Schanberg, Sydney, 143
Semino, Elena, 20, 22
Senate Intelligence Committee, 65
Shapiro, Michael, 134
Silberstein, Sandra, 23
Silverstein, Michael, 35, 71, 85, 141
sound bite, defined, 87
speech chain, 84–86, 97, 136, 137
Spitulnik, Debra, 113, 132
stare decisis, 78
State of the Union, 12, 28, 51, 79, 87, 88, 119
Stauber, John, 108
stay on the offense, 13, 90–92
Stelma, Juurd, 20
Stevenson, Seth, 49
strategies of entextualization, 86, 103

symbolic authority, 134, 159

tactics of intersubjectivity, 65, 66
talking points, defined, 87
Tannen, Deborah, 10, 11, 21, 22
Talbot, Mary, 87
Taylor, Charles, 18, 41
Tedlock, Dennis, 9, 132
Terkel, Studs, 36
terrorists and tyrants, 13, 35, 87–89
text, defined, 8–10
thinking-in-complexes, 71
time
    clock time, 45
    human time, 45
    narrative time, 142
Tovares, Alla V., 11
Towns, Alison, 59
Trew, Tony, 73

United Kingdom (UK), 7
United We Stand, 66
USA PATRIOT Act, 118

Van Dijk, Teun, 4, 22, 28, 37, 74, 83, 106
Van Leeuwen, Theo, 14, 112
Vietnam, 13, 17, 125, 129, 131–152
Voloshinov, V.N., 8, 16, 22, 23, 86, 90, 112
Vygotsky, Lev, 71

Wall Street Journal, 13, 101
Wallace, Chris, 95, 96, 107, 109, 110
Wallat, Cynthia, 21, 22
war on drugs, 46, 114, 115, 117
Washington Post, 13, 102, 105, 159
weapons of mass deception, 13, 108
weapons of mass destruction, 6, 13, 70, 72, 73, 77,
    90, 94, 95, 108–110, 121
weapons of mass distraction, 13, 108
weapons of terror, 90–95, 108
Werth, Paul, 21
White House, 11, 12, 23, 65, 82, 87, 88, 109, 127,
    137, 160
Wilce, James M., 16, 86, 103, 104
Williams, Princess L., 143
Williams, Raymond, 154
Wilson, Scott, 159
Wittgenstein, Ludwig, 39
Wodak, Ruth, 4
Woolsey, James, 94, 95
Wortham, Stanton, 9

Young, Katharine, 4, 45
Yule, George, 6, 82, 122

Zawahiri, Ayman al, 145–146
Zinken, Jörg, 20, 21